THE TRANSPARENCY OF SPECTACLE

Meditations on the Moving Image

WHEELER
WINSTON
DIXON

STATE UNIVERSITY OF NEW YORK PRESS

Published by
State University of New York Press, Albany

© 1998 State University of New York

For information, address State University of New York Press,
State University Plaza, Albany, N.Y., 12246

Production by Marilyn P. Semerad
Marketing by Fran Keneston

Library of Congress Cataloging-in-Publication Data

Dixon, Wheeler W., 1950–
      The transparency of spectacle : meditations on the moving image /
   Wheeler Winston Dixon.
            p.   cm. — (The SUNY series in postmodern culture)
      Includes bibliographical references and index.
      ISBN 0-7914-3781-7 (alk. paper). — ISBN 0-7914-3782-5 (pbk. :
   alk. paper)
      1. Motion pictures. 2. Spectacular, The. 3. Cinematography-
   -Special effects. 4. Motion picture audiences—Psychology.
   I. Title. II. Series.
   PN1995.D52 1998
   791.43'75—dc21   97-24037
                                                                                          CIP

10 9 8 7 6 5 4 3 2 1

THE TRANSPARENCY
OF SPECTACLE

THE SUNY SERIES IN
POSTMODERN CULTURE

*For Elaine, Madeleine, Mary C., Zoe,
and Jean-Marie Wheeler,
for their many blessings
throughout the years.*

CONTENTS

ACKNOWLEDGMENTS

In creating this text, I want to thank the many people who over the years have continued to shape my interest and discussion of the moving image, including David Desser, Dennis Coleman, Ian O'Sullivan, Mandy Rowson, Janet Moat, Oyekan Owomoyela, Steven S. Gale, Lili Berko, Anna Everett, Lester Friedman, Lloyd Michaels, Ira Jaffe, Deac Rossell, Tony Williams, Marcia Landy, Mark Reid, Stephen Prince, Bert Deivert, Stephen Buhler, Gwendolyn Foster, Laurence Kardish, Howard Guttenplan, and many others. In addition, I wish to thank Dr. Linda Ray Pratt, Chair of the Department of English at the University of Nebraska, Lincoln, for release time to complete this volume. I also wish to gratefully acknowledge the support and continued good wishes of my many colleagues in the Department of English, as well as a number of readers (both anonymous and identified) who read and commented on various aspects of the many drafts of this volume.

Sections of this manuscript appeared in substantially different forms in the following publications, under these titles: "The Commercial Instinct: New Elstree Studios and the Danziger Brothers, 1956–1961," *Popular Culture Review*, forthcoming; "The Colonial Vision of Edgar Wallace," *Journal of Popular Culture*, forthcoming; "Moving the Center: Notes Towards the Decentering of Eurocentric and American Cinema," *Popular Culture Review* 8.1 (February 1997): 3–16; "Gender Approaches to Directing the Horror Film: Women Filmmakers and the

Mechanisms of the Gothic," *Popular Culture Review* 7.1 (February 1996): 121–134; "Maureen Blackwood, Isaac Julien and the Sankofa Collective," *Film Criticism* 20.1/2 (Fall-Winter 1995–96): 131–143; "The Digital Domain: Image Mesh and Manipulation in Hyperreal Cinema/Video," *Film Criticism* 20.1/2 (Fall-Winter 1995–96): 55–66; "The Site of the Body in Torture/The Sight of the Tortured Body: Contemporary Incarnations of Graphic Violence in the Cinema and the Vision of Edgar Allan Poe," *Film and Philosophy* 1.1 (1994): 62–70; "*Femmes Vivantes* and the Marginalized Feminine 'Other' in the Films of Reginald LeBorg," *Cinefocus* 3 (1995): 34–41; "The Eternal Summer of Pinter and Losey's *Accident*," in *The Films of Harold Pinter*, Steven S. Gale, ed., forthcoming, State University of New York Press; "The Romance of Crime," *Proceedings of the Fourth Annual Kent State Conference on Film*, Dr. Douglass Radcliff-Umstead, ed., Kent State University, Ohio (Spring 1987): 70–74; "Archetypes of the Heavy in Classical Hollywood Cinema," in *Beyond the Stars: Stock Characters in American Popular Film*, Dr. Paul Loukides and Dr. Linda K. Fuller, eds., 201–211; "The Curious Case of John H. Collins," *Classic Images* 261 (March 1997): C8–11, Robert King, ed.; and "In Defense of Roger Corman," from *The Velvet Light Trap* 16, 11–15, by permission of University of Texas Press. My sincere thanks to the editors of these publications for permission to reprint these materials here.

In this volume, then, I wish to consider the ephemeral nature of the cinematic experience as we now apprehend it, and examine the ways in which this experience has changed over the course of the last thirty odd years. Cinema studies in the 1960s have given way (thankfully) to moving image studies in the late 1990s; as we approach the end of the century, a host of new technologies are springing up, most of them in their infancy, as the cinematograph was itself in the late 1890s, one hundred years ago. Already, in the past several decades, we have seen the obsolescence of 16mm as an independent production format, the rise of VHS home video and a host of related LaserDisc formats (bringing most films within the reach of the assiduous collector), and the creation of the Internet and the World Wide Web as new disseminators of both text and moving images (which can be downloaded with impunity across international boundaries in a way that few people envisioned only ten years ago). This new method of moving image distribution will, I feel, continue to grow, and will eventually (with fiber optic "wiring") replace much of the contemporary distribution network that we are currently familiar with.

This text thus considers not only these new technological advances (as well as the continually evolving world of computer-generated imagery, which seemingly makes quantum leaps in efficiency and capability with each passing day, rendering that which was impossible a few months earlier a matter of routine practice in the here and now), but also our changing idea of what constitutes a film, a video, or a televisual presentation, and how the genres we take for granted (never more so than in the present, when most commercial filmmaking has become strictly genre-driven, due to cost factors alone) have been transformed by these new methods of production, distribution, and reception. In so doing, I will look back over the past of cinema (and, tangentially, some selected critical and popular literary texts) and explore the ways in which these flickering images and fleeting words have shaped our collective consciousness. This overview of the corpus of the image/word spectacle in the late twentieth century is not designed to be comprehensive, being a highly personal examination of key texts, authors, and critics whose works command my attention in the waning days of the millennium. Hopefully, however, this text may suggest some fruitful areas for further inquiry, and gesture in the direction of new work to come in these fields. The television is our new electronic hearth, as I observed in *It Looks at You: Notes on The Returned Gaze of Cinema*; in this volume, I will examine the changes, influences, and consequences of some of the shifting images we apprehend as we gaze into the electronic flames.

CHAPTER ONE

Moving the Center:
The Reconfiguration
of the Moving Image

Those who expect this text to be a polemic exercise will be at least, I hope, partially disappointed. Although I wish to seriously examine the condition of cinema at the crossroads of interfacing with the next generation of imagistic recording, reproduction, and distribution (the net, the web, digital tape and discs, cable and satellite, videotape, LaserDiscs, and new systems not yet known but certain to be invented, not the least of which may be a simple chip encoding all the information necessary to reconstruct the sounds [images of a "feature film"]), I do not believe that cinema as a medium is defunct, although these days it seems almost fashionable to assert that it is.

I could argue that the cinema as we now know it is dying, rendered moribund by the rise of alternative imaging systems and reproduction/storage methods, including but not limited to CD-ROM technology, the web, and the Net, and the concomitant rise in production costs of traditional features films. When low-budget breakthrough films are made today, such as *El Mariachi* (1993) or *The Brothers McMullen* (1995), their makers hope to graduate immediately to large-scale Hollywood films, thus rendering the independent cinema nothing more than a potential proving ground for future masters of the dominant cinema. I could also argue that the model of theatrical feature filmmaking foregrounding the director as auteur is similarly obsolete, as directors now serve merely as "traffic cops" (no matter how stylish their technique) for producers whose interests are solely directed to the bottom line. Though borderline "personal/commercial" films continue to be made, such as *Everything Relative* (1996), *Paris Was a Woman* (1996), or *Champagne Safari* (1996), these more adventurous films seldom achieve national distribution, and concomitantly national impact, because their release patterns are confined to major United States and foreign cities (New York, London, Berlin, Paris). Seldom are films such as these allowed the luxury of a "wide break" (opening in one thousand theaters or more), which is so essential to both the critical and commercial reception and/or impact of a contemporary theatrical film. These "Indie" films must thus earn back their production and exploitation expenses in limited release patterns, despite favorable reviews in major metropolitan journals. The financial risk on even the most modest of these productions runs into several hundred thousand dollars; even a truly fringe effort such as Lisa Rose Apramian's *Not Bad for a Girl* (1996), a documentary on such pioneering feminist rock bands as L7, Babes in Toyland, Hole, Lunachicks, and others, costs nearly a hundred thousand dollars in production and post-production expenses, even with much of the initial image gathering for the project being accomplished through the relatively inexpensive medium of video.

THE DEATH OF THE AVANT-GARDE FEATURE FILM

The days when Ron Rice could direct *The Flower Thief* (1960) for less than $1,000 to final 16mm optical track print are long gone, as are the production methods that rendered *The Chelsea Girls* (1966) possible (direct sound recording on film with an Auricon camera). In their place has come a wave of video-produced films such as *Jupiter's Wife* (1994) (but even this low-budget "documentary" video was made with the express intention of being presented as a Showtime original movie, with its own interest in being both safe and profitable). The cost of cinema production has made even a seven-minute film (shown in color negative) run to $7,000 or so for even a modest production, with the demise of reversal film technology and the relative death of 16mm for more convenient, but image-degrading, formats.

Video represents the future, with every person having access to a Camcorder; we are provided with images of events such as the 1989 massacre in Tiananmen Square, the Rodney King and Reginald Denny beatings, and other events that demand to be recorded as part of the zone of visual justice. But the truly terminal nature of the theatrical cinema experience is perhaps best exemplified by the opening of a multiplex theatre in August, 1995, in Valley Stream, Long Island, where the patrons must pass through metal detectors and body searches to get to their assigned seats, and are repeatedly warned by a recorded tape played through the public address system that they are under surveillance at all times. The shared communality of the theatrical cinema experience is thus rendered an obsolete social contract, as movies on video encourage us to stay within the social sphere of our own home. The commercial cinema, as Godard predicted in *Le Mépris* (1963), is dead. It remains only to bury the corpse in an avalanche of $95,000,000 genre thrillers, where even the most compliant and creative directors are hard pressed to create an individual signature in the face of ever-tightening narratological requirements.

This argument has a great deal of support from both theoreticians and practitioners within cinema/video. Certainly the "independent cinema" (whatever this term might mean) is locked into a period of serious retrenchment. Even a seasoned producer such as Ted Hope, co-president of the New York Production Company Good Machine, whose credits include *The Brothers McMullen* (1995), *Safe* (1994), *The Wedding Banquet* (1993), and Hal Hartley's later film *Flirt* (1995), flatly asserted in an article in *Filmmaker* that "Indie film is dead" (indeed, this is the title of the text). Hope goes on to claim that

> The marketplace is nasty and brutal[,] remembering only the latest successes and never forgetting its failures. It allows no room for taste beyond the mainstream. Truly

unique films cannot get screens, let alone hold them for more than a week or two. There is virtually no American audience for art films, political films, or non-narrative films. The specialized distributors have morphed into mass marketers, not niche market suppliers. Monopolistic business practices drive most corporate strategies. (18)

Thus, under Hope's model, although the mainstream cinema continues to proliferate, and mainstream, mass-audience films such as *Batman Forever* (1995) and *Liar, Liar* (1997) capture huge theatrical audiences, the cinema itself is going through a period of radical change at the end of its first century, coexisting with CD-ROM interactive "movies," video cassette and LaserDisc distribution, cable television, satellite television, video games, and a host of competing sound/image constructs. While such films as *Virtuosity* (1995) demonstrate the limitations of interactive video systems rather than herald a seemingly limitless figurative horizon, the 1995 production of *Mortal Kombat* is a spin-off of a wildly popular video game, and owes whatever temporal popularity it achieved to its source material. The *Wayne's World* films (1992 and 1993) are spin-offs from characters created for the television comedy series *Saturday Night Live; Super Mario Brothers* (1994) is yet another noninteractive version of an interactive original. Low-budget films such as *The Brothers McMullen* (1995), *Clerks* (1994), *Go Fish* (1994) and other fringe enterprises may momentarily capture the public's fancy, but in every case these productions are now seen as stepping-stones to larger-scale Hollywood films rather than individual achievements in and of themselves. The exponentially rising cost of film production (not to mention distribution and publicity) helps to ensure the hegemony of the dominant industrial vision in the middle-American marketplace, and the super conglomeration of existing production, distribution, and exhibition entities further assures the primacy of the readily marketable, pre-sold film, as opposed to a more quirky, individualistic vision.

Theatrical distribution, the mainstay of motion picture distribution for more than a century, is obsolete. Target audiences are increasingly younger, and these viewers perceive the experience of seeing a film primarily as an escape from the mundanity of their pre-packaged communal existence, as witness the popularity of such lowest-common-denominator films as *Clueless* (1995), *Dumb and Dumber* (1995), *Forrest Gump* (1994), *Operation Dumbo Drop* (1995), and others too numerous to mention. European films are no longer distributed in America; they are remade in Hollywood, in English, with American stars—and then distributed overseas in this revisionist format. The few foreign films that attain moderately wide release in the United States are lavish costume spectacles. As we approach the millennium, it is apparent that people today go to the movies *not* to think, *not* to be challenged, but rather to be tranquilized and coddled. This means that more thoughtful, introspective works are increasingly pushed beyond the margins of moving image discourse into the phantom zone of commercial limbo. In response to an interviewer's suggestion "that combining both educational and spectacular elements would give you a wider audience," Roberto Rossellini responded, "spectacular in what sense? Sensational? Sensationalism is the first lie. You can't arrive at the truth through lies. I think we must evolve to a new kind of spectacularity, and what greater spectacle is there than knowledge?" (di Bernardo, 151). And yet for audiences without any historical context, films must be devoid of anything that threatens, or any referent to a past (forgotten) historical event. Films such as *The Last Days of Pompeii* (1935) have been replaced by *Volcano* (1997), *Anaconda* (1997), *Dante's Peak* (1997), and other films that operate in the eternal present, assuming no familiarity with any historical referent other than contemporary popular culture, identifiable by a single word as to intent and content.

Sequels, particularly, are safe bets for exploitation, provided that the original film performs well at the box office; it is for this reason alone that nearly every mainstream film today is designed with an open ending, allowing the film to be franchised if the parent of the series captures the public's fancy. Television has become a wilderness of talk shows and infomercials, with time so precious that even the end credits of series episodes are shown on a split-screen with teasers from the upcoming program, to dissuade viewers from channel surfing, which is nevertheless rampant. Much new television programming is simply advertisements for upcoming movies or television shows; the *E* Entertainment channel regularly runs a program entitled "Coming Attractions," composed of nothing but the theatrical "trailers" (or "previews") from upcoming feature film releases. The host of the program blandly assures the audience that the show is devoted to "the best part of going to the movies . . . the previews," a direct acknowledgment that the previews are often better edited, better produced, and certainly more interesting than the films they profess to announce. The content of contemporary mainstream films is almost incidental to the production/distribution/exhibition process, since cinema patronage is essentially a non-refundable experience. All that is required is to get the audience into the theatre; once delivered, the audience need not be satisfied, only satiated.

Psychic hotlines offer spurious counsel at $3.99 a minute; shopping channels commodify the images we see into discrete, marketable units; "no money down" real estate brokers hope to dazzle us with their varying formulae for success. The cable movie channels run only current fare, or thoroughly canonical classics, avoiding subtitling and black-and-white imagery (with rare exceptions) at all costs. Revival houses screen films in only a few major cities, particularly Paris and New York, and even these are closing (witness the firing of curator Fabiano Canosa from the Public Shakespeare Theatre Film program, and the closing of the Film Theatre itself, Taubin, 8–9; Canosa has since found a new home with Anthology Film Archives as a curator of film exhibitions, at least for the present). Indeed, it seems very much as if the first century of cinema will now be left to the often fugitive ministrations of museum curators and home video/LaserDisc collectors, rather than remaining a part of our shared collective cultural heritage.

With mainstream contemporary films so banal, it is any wonder that more adventurous viewers/auditors are turning to the Internet, e-mail, the nascent world of cyberspace, in search not only of a cheap medium of expression, but also human contact? For this last is what the cinema inherently denies us; sealed in a can, projected on a screen, we watch it, and it watches us, but the connection between viewer and viewed is gossamer thin. CD-ROM and cartridge games offer a more concrete, though still synthetic connection to the spectacle witnessed by the viewer/participant—an illusion, in fact, of control and interactivity.

THE INSULARITY OF SPECTACLE

The limits of this insular spectacle are striking, and the technology at present is clumsy and expensive. But the experiential horizon is there, and the strip of film that runs through a conventional 35mm projector is an archaic *aide de memoire* of an era of puppet shows and magic lanterns. To satisfy us, the spectacle must engulf us, threaten us, sweep us up from the first. The "plots" of most interactive games are primarily simple— kill or be killed. These games achieve (at home and in the arcade) a wide currency among viewers bored by the lack of verisimilitude offered by the conventional cinema. And because of this lack, the cinema, many argue, is dying. Laura Mulvey asserted that the Hollywood studio system film

> . . . is really a thing of the past—I mean, it's like studying the Renaissance. But at the same time I think perhaps, like the Renaissance, it's something that doesn't go away and still stays a source of imagery and myths and motifs . . . although we could say that the studio system is dead and buried, and that Hollywood cinema, however very powerful it is today, works from very different economic and production structures, at the same time, our culture—MTV images, advertising images, or to take a big obvious example, Madonna—all recycle the images of the old Hollywood cinema, all of which have become points of reference, almost as though they've become myths in their own right, which are then taken over, absorbed, and recycled every day in the different media. (Súarez and Manglis, 7)

And yet, it seems to me, an equally strong case can be made for precisely the opposite contention: the cinema is not dead, but rather reconfiguring itself, emerging from the chrysalis of variant new technologies to reassert itself as the dominant form of image manipulation/discourse, no matter what delivery system is ultimately employed for these images. Nor is Mulvey alone in this view. In his 1995 article, "The Eternal Return," Michael Atkinson argued that although we now have unprecedented access to "a full century of cinema . . . on video, on cable, [and] in revival houses," the "serious revivalism" of cinema is imperiled by the closing of theatres that cannot compete with the inroads Blockbuster Video has made into mainstream American consciousness (4). Further, as Elliott Stein notes, when films are screened theatrically, even in a major metropolitan center such as New York, print quality is so variable as to vitiate the film-going experience, offering patrons "one day, a great mint print of a classic; the next day, a beat up 16mm print, fit for junking . . ." (5). Even commercial houses in New York's Chinatown that specialize in foreign "action" imports from Hong Kong are closing due to the impact of near-instantaneous (and often illegal) videotape competition (Wice, 14). What can we offer to counterbalance this grim view of the collapse of the classical cinema?

Firstly, we must embrace the future of cinema/video representation and reproduction, rather than seek to ignore and/or avoid it. As has been necessary through time with sound-on-film, color, CinemaScope, television, and the more recent technological developments previously mentioned, we should above all welcome these changes in the medium we share as scholars and practitioners. Cybertechnologist Bert Deivert published a superb commentary in *Cinema Journal* on film research on the Internet, detailing a variety of visual and/or textual research materials readily available through the net and the World Wide Web (see Deivert, 103–124, for further details). Anna Everett notes that to secure our collective future within the world of cyberspace "we must become programmers, software developers, and whatever else it takes . . . a whole new lexicon has emerged" (10) in the study of cinema through computer-aided access. And video cassettes and LaserDiscs give us as scholars, researchers, or casual viewers wider and cheaper access to cinema/video moving image constructs, both old and new, than ever before.

As cited by Scott Heller, Henry Jenkins of M. I. T. declared that "we [in academe] are paying a tremendous price for our intellectual and aesthetic conservatism . . . there is enough work [in the new media environment] to keep us all investigating and theorizing . . . for decades to come" (A17). The newest phenomenon in moving image distribution is the use of the World Wide Web as a cheap, global disseminator of short films from Africa, China, and other Third World and/or Asian countries. Hollywood has jumped on the web bandwagon eagerly: nearly every new film now released has a web site of its own, displaying the trailer and other promotional materials for each new release. The web may indeed be the place where 1960s experimental cinema is re-invented, as it is cost effective, pervasive, and readily accessible. The introduction of Netscape 3.0 makes downloading films to your computer hard drive relatively quick and efficient; saved as simple text documents, a fifteen-minute film can be downloaded in roughly that same amount of time. MPEG videos offer even greater quality, and a number of new programs are experimenting with the dissemination of full-screen MPEG imagery with sound (such as the "Toob" format). Undoubtedly, the ease with which one can access full-screen moving images on the web will increase almost daily; it will probably be less than a year before films can be routinely distributed in this manner.

THE "NICHE" FEATURE

Despite claims to the contrary, "niche" features are a growth industry for a variety of reasons. When Arnold Rifkin took over as head of "the William Morris Agency's motion picture division . . . he set up a special division . . . to stitch together the sort of movie projects that top Hollywood agencies traditionally disdain" (Bart, 89), developing films such as Quentin Tarantino's *Pulp Fiction* (1994), David Twohy's *Shockwave* (1995), Desmond Nakano's *White Man's Burden* (1995), and Kevin Spacey's *Albino Alligator* (1995). One of Rifkin's top lieutenants, Rick Hess, noted that "despite what anyone may tell you, there's a voracious appetite for niche product out there" (Bart, 94). As testing grounds for newer talent, or zones of rejuvenation for actors or directors who have had a few box-office failures (Bruce Willis sought out small but flashy roles in a variety of niche films after the failure of *Hudson Hawk* [1991] at Rifkin's suggestion), these modest and compact films are one manifestation of the future of cinema. More women are making films today than at any time since the silent era, with such directors as Julie Dash, Kathryn Bigelow, Jane Campion, Amy Heckerling, Patricia Roszema, Mira Nair, Chantal Akerman, Marta Meszaros, Allison Anders, and many others making feature films, on both modest and grandiose budgets. Gregg Araki, Hal Hartley, Abel Ferrara, and Jim Jarmusch create low-budget films with regularity and rapidity, assuring their careers while simultaneously operating at the margins of commercial cinematic discourse.

CD-ROM films are another new medium whose potential has barely been tested. Confined in the past to interactive "shoot and kill" games, the medium may be moving into the zone of true narrative signification, as stars such as Margot Kidder, Tim Curry, Christopher Lloyd, Donald Sutherland, and Christopher Walken venture into the ever more plot-driven, yet still exceedingly low-cost, medium ($2.5 million is considered a lavish budget; Steinberg, 114). The routine use of computer-generated imagery is becoming so prevalent, and cost-effective, that sets, costumes, locations, and even supporting players can be conjured up with a whisk of the electronic paint box. All of these new technologies raise serious questions about their use and/or reception by practitioners/viewers, but these are precisely the areas that we should seek to explore in the coming years—indeed, this new territorial domain of the cybervisual is one of the most vital fields of contemporary cinema/video/moving-image research.

And yet, there is much information that can easily be cited to chronicle the actual *death* of the cinematic image experience as we have to come to appreciate it. Like the movie palace theatre seats in Godard's *Alphaville* (1965), which electrocute patrons during the projection of a film and then unceremoniously dump their lifeless bodies into a disposal pit below, the theatrical cinematic experience of the past is being replaced by the glow of the twenty-first-century hearth, the video terminal/television screen. In an oft-cited opinion piece, "The Decay of Cinema" in *The New York Times Magazine,* Susan Sontag mourned the death of "cinephilia," an unrestrained, auteurist-driven passion for the classical, narrative cinema which flourished in the critical discourse of the '60s and '70s. In many ways, Sontag's assertion is correct. The Sarrisinian model of film appreciation fueled by such early cinema-based texts as *Film Form* and *Film Sense* has been replaced by a new teleculture which embraces the entire panorama of moving image studies—including film, video, and images transported through cyberspace on the World Wide Web. At the same time, cinema study (seen in the most reductive sense of that term) has experienced a proliferation of texts and new critical methodologies, as alternative fields of study prove their efficacy in analyzing the moving image construct. Concomitantly, we are also witnessing a move away from European/American dominated modes of visual discourse, and an embrace of African, Asian, and Queer Cinema practice, even as national and international boundaries crumble in the wake of Internet image dissemination. Finally, the archival hegemony of the traditional Hollywood cinema is being challenged by a post–New Wave movement of feminist and Third World moving image practice, although the major studios still seek to maintain their stranglehold on the international theatrical box office. One studio executive predicts that while four thousand prints (on average) of a hit movie such as *Braveheart* (1995) may suffice for international distribution in the current marketplace, entirely new mechanisms of image delivery will increase the demand to eight thousand prints by the turn of the twenty-first century, as new markets (primarily in Asia and Africa) are penetrated by the neocolonialist project of the traditional Hollywood narrative cinema. That is, of course, assuming that alternative methods of visual reproduction are not already in common use by that time; today 35mm film, tomorrow digital videotape, or finally, a computer chip encoded with all the glyphic data necessary.

CONTEMPORARY MOVING IMAGE THEORY

An entirely new set of values and concerns mark contemporary moving image critical discourse. Mark Seltzer's *Bodies and*

Machines argues for the primacy of the inextricably laced link between the human corpus in motion and the task/objective of the motion picture apparatus. Gwendolyn Audrey Foster's *Women Film Directors* persuasively and exhaustively chronicles the thorough marginalization of the works of women filmmakers in the traditional cinematic canon. The previously under-appreciated work of the German cinéaste Valie Export has been documented in the critical study *Valie Export: Fragments of the Imagination* by Roswitha Mueller. In *Risking Who One Is; Encounters with Contemporary Art and Literature*, Susan Rubin Suleiman argues that it is the "self" that is at risk when one contemplates the cultural project of contemporary visual discourse. David Curtis has compiled a directory of previously marginalized British cinema and video practitioners (*A Dictionary of British Film and Video Artists*) that highlights the work of Susan Collins, Steven Dwoskin, Sandra Lahire, Juliet McKoen, Pratibha Parmar, and others. In *The Location of Culture*, Homi K. Bhabha interrogates the cultural hegemony of moving image production and dissemination as practiced by the West, thus ensuing the erasure of textual/visual practice, and discouraging the creation of self-identity in the Third World. A group of American independent theorists/practitioners have gathered their critical writings and manifestoes in a document entitled *Angry Women*—a platform for the post-feminist discourse of such artists as Avital Ronell, Susie Bright, bell hooks, Sapphire, Karen Finley, and other media practitioners who work at the frontiers of corporeal visual image discourse. Simultaneously, markers of the decline of Hollywood's domain over the collective imaginations of the transgendered spectator constructed by the hegemony of the dominant cinema may be observed in essays such as Michiko Kakutani's "Designer Nihilism." In this essay Kakutani persuasively argues that the contemporary viewer has lost faith in traditional patterns of narrative closure, and, in the age of AIDS, believes only in the finality of self-annihilation, configuring the zone of the living as a location of pain and self-denial rather than a site of possibility and pleasure.

As cinematic/moving image practice thus becomes more reflexive and self-referential, audiences who desire only an escape from the predestined patterns of their shared commonality embrace films that are airbrushed and digitally manipulated to artificial perfection (*Forrest Gump* [1994], *Jurassic Park* [1993]), and choose the mindless reductivism of *Happy Gilmore* (1996) over the chic cynicism of *Leaving Las Vegas* (1996). (Kakutani correctly identifies *Leaving Las Vegas* as the logically fatalistic plague-era extension of Billy Wilder's *The Lost Weekend* [1945]. That film ended with Ray Milland resurrecting himself from the self-destructive cycle of alcoholism through the agency of a heterotopic union with a "redemptive woman"; in contemporary critical/practical discourse, we seek only a collective exit from the zone of corporeal existence, as Nicholas Cage demonstrates in *Leaving Las Vegas*. Both actors, it should be noted, won Best Actor Academy Awards for their respective performances. If one seeks a discrete symptomatic display of the loss of hope as a shared cultural conceit in the repressive, neo-Victorian social climate of the late 1990s, this consensual, canonical certification of Cage's relentlessly self-loathing fictive construct might well serve as a unique example.) The gritty, yet blender-processed imagery of *Leaving Las Vegas* (the city itself being a spectacular site of Western cultural decay and commodification) is counterbalanced in Hollywood discourse by films such as *Father of the Bride II* (1996), *Happy Gilmore* (1996), *Sgt. Bilko* (1996), and other paeans to the established, though collapsing, social order, in which all threats to the established locations of American culture are comfortably burlesqued, thus ensuring the final and inevitably artificial re-establishment of the patriarchal social order.

As John Frow argues in his study *Cultural Studies and Cultural Value*, "the formation of the knowledge class characteristically takes place around the professional claim to, and the professional mystique of, autonomy of judgment; this forms the basis both for the struggle over the organization of work and for individual self-respect (that is, for a particular mode of subjectivity) grounded in this relation to work" (125). Thus what is at stake in cultural studies in the late 1990s is the right to self-actualization and the creation of alternative forms of self-representation in direct opposition to the "normative" identity constructs proffered with increasing insistence by the hegemonic mainstream cinema. The proliferation of video cameras, more than any single other factor, has assisted the individual in reclaiming a personal space of self-representation within the sphere of visual/social identity. The Camcorder has brought us detailed documentation of the Rodney King beatings, of the riots in mainland China, and of the relatively recent disastrous satellite launch in that same country which resulted in the destruction of a large civilian living area (these images were suppressed by the Chinese government, only to be recorded and then smuggled out of the country by a visiting Israeli engineer). Yet it is not surprising to note that programs such as *America's Funniest Home Videos* seek to undermine this creation of an alternative self through the same medium—real-time, synchronous sound, portable home video cameras—by reducing common daily experience to a series of embarrassing, discontinuous incidents "excerpted" from the flow of temporal human existence. At the other end of the scale, such TV shows as *Cops* revel only in the most grotesque and violent images culled from several days of surveillance by a professional video crew. In these shows, life has become the zone of buffoonery or brutality to the exclusion of all else. In *Hegemony and Power*, Benedetto Fontana holds that the "opaque quality of the culture and con-sciousness of the people implies that political knowledge, when related to the life and practice of the masses is a knowledge whose function it is to mask—*velare*—the technique and science [of political discourse]" (159). It is the "opaque quality" that makes self-actualization through the visual so problematic, lacking any "solid ground" of shared telecultural space, and yet simultane-ously calls our collective attention to the desperate urgency of this project, in the face of numerous competing social and com-mercial imagistic discourse models, all of which seek to erase the individual in the service of the global economy of image produc-tion and exchange.

It is the project of international cultural displacement that makes the potential work of the Internet and the World Wide Web so inherently crucial to twenty-first-century moving image production, dissemination and reception, and simultaneously signals why governmental agencies on an international scale so desperately seek to control the international flow of information afforded by this medium of cultural exchange. We are in the dawn of a re-invention of the moving image construct, either as a narrativist methodology, or a conglomeration of individual glyphs that seek to form a separate self-identity through the medium of cyberspace. Static web pages, much like early "magic lantern" projection systems of the late nineteenth century, are already perceived as passé by even the least sophisticated auditors of the Net; Shockwave imagery, still in its infancy, must be compared to the zoetrope—a device that prefigured the invention of paper "roll film" by George Eastman in the late 1880s—in its infancy. As the Internet moves from telephone lines to fiber optic transmission cables, and the quality of QuickTime and/or MPEG video/cinema imagery improves (particularly with the new MPEG "Toob" format, a pioneering attempt to present full-screen sound/image 30fps video through the existing ethernet facilities), one might persuasively argue that the large-scale computer screen may well replace the traditional configuration of TV/cable/satellite/digital dish delivery, as passive viewers are replaced with individualized, self-constructed auditors who select, modify, and program their own schedules of narrative/glyphic imagistic discourse. The primary concern in this area, however, is the cost factor, which is prohibitive—as it was in the early days of conventional broadcast television. Yet it seems inevitable that mass production and the global embrace of these new technologies will bring the web within the reach of nearly everyone who now owns a conventional television receiver, and the stage will then be set for the central site of cultural struggle in the century to come: that is, who will control the images that are created, and "published," on home pages throughout the Internet. While commercial web sites are now commonplace on the web, it is the personal/educational "home pages" where the truly important disruptive and discursive work of the Internet is being accomplished, and it is for this reason that the hegemonic social order finds these individual sites of social expression so disconcerting and threatening.

MOVING THE CENTER OF CULTURAL DISCOURSE

When we speak of "moving the center," we are discussing not only the displacement of American/European culture from the center stage of moving image studies; or the ascent of the video/chip image over the traditional photographic medium of 35mm film; or the explosion of cultural artifacts in the form of critical texts that seek to explicate the word obtained by the domain of the visual over our contemporary telecultural existence. We are also speaking of the rebirth of the individual vision, of the potential for self-actualization through the creation of a series of visual constructs that reposition the creator/viewer at the center of imagistic discourse, and the subsequent (and consequent) "freeze" of Hollywood cinema into a ritualistic medium of operatic self-referentiality, seeking to support itself through the rule of the look alone.

As Henry A. Giroux argues in *Disturbing Pleasures*, "a pedagogy of representation [within academic discourse] would give students the opportunity not simply to discover their hidden histories but to recover them" (89), thus educating spectators on how to both analyze and respond directly to the fictive constructs that have unanswerably dominated our spectatorial consciousness since the invention of the theatrical motion picture. Steven Shaviro (in *The Cinematic Body*), Bill Nichols (in *Blurred Boundaries*), and Steve Redhead (in *Unpopular Cultures*) have all argued for a new aesthetic that views the cinema as a site of primary cultural discourse, a being possessed of its own phantom authority and corporeal resonance. Cinema, they have contended, simultaneously signals and interprets the landscape of popular culture in a mimetic medium that derives its primary authority from the continual oscillation between the figurative and the physically constituted domain of corporeal discourse; the moving image becomes a living being, transmitting and translating the circumstances of our proscribed existence into the shared domain of the transcultural glyph. Moreover, as I have argued in *It Looks at You: The Returned Gaze of Cinema*, the cinema/video image (particularly as constituted through cyberspace, where each auditor of a given image is in turn addressed, indexed, and reciprocally watched by the image she/he views) creates in contemporary culture a zone of societal control and panopticonic dominion as an ineluctable coefficient of its presentation/reception to all members of its intended audience. Futurists Arthur and Marilouise Kroker, particularly in their works *The Last Sex: Feminism and Outlaw Bodies* and *Hacking the Future: Stories for the Flesh-Eating 90s*, argue that the body has transcended the traditional corporeal dimensions of gender constructs and fleshly existence to enter the zone of the cyberbody, in which the human and the technological are virtually wedded in an ecstatic, all-encompassing fusion of the post-cybernetic corpus. Indeed, as the texts collected in *The Last Sex* persuasively argue, contemporary culture has moved of its own accord beyond the artificially fixed ground of societally sanctioned sender constructs into an "interzone" of transgenderal expression and corporeal reconstitution, in which we construct for ourselves the bodies and cultural identities we wish to possess. This idea is also expressed in the anthology *Cruising the Performative*, which deconstructs gender and the cultural signification of such personal accouterments as clothing, hairstyling, the use of rings and body piercing, as "interventions into the representation of ethnicity, nationality, and sexuality" (as declared by the subtitle of the text itself). Robyn Wiegman's *American Anatomies: Theorizing Race and Gender* proceeds along similar lines, seeing both contemporary and canonical social discourse as a clash between the exigencies of individual identity, and the concerns of a society that seeks to de-gender and virtually disempower the authority of the human versus the controlling interests of an inherently corporate social order.

Nor is this work new. A renaissance of intense interest in the work of Andy Warhol (as seen in Shaviro's *Cinematic Body*, as well as the cultural texts *Pop Out: Queer Warhol* and *Bike Boys, Drag Queens and Superstars* [this last text linking Warhol's "subversive" gay films of the 1960s with the pioneering work of queer cinéastes Kenneth Anger and Jack Smith]), who sought to disrupt not only traditionally received notions of gender construction and authorial discourse, but also to undermine the primacy of the "humanist" in the plastic arts by declaring himself a "machine" engaged in the replication of still and moving images for popular consumption. Warhol's factory may be seen as one of the earliest sites of cybernetic moving image discourse, in which the bodies of Warhol's performers/subjects were ineradicably linked with the mechanistic processes that reproduced them (either Warhol's silk-screen painting method, or his use of a static 16mm movie camera, most often loaded with 1200' of film for an uninterrupted thirty-five minutes of reproduction). This embrace of the mechanistic and mundane extension of the human corpus into the domain of the cybernetic machine was shared by Michael Snow, Hollis Frampton, Ernie Gehr, and other "Structuralists" of moving image production in the 1960s through the present.

In *Nothing Happens: Chantal Akerman's Hyperrealist Everyday* by Ivone Margulies, and *Landscapes of Resistance; The German Films of Danièle Huillet and Jean-Marie Straub* by Barton Byg, the authors argue that this linkage of the human and the mechanical is an inherent coefficient of the moving image production/exhibition/reception process, and that in their films from the 1960s to the present, Straub/Huillet, Akerman and other "Postfilm" (to use Mas'ud Zavarzadeh's term) practitioners are signaling the collapse of the filmic narrative and the ascension of the real-time machine-generated construct as the dominant mode of moving image discourse, and simultaneously creating a new model of unparalleled economy in the creation of post-narrative cinema, as befits films that acknowledge their intrinsically mechanical nature with each frame of their flickering, fugitive existence. These films, the authors argue, are sites of sexuality and loss, of pleasure denied and transformed; they are zones for the reconfiguration of gender roles and the increasingly rigid normative standards espoused by a political hegemony desirous of masking its own bid for authority, while seeking to assure an international viewing (and voting) constituency that the repression of desire, and the substitution of despair and loss for the pursuit of individual reconfiguration, are necessary to uphold the existing visual hegemonic order, and to deny the sexuality of human experience.

The link between our current neo-Victorian society and the values espoused by the original Victorians in late nineteenth-century America and Britain is, indeed, a hot topic in current moving image cultural studies. The late Victorian era witnessed the "unfreezing" of the still image into the phantom sarcophagus of the infant form of the motion picture; in much the same way, as I have remarked, images on the Internet are now haltingly being brought to artificial life through a variety of metanetric digital devices. As Carol Mavor notes in her discussion of the work of Julia Margaret Cameron in *Pleasures Taken: Performances of Sexuality and Loss in Victorian Photographs*, Cameron's images, phantasmally blurred daguerreotypes of mothers and their infant offspring (living and dead), map a zone of bodily recovery, memory, and sexual desire that constitutes the intrinsic domain of the human body, a domain that the nearly instantaneous medium of wet-plate photography allowed women and men to inhabit for the first time. As our corporeal selves are exposed to increasing risk through AIDS, fugitive viral infections, and the random exigencies of a social system in collapse, the artificial extraction of temporal/spatial moments of respite and repose from our collective existence becomes all the more pressing—indeed, it reveals that the primary function of the cinematographic apparatus is to enable us to remember, recapture, and vicariously re-experience selected zones of pleasure, fear, desire, and communal longing. It is this desire to confront the prison of our bodies through the medicine of the moving image which, above all, fuels the current discourse in moving image cultural studies. As we contemplate the transience of human existence, and beyond the fragility of our own corporeal being the delicate transience of even the most permanently engraved life-glyph, the study of the visual arts becomes a consideration of the physics of serial mortality, as our bodies are transubstantiated into filmic/video/digital simulacrum for the contemplation of a generation of spectatorial voyeurs as yet unborn, and the critical scrutiny of a society whose values will be wholly different from our own.

POSTFEMINIST CRITICAL THEORY

Signaling this shift in cultural perception, postfeminist cultural theory has entered a new phase of critical discourse, in which considerations of feminist text/image production are being re-evaluated in light of contemporary archival discoveries. Beverly Skeggs's *Feminist Cultural Theory: Process and Production* offers compelling insights by a number of theorists on the values espoused by competing sites of social/cultural discourse, as well as reconsiderations of marginalized figures in moving image history. Notable are Pat Kirkham's perceptive consideration of Ray Eames, the wife of designer/filmmaker Charles Eames, whose entirely *co-equal* contributions to the culture of visual literacy have yet to be fully assessed in the same volume, and Jackie Stacey's consideration of the shift in viewer perspective in postmodern feminist moving criticism in the concisely considered essay, "The Lost Audience: Methodology, Cinema History, and Feminist Film Criticism." Myra Macdonald's *Representing Women: Myths of Femininity in the Popular Media* explores how feminist discourse is decentered in the dominant contemporary commercial domain of televisual culture. In *Feminist Subjects, Multi-Media, Cultural Methodologies*, Penny Florence and Dee Reynolds have chosen essays that examine current totemic exemplars of supposed feminist discourse, including Jane Arthurs's properly skeptical critique of *Thelma and Louise* (1991) (which can be seen as espousing feminist self-actualization through ritual self-destruction), and Annette Kuhn's consideration of her own "gendering" through the guidance of her mother in a haunting autobiographical text, "A Credit to Her Mother." All of these critical investigations into the hegemonic power of the visual domain of the moving image significantly advance the constituted body of critical thought in this area.

This long overdue effort towards canonical expansion, or revision, or perhaps elimination, places feminist moving image practice within the body of received knowledge which has become identified as the collective corporeal output of the video graphic/cinema to graphic apparatus. In its totality, it signals what Kathy Acker has aptly termed "The End of the World of White Men," and what Third World theorists such as Manthia Diawara (in his classic study *African Cinema* and his feature-length video project, *Rouch in Reverse*, which feeds the work of the favored colonial ethnographer back upon itself to devastating effect), Mas'ud Zavarzadeh, and others argue for in their textural and visual projects. Even at the introductory level of moving image studies, basic survey texts now boast an inclusiveness and exhaustive attention to detail which was unimaginable even a half decade ago. Thompson and Bordwell's new film survey text, *Film History: An Introduction*, aimed at college undergraduates, manages within its compact duration to discuss the cinemas of Cuba, Angola, Burkina Faso, China, Japan, and the former Soviet Union, along with the more traditionally known works from Western European countries, and Hollywood films. Women and men are presented on an entirely egalitarian basis; within this text, the concept of "canon" is rendered virtually meaningless through the systematic inclusion of literally thousands of moving image practitioners on a global, century-spanning scale. Anything less than this universal overview of the international cinema would seem both reductive and retrograde. As evidenced in this text alone, moving image studies have progressed considerably from their initial inception in the mid-to-late 1960s.

Another indication of this non-colonial, non-canonical revision is the work being done in the studies of national cinemas, with particular attention to Asian and African cinemas, in the work of David Desser, Lester Friedman, Linda Ehrlich, Deac Rossell, Klaus Eder, Manthia Diawara, and many others. The work in this area is only just beginning, and it seems obvious that only the twin colonialist threads of Orientalism and cultural exploration have prevented the works of Ousmane Sembene, Maria Navaro, Lucian Pintille, Tahehiko Nakajima, Idrissa Ouedraogo, Zhang Yimou, Ulrike Ottinger, Tomas Gutierrez Alea, Ildiko Enyedi, Márta Mészáros, Pavel Lounguine, Nobuhiko Obayashi, Sarah Maldoror, Désiré Ecaré, Ababacar Samb, Mahama Johnson Traoré, Xie Fie, U Lan, Ann Hui, and many other gifted artists from reaching the wider audience they so clearly deserve—that, and perhaps the tendency of some to accept existing canons for the sake of convenience, and to refuse to move beyond the Eurocentric vision that informed moving image studies in the 1960s through the early 1980s.

Finally, there are the many moving image information sites available on the World Wide Web. These sites not only offer encyclopedic information on the texts and practitioners of moving image production/reception, but also afford the viewer actual films and videos (downloaded in either QuickTime and/or MPEG formats, from a variety of national cinemas), a wide variety of software with which to view these videos, and detailed critical studies of the works in question. Taken as a whole, this unceasing revision of the field of moving image studies reminds one of the perceptive words of Todorov: "democracy is a *negative* society; it defines itself by the rejection of what had guaranteed the good working order of the old society" (179). Those artificial limits that guaranteed the "successful" operation of the mechanics of moving image studies have, ultimately, collapsed under the weight of their own exclusionary tactics. What we are left with is the knowledge that although we cannot possibly know every work, every text and every person, of every race and every nationality, in the history of moving image studies, this is nevertheless the task—the only task—we must set for ourselves. To do anything less is a betrayal of the artists and the works that make up the combined history of our wakeful, dreaming consciousness, a shared commonality of visual experience which increases exponentially on a daily basis. Perhaps the Web will make this information available to all. As critics and scholars, we should demand nothing less than complete and total access to all film/video/digital works that have been created in the totality of cinema history, and to ceaselessly question all judgments that privilege one work or one artist at the expense of another.

THE UNRELIABILITY OF THE
MANUFACTURED IMAGE

For all of the benefits of these technological advances, it is impossible to overstate the impact, both in terms of image production and image reception, of digital special effects (and the use of digital production method as a kind of overall "finishing process" for filmmaking as a general practice), which have effectively (and surreptitiously) changed the language of what we have come to know as "motion pictures." This now-antiquated term conjures up images of Georges Melies or Augustin Le Prince patiently hand-cranking their wooden box cameras to expose frame after frame (or plate after plate) of conventional photographic film, essentially engaged in the process of recording that which is seen, that which exists. Gradually introduced over the last five years, digital special effects have transformed the landscape of the visual in film, transporting the viewer seamlessly beyond that which is real into a synthetic world where computer animation, morphing, and digital effects blend the actual with the fantastic. Perhaps one of the most disturbing aspects of the new wave of digital effects films is that they do not seem—at first glance—to contain any effects at all.

Jan de Bont's *Twister* and Brian de Palma's *Mission: Impossible*, two of the biggest box office movies of the summer of 1996, rely almost entirely on computer-generated imagery to seduce their audiences into entering into the constructed reality of the spectacles they present. These images, coupled with a heavily channeled, bass-boosted, digitally recorded soundtrack designed to enhance the supposed verisimilitude of these manufactured images at key syntactical points within the film's respective narratives, constitute, in fact, the only reason for their existence. The implicit contract with the intended audience is clear: we will show you that which you will never be able to witness, and make it appear real; we will intensify this illusion through the use of overloaded soundtracks in a (vain) attempt to concretize the digital spectacle we present. Both *Twister* and *Mission: Impossible*, however, foreground these computer-generated effects as the sole substance of the moving image construct the audience collectively witnesses. These films acknowledge that much of their effect will be lost on small-screen video, in yet another attempt to lure audiences out of their homes and into the Multiplex (as with 3-D, CinemaScope, Cinerama, and other related "spectacular" processes). What happens when these same computer-generated effects are more insidiously, or perhaps less pronouncedly, employed in the service of a conventional narrative?

Forrest Gump (1994), a hugely popular Capraesque film designed as an intentionally banal everyman success story, seems to be a rather straightforward film from a visual standpoint. There are several obvious trick sequences in *Forrest Gump*, most notably when Gump meets Presidents Kennedy, Johnson, and Nixon during a series of White House ceremonies. These scenes skillfully blend archival newsreel footage and blue-screen plates of Tom Hanks into an artificially congruent imagistic whole. Yet, the cultural/spatial displacement of Tom Hanks's persona in juxtaposition with thirty-year-old newsreel footage immediately signals to most audiences the intentionally duplicitous construction of these scenes (assuming that this hypothetical audience has the historical frame of reference to identify these scenes as faked). More disturbing, it seems to me, are the numerous scenes in *Forrest Gump* that seem to be straightforwardly photographed, but that in fact involved many hours of digital effects work.

The opening scene of the film, in which a feather floats through the air to land at Gump's feet, features a digitally manipulated feather which looks for all intents and purposes quite real. To film the scene at the reflecting pond near the Washington Monument in which Forrest is reunited with Jenny, his high school sweetheart, a mere one thousand extras were used. In final editing these one thousand extras were copied by computer and pasted in around the perimeter of the reflecting pond, resulting in an illusion of nearly one hundred thousand people gathered together in one place. Gary Sinise's character in *Forrest Gump* has his legs blown off during the Vietnam War; subsequent scenes of the legless Sinise in a wheelchair are accomplished by using a digital airbrush to remove the lower portion of the actor's anatomy. In the film, Forrest Gump becomes a ping-pong champion while recuperating from wounds received in Vietnam. Forrest's spectacular playing technique was mimed by Tom Hanks in front of a blue screen, and the ping-pong ball (and the various tournament backgrounds) were added later. Shadows are added to scenes in peaceful country lanes; violent explosions are digitally enhanced for greater effect.

All in all, it's a perfect world, even if it doesn't exist. The director of *Forrest Gump* is no stranger to the world of digital special effects; indeed, he is deeply in love with the illusions they can help him create. Robert Zemeckis, a protege of Steven Spielberg, has done almost nothing *but* effects pictures since coming into his own as a director; his films include *Back to the Future I, II* and *III* (1985, 1990, and 1990, respectively) and the highly acclaimed *Who Framed Roger Rabbit?* (1988). Zemeckis also directed another heavily digitized film, *Death Becomes Her*

(1992). In that film, Zemeckis seemed curiously interested in how grotesquely he could contort and distort the bodies of Meryl Streep and Goldie Hawn by twisting their necks, putting holes through their torsos, and mangling their arms and legs in post-production. Several years ago, Zemeckis recycled a series of images of Humphrey Bogart for a hybridized *Tales from the Crypt* episode, *You, Murderer,* first broadcast on HBO on February 15, 1995. Interestingly, the long-dead Bogart received top billing in the credits over John Lithgow and Isabella Rossellini, offering proof that an entire performance can now be created out of cannibalized imagery. In *You, Murderer,* "Bogart" interacts with his living colleagues just as if he were playing a scene with them in real life. The effect is both disquieting and a harbinger of things to come.

The verisimilitude of these manufactured images comes as a shock to the viewer conditioned to spot conventional movie trickery. Old-fashioned photographic processes, such as the movable matte, rear-projection, stop-motion animation, and forced perspective miniature work are easy for the sophisticated viewer to spot. One of the implicit safety zones of such films as *King Kong* (1933) is the unabashed crudity of the special effects work, which was nevertheless highly complex for its time. Such pioneer model animators as Willis O'Brien, Ray Harryhausen, and Jim Danforth created wondrous visions with the tools at their command. With the release of *Terminator II* (1991), generally acknowledged as the first feature film that made extensive use of digital effects, all of these time-honored filmic techniques became obsolete.

With digital effects there are no telltale matte lines around a figure artificially incorporated into a new background, as there are in Tod Browning's 1936 production *The Devil Doll,* which used oversized props and movable matte work to create the illusion of a troupe of miniature dolls intent on murder. No longer can one instantaneously spot the jerkiness of stop-motion animation that one sees in the model work of *20 Million Miles to Earth* (1957), *Jason and the Argonauts* (1963), or *Clash of the Titans* (1981), all films with special effects by Ray Harryhausen. The original *Godzilla* (or *Gojira*) was a man in a monster suit; Inoshiro Honda's 1954 film couldn't afford the many months of work involved in stop-motion animation, and relied instead on a rubber bodysuit and a miniature set of Tokyo (coupled with slow-motion photography) to create the illusion of rampant urban destruction. None of these methods are practicable anymore. They have lost their power to astonish.

With the advent of digital effects, these purely representational methods of achieving filmic illusion (involving the photography of concrete objects, and their subsequent re-integration into an artificial whole) have become clumsy and expensive, and have lost the power to convince audiences of their counterfeit reality. As indirect proof of this, the classic film monster Godzilla is being resurrected in an entirely digital production, "whose title character will be completely computer generated" (Parisi, 1); that is, lacking any actual physical substance at all. As with the digital dinosaurs (the velociraptors) who chased the protagonists of Steven Spielberg's *Jurassic Park* (1993) around the chrome and steel kitchen of Sir Richard Attenborough's mythic theme park, the new Godzilla will be created out of nothing at all. The new Godzilla will consist of pixels, shading, and computer animation techniques—afforded physical presence where none actually exists. As currently projected, Roland Emmerich (the director of *Independence Day* [1996]) and producer Dean Devlin will re-team to director/produce the new *Godzilla* for release in 1998.

THE NEW *GODZILLA* AND ITS PROGENY

The digital effects for the forthcoming *Godzilla* will be handled by one of Hollywood's newest and largest digital effects firms, the aptly named Digital Domain. To one of the producers of the new version of *Godzilla*, the production of the film marks a significant milestone in cinema history, as noted by industry observer Paula Parisi:

> "This is the first film of this magnitude where the lead character, who spends a good deal of time on screen, is virtually 100% computer animated," [says] one of the project's producers, Robert Fried. "The dinosaurs of *Jurassic*

Park were on screen for less than 15 minutes" . . . Godzilla's nemesis, the Griffin, will also be computer-generated, and will also involve numerous digitally generated morphing effects . . . The film will have an estimated 500 effects shots and an effects budget of $38 to $50 million . . . by comparison, *Apollo 13* [1995; directed by Ron Howard] had about 150 digital shots, as did *True Lies* [1994; directed by James Cameron], 104 of which were done by [Digital Domain]. *Interview with the Vampire* [1994; directed by Neil Jordan], another film on which Digital Domain handled the special effects] has 42 [digital shots]. (1, 29)

To many observers, Digital Domain and George Lucas's pioneering effects company Industrial Light and Magic are the two front-runners in the new digital effects industry, with Digital Domain now being given the leading edge in the competition. Domain was started up by director James Cameron after the success of his feature film *Terminator II*; with it, he hoped to keep digital effects production on *True Lies* under closer personal control. Special effects analyst Don Shay notes that

Cameron was among [Digital Domain's] creative principles. In partnership with Stan Winston and Scott Ross— and with corporate underwriting by International Business Machines [IBM]—Cameron has chartered Digital Domain with the goal of making it a first-rate effects facility . . . (37)

Since its inception, Digital Domain has been involved in a number of modest yet high-profile projects, including the 1994 Rolling Stones *Voodoo Lounge* video in which the band members are digitized into eighty-foot giants, nonchalantly strolling about the environs of New York City. For the *Godzilla* contract, Domain must cooperate with two rival effects houses to complete the job: Imageworks and Video Image. Parisi notes that

as a function of the [*Godzilla*] collaboration, the firms will be sharing computer software, a practice virtually unheard of in this competitive market [where new technological innovations are jealousy guarded by their creators]. "It's

hard to believe this is going to work" [an] effects observer
noted. "First of all, these companies all hate each other!" . . .
One source on the project who requested anonymity [said]
"the truth is, [most] effects houses in town would probably
have a feeling of awe. They didn't pay their dues, work their
way up from a small company. They came out of nowhere
and are now the biggest guys in Hollywood. And to top it all
off, they stole everybody's talent." (29)

Indeed, the field of digital effects is crowded with fledgling
companies. Current digital effects companies include VIFX (digital effects for *Timecop* [1994]); Sony Pictures's Imageworks (which
did some of the "jumping bus" digital effects for *Speed* [1994]);
Fantasy II Film Effects, Pacific Title Digital, Light Matters, Pacific
Data Images (all of which worked on *True Lies*); Dream Quest
Images Digital (whose credits include work on *The Crow* [1994],
The Mask [1994], *Coneheads* [1994], and *The Three Musketeers*
[1994]); Digital Magic (*Blown Away* [1994]); Electron Film Works
(also contributing to *Blown Away*); Buena Vista Visual Effects (the
Disney digital effects arm); Electric Image (which specializes in
main titles [the *Dateline NBC* series, the titles for *The Mask*], and
also did the "tornado" effects for *The Mask*, in which star Jim
Carrey becomes a blur of light and motion as he streaks about the
screen); the Digital Film Group (*The Shadow* [1994]); Cyberware
(specializing in "three dimensional digital scanning for models
and computer special effects" on everything from *Robocop II*
[1990] to the Clint Eastwood vehicle *In the Line of Fire* [1993]); as
well as Blue Sky Productions, Cineon (the Kodak digital effects
arm), Todd–AO Digital Images, Shockwave Entertainment, and a
host of other companies.

Even from this cursory overview, it is obvious that everyone
is jumping on the digital bandwagon. From the standpoint of cost
efficiency, creative flexibility, and apparent filmic verisimilitude,
digital imagery offers a nearly limitless list of possibilities for the
plastic manipulation of the cinematic image. Compared to
model animation or conventional process photography, the ease
of digital effects work is prodigious. All it takes is a computer,
one or two technicians, a light pen, a device to download the
35mm original film to videotape, and then a high-resolution

scanning system (such as the Solitaire Cine III Digital Film Recorder, used on *Jurassic Park, Batman Returns* [1992], *Hook* [1991] and *Terminator II*) to transform the videotape back into film, and presto—you have whatever effect you might require. The ease of special effects production under this new system is so pronounced that producer/director George Lucas announced in November of 1994 that he would shoot three new *Star Wars* films *simultaneously* in 1997 to 1998, with digital effects replacing nearly all of the model animation and matte work utilized in the original productions. Shrewdly, to pique audience interest in the new films, Lucas first re-released the original three *Star Wars* films in January and February of 1997. These had enhanced digital effects to "pump up" the older matte and model effects, which no longer impressed contemporary audiences. This complete replacement of the real (or even the models and puppets used in the first three films) would never have been possible with conventional special effects technology.

In addition to the special effects capabilities, as director Rachel Talalay observed in a telephone interview with me, routine digitizing of images straight from the camera "gets rid of all your problems." Talalay, director of the 1995 film *Tank Girl*, and before that producer and sometime director on a number of the *Nightmare on Elm Street* films and 1994's *Ghost in the Machine*, marveled that

> you can fix anything. We shot a lot of material in sand storms, and there were scratches in the negative, which at one time would have meant re-shooting. Now, we just feed the image into a computer, get rid of the scratches through digital technology [a distinct improvement over the old-fashioned "wet gate" printing method of rephotographing the offending negative to remove the scratches], and we can use that material in the film. Digital effects can take a shot that's too dark and make it absolutely perfectly illuminated; you can fix a performance by adding a smile where there wasn't exactly the reaction you wanted. Once upon a time, you would shoot material on the set and if it didn't come out exactly as you wanted it, you were stuck with it. Now, you can fix anything. (Dixon interview)

And so *Tank Girl* joins the growing list of films that are "processed" as a final step on their way to the marketplace, to achieve an almost supernatural perfection of stylized imagery.

THE DARK SIDE OF DIGITAL IMAGING

So it's a revolution—digital effects have taken over. Occasionally someone will use traditional cel animation as a double-reflexive effect, a special effect that calls attention to its inherent artificiality, imbuing the resultant image with a nostalgic glow. But for the most part, the digital effects revolution has entirely displaced the traditional methods of special effects production. And, in a sense, so what? Digital effects look slicker, the dinosaurs and automatons seem entirely believable, reality and fantasy (as in *Roger Rabbit* and the less successful *Cool World* [1993]) can be intertwined with vigor and impunity. And just like sound, color, television, home video, interactive video games, push-button telephones, magnetic tape recording (rather than optical sound recording on the set), CDs, e-mail, word processors and a host of other technological advances (not the least of which is the motion picture medium itself), the advance and development of digital special effects is yet another step in the evolution of image and sound recording and reproduction. So why resist it? Should we resist it? What's the downside of this technological shift, if any?

One immediate problem is the rights of actors over their own image and their past performances. The much recycled Humphrey Bogart was lifted out of a clip from *Sirocco* (1951) and plunked down in a police station in *The Last Action Hero* (1993). No doubt Bogart's estate approved the use of the late actor's image. But what would Bogart himself have thought of this use of his iconic presence? Several years ago, a series of soft drink commercials used the images of Cary Grant, the Marx Brothers, Marilyn Monroe, and other deceased celebrities to endorse their product; more recently, recycled images of Fred Astaire have been used to sell Dirt Devil vacuum cleaners, and clips from old John Wayne films have been manipulated into an advertisement for beer. Again, I'm sure that the proper legal clearances were obtained, but isn't the presence of these actors within the context of the commercial an implied endorsement of the commodity being sold? Allied aesthetic objections have been raised to the practice of "colorization," an early and now routine use of computers to add color (of a sort) to existing black-and-white films. One might argue from a strictly commercial point of view that the colorization of black-and-white films gives those films a new life for a generation of viewers for whom black-and-white cinematography itself has become an effect (in music videos, or an overall framing device in films such as Tim Burton's *Ed Wood* [1994]). But colorized versions of *The Maltese Falcon* (1941), *The Big Sleep* (1946), and *White Heat* (1949) ignore the carefully planned black-and-white camerawork that made these films so memorable and effective, destroying the vision of the original film in the process. When you clone one thousand extras into a hundred thousand, aren't you denying that many extras a job? And when you use a body double and paste a dead performer's face over it to finish a film (as was done in 1994's *The Crow*, when the film's star Brandon Lee died during production), aren't certain aspects of a performer's rights being potentially violated?

When Jean Harlow died during production of *Saratoga* in 1937, the film was finished with doubles, out-takes, and other makeshift measures. The same thing happened with Lionel Atwill (*Lost City of the Jungle* [1946]), Robert Walker (*My Son John* [1952]), and Natalie Wood (*Brainstorm* [1983]). The difference between these examples, however, and *The Crow*, is that with the technology currently available (and/or to be developed) an entire performance by a deceased actor could be fabricated to create an entirely new production. This is already happening with the TV "talk show" series *Space Ghost*, in which a digitally cannibalized cartoon character is morphed into a celebrity interviewer along the lines of Tom Snyder or Larry King. No new footage of the Space Ghost character is needed. All the visuals are lifted from old episodes of a Hanna-Barbera cartoon series. In many ways, Space Ghost is the ideal talk show host of the digital future. He will say whatever his producers want him to say, he will never ask for a raise or go on strike, and he will never seek ownership of his program. He needs only a voice and a script.

This is the essence of the digital future at its most extreme: a voice, a script, and entirely synthetic (recycled) imagery. Only the guests are live. Still, Space Ghost is just a cartoon character, and this pioneering recycling effort (which began as a cost-cutting measure to produce "new" programming out of old; see Meisler, 44–45, for more on the "production" of the *Space Ghost* talk show) might be said to compromise no one. But as Tom Cruise and other actors have complained, the appropriation of an actor's likeness without her or his consent represents a new grey area that needs to be legally and aesthetically addressed.

There is also the specter of an entirely synthetic star being digitally constructed as a franchise possession by a studio or digital effects firm, as was posited by Michael Crichton in his 1981 film *Looker*. When John Candy died during the production of *Wagons East* (1994), it was a foregone conclusion that the film would be completed. With the technology now so readily available, who would do otherwise, particularly given the enormous investment involved? Similarly, it is more than a little disturbing that the actual lips of Presidents Kennedy, Johnson, and Nixon can be manipulated through the use of a light pen and a desktop computer to perfectly enunciate words they never spoke in real life, as happens in *Forrest Gump*. The "writing in" of Gump during desegregation efforts in the South (by placing Gump within the flickering frames of old newsreel footage) also raises serious questions about the manipulation of archival footage for historians and scholars. Image manipulation through external montage is one matter, in which shots are intercut for emotional or associative impact. But Digital Domain, ILM, and their brethren are creating a new sort of montage—montage within the frame, without the familiar warning, or "limit" signals we have been trained to look for (wipes, matte lines, differences in film stock grain, inaccurate image-sizing and other flaws). These visual cues alerted us to the artificiality and constructedness of the manufactured image we see on the screen; now these cues are absent. Images within images are nothing new. Images seamlessly bonded to images within the same frame are a different matter altogether.

But by far the most radical extension of digital imaging is the idea that entire films and television shows may well be created without the use of actors, sets, props, costumes, lighting, or any other physical production apparatus, other than a computer. There will be no need for a conventional film or video camera. The entire production will be synthetically created through computer digital imaging. At this point, the technology to do this already exists—even the actors' voices can be electronically simulated, although this part of the process is primitive at the moment. Total digital production would directly affect directors, actors, set designers, costumes, directors of photography, gaffers, grips, extras, assistant directors—nearly everyone involved in the physical production of a motion picture as we now know it. Only producers, writers and post-production personnel would be exempt—for editing, sweetening (sound effects), music scoring (much of which is already done with a synthesizer anyway, throwing many hundreds of talented musicians out of work)—along with the women and men who control the financing, production, and distribution/exhibition of the finished product. All other personnel would be expendable.

Far from being a worst case scenario, many industry analysts see this as precisely where the cinema is heading, as a means to control soaring production costs. Film as a projection medium is already antiquated; soon it may be replaced with the much cheaper medium of digital videotape, and after that, a chip. Why spend one to two thousand dollars per print for one thousand prints of a film, when one thousand copies of a digital (as opposed to analog) videotape of the same production would cost twenty dollars each? The cost-conscious producer could also do away with conventional sets. While the budget for the new *Godzilla*, for example, allows thirty-eight to fifty million dollars for digital effects, total physical production will cost between one- and two-hundred million dollars (Parisi, 29). Even if you tacked on another ten million dollars to the effects budget to create the sets, costumes, extras and the like out of the digital ether, you would still be saving money. Total digital production would significantly reduce shooting costs, as there would be no bad takes. Everything coming out of the computer would be perfect. With the costs of digital production dropping exponentially, the price of creating a digital universe can be expected to diminish significantly as technology evolves and becomes more widespread.

Certain actors (star commodities, in particular) might even welcome the digital revolution. Stars might be asked to pose for a generic imaging session, which would inventory all their physical characteristics. Then digital image operators would take over to create their performance. Producers in an increasingly cost-driven hit or miss business will inevitably embrace any production method that saves them money, and simultaneously offers them a degree of physical control hitherto unimaginable. No more temperamental stars, cost-overruns on catering, or perfectionist directors. Audiences would never know the difference. See it, believe it. Viewers are conscious of a degree of image manipulation in the films they witness when the visual juxtapositions are transparently unreal, but more subtle digital transpositions go unnoticed.

Thus, the digital world seems destined to become seamlessly meshed with the mass-produced photographed/videotaped image. This image mesh will be woven ever tighter in the years to come. Cinema video space will become the zone of the eternally hyperreal. Audiences will demand a souped-up, picture postcard vision of existence for entertainment consumption, while the actuality of their physical lives becomes ever more marginalized. When Forrest Gump suddenly decides to walk across the United States from coast to coast, the America he sees is a Norman Rockwell vision of epic sunsets, cloud-free mornings, small-town bonhomie, and return-to-the-past contentment, entirely in keeping with the reductionist tone of the film. Much has already been written about the ways in which Forrest Gump attempts to re-visualize and rewrite American history, reducing (for just one example) the antiwar movement during the Vietnam era to a group of violent, misogynist misfits. There are no slums in the world of Forrest Gump, or if they exist, they are sentimentalized. In this fictive zone of non-being, only phantoms can flourish. Viewers embrace the vision of Forrest Gump in the increasingly narrow world of the 1990s as a place of safety and escape, because these phantoms offer them unconditional reassurance.

The reductive mindlessness of Gump is seductively complex; it meshes actual incident with revisionist embellishment in a ceaseless swirl of reconstructed "history" that deludes the viewer into accepting Zemeckis's fiction as historical fact. On the one hand, the incidents of blatant manipulation distance us from the film, reminding us that we are witnessing a fable; in opposition to this, Gary Sinise's amputated limbs seem terribly real, casting perfectly formed shadows on the floor of his dingy apartment. The bucolic Americana of Forrest's epic walk across the country seems as authentic as any store-bought pictorial souvenir. Perhaps *Forrest Gump* can serve an indicator of the future of digital imagery in film and video: Realest when it pretends to be fictional, most manufactured when it strives for naturalism, *Forrest Gump* is in every way the perfect digital film. It sweeps unpleasantness under the rug, and shows us only that which we will find soothing or melodramatically tragic (the death of Jenny, or of Forrest's mother). All the rough edges are rounded off, airbrushed to perfection.

It would be nice to suggest that as digital imagery becomes cheaper, the process of creating digital imagery will find a more democratic leveling point, where everyone can make a film because no physical elements are required. But such an argument ignores the reality of distribution. The major companies will still get to control what we see and hear. Within the digital imaging industry itself, there are already only two real players: Industrial Light and Magic (ILM) and Digital Domain. Both companies seek to further consolidate their market shares, as businesses will. Just as most of Hollywood's talent pool has been taken over by an elite group of agencies (CAA, William Morris, and ICM), and Hollywood, in turn, has monopolized the world's box office, so digital production may well completely supplant film and video creation as we know it today, and as we have known it to be. Whether we like it or not, we are approaching the frontier of hyperreal image production with increasing velocity. As the costs of labor and materials continue to spiral, we will cross over into this phantom zone of signification with hardly a glance over our collective shoulders. What we cannot create, we will envision and give artificial substance to; what we wish to be, the new mass-media films will become.

REVOLUTION AND "REALIST" CINEMA

In the face of this digital image creation and consumption, what alternatives do we have as a return to some sort of tactile "realism" within the apparatus of the cinematograph and its related image capture and reproduction systems? As cited by Kathleen Murphy in her commentary "Recent Iranian Cinema," a critic for the *Economist* predicted that "the next breakthrough in world cinema—-not commercial, but artistic—may come from Iran," and noted that Iranian films seem "avant-garde because they endorse the notion of absolute values that has lost favor in the secular West . . . underpinning all Iranian movies is a sense of justice and morality" (Murphy, WR 2, 7). It is precisely this embrace of the egalitarian that informs the best of Iranian cinema, and constitutes its fresh vision of human affairs, as opposed to the tired generic path beaten to death by the contemporary commercial Hollywood cinema.

Perhaps understandably, of all the contemporary Iranian films, it is Jafar Panahi's feather-light first feature film *The White Balloon* (1995) that has thus far achieved a sort of arthouse breakthrough in a number of major American cities. As the Iranian journal *Film International: A Cross-Cultural Review* notes, the film (based on a screenplay by Abbas Kiarostami), was originally conceived as a "short 16mm film," and benefits from Panahi's long apprenticeship in the cinema to Kiarostami. *The White Balloon* uses non-professional actors, and is, in contrast to some of the other Iranian films discussed here, a rather slight work. Other Iranian films, such as Azizollah Hamidnezhad's *Earthly Stars* (1995), Dariush Mehrjui's *Pari* (1995), Behrouz Afkhami's *The Day of the Devil* (1995), Yassaman Malek Nassr's *Common Plight* (1995; Nassr, a graduate of USC's film program who returned to Iran to make films, is one of eight women currently directing feature films in Iran), Massoud Kimiaee's *The Business* (1995; a film documenting the plight of expatriate Iranians in Germany), and Mohsen Makhmalbaf's *Salaam to Cinema* (1995; a tribute to the first century of the cinema, using screen tests of prospective actors for a film he intended to produce after a more traditional narrative style, then abandoned when the tests proved more interesting than any artificially contrived script), demonstrate that the Iranian cinema is simultaneously daring and innovative, aiming for the same sort of iconoclastic brilliance that was the hallmark of the best of Godard and Truffaut during the '50s and early '60s, or Rainer Werner Fassbinder during his most prolific period. What we're being allowed to see of contemporary Iranian cinema in the United States is just the tip of an avalanche of alternative cinematic visions, ways of seeing which will substantially alter that which we now call a contemporary fiction film.

Werner Herzog declared at the Telluride Film Festival that Iranian cinema was one of the two really consequential cinemas currently operating in the world today. But will it get the international, or even national distribution that it deserves? Abbas Kiarostami remains the best known of the current wave of Iranian cinematic practitioners. The Iranian cinema is vital because it carries with it the wave of conviction inherent in any cultural revolution; these are filmmakers, much like the Soviets of the 1920s, who believe absolutely in the message that they convey in their works. And yet, unlike the often didactic films of Eisenstein and Pudovkin, which dazzle the eye but leave much to be desired beyond the most rudimentary narrative framework, the products being created by the current wave of Iranian filmmakers are simultaneously engaging and politically charged; it is also surprising that a number of women are working as directors within the Iranian cinema, and that, despite a cut in government subsidies, the Iranian cinema remains as vital as ever.

Of the Iranian films made under the new regime, I would single out Shahram Asadi's *The Fateful Day* (1995), Mohammed-Ali Talebi's *The Boots* (1993), Bahram Beizai's *Travelers* (1992), and Kamal Tabrizi's *End of Childhood* (1994) as being unique exemplars of a cinema industry that is flourishing both commercially and critically, although many of the values it espouses are foreign to Western sensibilities. Shahram Asadi's *The Fateful Day* is already an enormous hit in its home country, winning numerous awards at the thirteenth Fajr Film Festival, including best makeup, best set design, best musical score, and best direction of a second feature film. The film is based on a screenplay by Bahram Beizai which went unproduced for more than a decade, and was completed only after numerous production delays; indeed, Asadi wanted to make *The Fateful Day* as his first feature film, and even shot some footage for the project, but he broke off to produce his first feature *Avinar*, which dealt with the plight of a group of wounded Iraqis traveling to Iran. Asadi learned his craft as a filmmaker at UCLA and at the School of Cinema and Television in Iran; his style is something like that of David Lean in its bold sweep and color, but the sensibility of the film is entirely Asadi's own. Shoja Noori stars in *The Fateful Day* as Abdollah, a young Christian man in fifteenth-century Iran who has converted to Islam, and who seeks to marry Raheleh, a young Muslim woman. Despite the objections of Raheleh's father, Abdollah persists in his quest, and eventually the date of the wedding is set. The film begins with the pageantry of the wedding ceremony and its concomitant celebration; the film is a swirl of color and motion, fabrics and earth tones, as Abdollah and Raheleh prepare to begin their life together.

Just as the wedding celebration reaches its climax, however, Abdollah hears voices telling him to rush to the aid of Moslem bin Aghil, the third saint of the Shiite sect, who is engaged in a battle that will eventually result in his martyrdom. Though Raheleh's father and her three brothers oppose Abdollah's hasty departure, Abdollah continues on with his quest through the desert, through a phalanx of warring factions who seek to impede his progress, only to arrive at the battle scene too late to prevent a slaughter of cataclysmic proportions. As Abdollah collapses on the battlefield from a combination of heat stroke and exhaustion, two suns rise in the sky over the battlefield, a sign of the disastrous and decisive events of the day. At the conclusion of the film, Abdollah realizes that he has been called to the scene not to give direct aid, but rather to bear witness to the massacre, so that he may return to Raheleh's family and tell them what he has seen.

Asadi's direction of the actors is assured and confident, and the cinematography is vibrant and flowing, with all the technical polish and competency that one associates with a commercial Hollywood film. Indeed, one of the key characteristics of all of the films discussed here is their technical mastery, coupled with sensitive and skilled direction of the actors, and narrative lines whose outcomes are difficult if not impossible to predict in advance. In this particular case, the tale is well known to Iranian audiences, and so the result of Abdollah's quest is, for the most part, a foregone conclusion. But Majid Entezami's pulsating and hypnotic musical score draws the spectator into the film, which is a visual and editorial tapestry of interlocking mutality of gazes, as Abdollah's quest becomes an endless trek of seemingly impossible proportions.

The political implications of *The Fateful Day* are inescapable, as is the message of Kamal Tabrizi's *End of Childhood*, in which the four members of a typical family are forced to flee across war-torn Iran in the beat-up family truck, abandoning the former security of their home to seek safety from the invading forces. The film resembles Steven Spielberg's *Duel* (1971) in a number of respects, as the family is chased by a jeep containing two American soldiers, whose faces we never really see (much of the chase is viewed through the truck's rear-view mirror). As the film progresses, the father is forced to abandon the truck to search for water in the hills to fill the truck's leaking radiator; as he departs, the father charges his young son with the protection of his wife and daughter. Clocking in at a tight seventy-seven minutes, the film depicts (with a series of sinuously interwoven Alain Resnais–style flashbacks) how the young boy learns, in the heat of battle, how to drive the family's truck to escape his would-be captors, and how he eventually kills one of the American soldiers with a primitive rifle to protect his mother and sister, while the soldier is armed with a rapid-fire Uzi-style machine gun. Perhaps the most sinister moments in the film occur in a protracted sequence in which one of the American soldiers, whose speech is limited to a series of guttural grunts, approaches the truck with the intention of slaughtering the young boy, his mother and sister, while tunelessly whistling the theme song from the Mickey Mouse Club as a sort of endlessly repeated mantra invoking the banality of American culture.

Mohammed-Ali Talebi's *The Boots* reminds one of Marcel Hanoun's *Un Simple Histoire* (1960) in its simplicity, its elegantly concise construction, and its depiction of a strong relationship between a mother and her daughter. The film's narrative strand is slight; a very young girl, perhaps four or five, wants a new pair of shiny red boots more than anything in the world, and eventually, after repeated entreaties, the mother capitulates to the child's demand. However, as mother and daughter return from their shopping expedition, one of the boots is lost on the bus. A young boy with only one leg, who is a neighbor of the little girl, eventually finds the lost boot just as it is about to be cut up into scrap rubber. As soon as he returns the boot to the young girl, the boy mysteriously disappears. The shortest of the films discussed here, *The Boots* runs one hour in length, but it contains enormous dramatic impact within its brief compass. It is also the most naturalistic of the films examined within the text of this piece, with a feeling of Rossellinian dailyness it both its settings and its utilitarian mise en scène.

An altogether different sort of film is Bahram Beizai's *Travelers*, which begins with a group of people preparing to travel to a wedding. As the members of the group leave their house, the woman who is the nominal leader of the group directly addresses the camera and tells the members of the audience that "we're all on our way to a wedding. But we won't arrive. We'll all be killed in a car crash." Thus the narrative sets up considerable tension from the first moments of the film, as the editorial syntax of *Travelers* cuts back and forth between the progress of the doomed group down the highway, and the members of the wedding household who await their visit. Eventually, the news of the crash reaches the members of the wedding, who transform the festive occasion into a time of mourning, with the exception of the family's grandmother, who remains convinced that the travelers will arrive. The doomed group had been carrying a mirror to the ceremony, an heirloom which has been in the family for generations, and as no fragments of the mirror were found at the supposed crash site, the grandmother remains convinced that news reports of the crash are in error.

Throughout the film, Beizai's Ophulsian camera movements glide between the various members of the household, increasing and mirroring the mounting tension as the viewer is forced to decide whether or not the grandmother is correct in her assumption, or (as most of the wedding guests surmise) hopelessly deluded. The film's triumphant climax occurs as the grandmother encourages the bride-to-be to don her wedding dress, as a sort of talisman to welcome the travelers, who do, finally, arrive at the wedding, to the astonishment of the rest of the company. But the conclusion of Beizai's *Travelers* is certainly open-ended: as the members of the supposedly doomed group glide into the room in a Spike Lee–like "trance dolly," they are bathed in a blinding bluish white light, carrying the mirror before them as a shield, or a sign, of their visit to the wedding. Beizai cuts to a series of mirror point-of-view shots to accentuate the spiritual powers of the reflecting glass, and resolutely refuses to tell the members of the audience whether we have witnessed a miracle (the return to life of the presumed dead), or whether, in fact, the police reports have been erroneous. Beizai's film affects us as viewers through the direct address of its imagery—what effects there are in the *Travelers* are achieved entirely "on the floor" (that is, during the actual shooting of the film), and not in post-production.

Nor is this renaissance of cinema confined solely to Iran. I would argue further that it is in the Middle East and Africa that some of the most affecting and effective filmmaking is currently being accomplished, usually on shoestring budgets. In Senegal, the cultural influence of the work of Ousmane Sembene looms large with such works as *Barom Sarret* (1964), a brutally economical short film about an African cart driver who daily struggles for both sustenance and self-respect; *Tauw* (1972), a half-hour film in which the protagonist, Tauw, seeks to build a new life for himself and his fiancée over the unreasoning objections of his father, and of a social system that conspires to keep him both unemployed and unempowered (in one sequence, for example, Tauw pays one hundred francs to gain admittance to a construction yard where day-laborer jobs are being offered; once inside, he is told there are no jobs available); and *Guelwaar* (1993), a leisurely yet impassioned comedy/drama in which the remains of a political activist are accidentally interred in the wrong grave. In addition, Sarah Maldoror's *Sambizanga*, made in Angola in 1972, offers a compelling tale of an underground political movement which seeks to overthrow its colonialist masters; Mahama

Johnson Traoré's *Njangaan* (Senegal, 1974) presents a searing indictment of the outdated and corrupt Koranic school system which exploits children without educating them (in the movie they are forced to beg for their physically abusive teachers, until the young protagonist is accidentally run over by the car of a government minister; in the final scene, two corrupt government officials decide that the boy's body should be used for medical experiments at the local hospital); and Désiré Ecaré's *Faces of Women* (Ivory Coast, 1985), which uses a two-part structure to partially mask the fact that the film was made over a ten-year period. Due to lack of funding, Ecaré was only able to complete the film in 1983, followed by two years of post-production work. The film was then presented triumphantly in the West at numerous festivals and special screenings. A sensuous and beautifully raw film, *Faces of Women* offers compelling evidence that a document of feminist self-empowerment can be constructed under the most difficult and precarious economic circumstances, while simultaneously sacrificing nothing in its untrammeled depiction of feminist desire and economic self-advancement. Ababacar Samb's *Jom: The Story of a People* (Senegal, 1982), uses a multi-leveled story structure to tell the tale of a *griot* (or storyteller). The storyteller relates to the members of his community tales of resistance and survivalist instinct from the period of colonial domination of that nation in the early part of the twentieth century in a series of dazzlingly beautiful tableaux photographed in lush, evocative color; four connected tales are presented within the brief compass of an eighty-minute running time. Such films as Cheick Oumar Sissoko's *Guimba the Tyrant* (Mali, 1995), a historical/political spectacle of immense scope and ambition, and Bassek ba Kobhio's *Le Grand Blanc de Lambarene* (Cameroon, 1995), a revisionist study of the work of Albert Schweitzer (which presents the physician as a cultural interloper and falsely paternalistic figure), carry forward this traditional of reinvention of identity and cinematic style, as directors from these various African nations seek a means and a method for presenting their shared histories to the members of their own nations, and then disseminating these visions to the world.

In the Middle East, such films as Shadi Abdes-Salam's *Night of Counting the Years* (Egypt, 1969), Abd al-Rahman al-Tazi's

Badis (Morocco, 1989), Kahlid Siddiq's *The Cruel Sea* (Kuwait, 1971), Maroun Baghdadi's *Little Wars* (Lebanon, 1981), Muhammad Lakhdar-Hamina's *Chronicle of the Years of Embers* (Algeria, 1975), Usama Muhammad's *Stars in Broad Daylight* (Syria, 1988), Youssef Chahine's *Cairo Station* (Egypt, 1958), and Nouri Bouzid's *Man of Ashes* (Tunisia, 1986)—to name but a few films from the emerging Arabian renaissance—combine to create a compelling vision of a world in which beauty, love, faith, desire, betrayal, loyalty, cruelty and mysticism intermingle with the daily struggle to survive, and a vision of the emerging character of these emerging nations. *Night of Counting the Years*, with its hypnotic "drone" soundtrack and coolly contemplative camerawork, reminds one inescapably of *L'Immortelle* (1963), Alain Robbe-Grillet's first feature. As in *L'Immortelle*, the past, present, and future are presented as one continuous strand of experience as *Night* traces the destinies of a group of tribal graverobbers who despoil the tombs of the dead, to sell golden ceremonial antiquities on the black market. Every move in *Night of Counting the Years* is measured, contained; it is the vision of a master of the cinema, an artisan with a supreme command of the medium of the moving sound/image construct. *The Cruel Sea* recounts how impoverished citizens of Kuwait had to make their living diving for pearls under impossibly dangerous conditions, before oil exploded on the international market as a dominant import; in its depiction of the plight of the men who go to sea for six months at a clip in search of the financial independence, the film is bleak and uncompromising, climaxing with the death of its protagonist, and suitably photographed in raw, documentary black and white. Abd al-Rahman al-Tazi's *Badis*, one of the most arresting of the new films from Morocco, recounts the tale of two young women who seek to escape an island prison camp, and thus free themselves from the continued abuse of the men who dominate and circumscribe the tedious days of their existence. Reminding one of Godard's *Le Mépris* (1963) in its audacious use of primary colors (particularly deep Mediterranean blues and reds) as part of its chromatic composition, *Badis* concludes with the flight of the two women across the beach, after they drugged their tormentors with Valium; the men of the village, aroused by the owner of a local cafe, successfully track the women down and ritually stone them to death. Mixing the sublime (in the scenes where the women dance for each other, demonstrating performative gestures of pleasure which they would never dare to present in public) with the barbaric (it is, ironically, the older women of the village who lead the final stoning which kills both women near the end of the film), *Badis* is a stunning and unjustly marginalized achievement that deserves the widest possible distribution.

There is thus a humanist rawness in the vision of the new Iranian, Middle Eastern, and African cinema that offers an appealing alternative to the hypercooked, intensely calculated, computer-generated non-reality currently being offered by Hollywood. The American cinema, with its new reliance on the artificial as hyperreal, seems to be ineluctably suggesting that the "real" no longer satisfies audience expectations of "spectacle." Places, persons, and objects directly photographed and reproduced have lost their power to convince us of their phantom reality, just as special effects sequences in such films as *Jumanji* (1996) must operate through an excess of spectacle to even momentarily divert the film's audience. As with enunciated special effects sequences, the actual in the classical Hollywood cinema is no longer "actual" enough, because we are directly aware that we are witnessing only an illusion, an unspooling of light on to the screen. As everything becomes possible, *nothing* becomes possible. An excess of spectacle has led to the collapse of the contract between the film and its audience.

SPECTACLE AT MILLENNIUM'S END

The cinema is not ending with the turn of the century, but is rather engaging in a process of continual renewal and transformation that will lead it beyond the realms of theatrical projection and/or home video into an entirely new arena of image construction, storage, and retrieval. We are in the age of "the moving image," no matter what delivery system is used to disseminate the finished products of our collective imagination. While nothing can replace the sweep and intensity of theatrical projection (whether 35mm, 70mm, or IMAX), we must recognize that this is only one of many possible ways to capture, analyze, and disseminate the images that move before our eyes like waking dreams. The future of cinema incorporates all known distribution methods, and extends beyond it into the Net, the web, and other methods/mediums we can now only hazard a guess at. We are certainly the custodians of the past of cinema, but we are also the heralds of the future of the moving image, whether on film, or video, or a chip, or a digital CD. The new technologies we are seeing now will only accelerate their hold on the public consciousness in the decades to come, and in the end, I think, the practice and reception of cinema will become more democratic because of it. The past of the moving image belonged to the few; the future, it seems, will belong to almost everyone with a Camcorder, or a computer with access to the web. It may not be the end of cinema, then, but the end of privilege, for now the methods of sync-sound image capture/reproduction belong to us all. With distribution on the web, and the use of concomitant delivery systems, more people than ever before will have a platform from which to present their vision of the world.

I certainly do not argue that this will create a utopia, nor do I claim that what is coming will be as comfortable and reassuring as the stories the moving image has brought us in the past; the independent theatrical films of today, such as Hettie McDonald's *Beautiful Thing* (1996), Larry and Andy Wachowski's *Bound* (1996), David Cronenberg's *Crash* (1996), Allison Anders's *Grace of My Heart* (1996), Doug Pray's *Hype* (1996), Michael Winterbottom's *Jude* (1996), Hirokazu Koreeda's *Maborosi* (1996), John McNaughton's *Normal Life* (1996), Adam Taylor's *Palookaville* (1996), Abel Ferrara's *The Funeral* (1996), and many other contemporary films offer us revisionist visions of the past and present not as we would wish it, but rather visions of bleak isolationism, meaningless violence, or unending human need. These highly personal visions are not designed to pacify or satiate, but rather to enrage and engage their audiences, and so, perhaps, cause them to question the finely contoured edges of their collective existence. The moving images that drift through the space of the Internet are even more unfettered by the inevitable demands of commercial production, no matter how modest the exponential scale. The personal is now the visual, and each of us is now an image maker, sharing the same ground once occupied by Ford, Hawks, Griffith, Arzner, Lupino, Crosland, Ulmer, Deren, and others who sought for themselves dominion over the darkness that constitutes the theatrical cinema projection device known as the "cinema."

The end of the classical cinema, when, as Andrew Sarris put it, films were constructed like Gothic cathedrals, brings with it the dawn of the individual as image maker. If the distribution mechanism afforded by the web can be equitably maintained (and this may be difficult), we can look forward to a turbulent yet transcendent future, in which TV viewing drops as computer use goes up, people interact with each other more on a global scale, and the dissemination and transmission of images moves beyond all known boundaries into the unknowable zone of the world as the simultaneous creator, and consumer, of the future of the moving image. If this model is not attained, we will be faced with yet another commercial transmission system controlled by such giant corporations as Microsoft, laced with heavy advertising, minimal context, shattering the individual "self" into a thousand uncontained segments, each one representing the death of an individual who is fragmented each time s/he logs on to the internet. Yet no one can argue that which we now call a "movie," or an evening at the cinema, is rapidly being reconfigured by a host of social and/or cultural factors, as well as the incessant impact of evolving technology. What form the final transformation of this thing we call a "movie" will take is at this point unknowable.

CHAPTER TWO

Images of Empire Lost
(Losey, Wallace, and the Danzigers)
and Empire Regained
(the Sankofa Collective)

JOSEPH LOSEY'S *ACCIDENT*

Of all of Joseph Losey's films, I have always admired *Accident* (1967) the most, even when placed side-by-side with *The Servant* (1963) or *These Are the Damned* (1962), Losey's two other key works of the 1960s. *Accident* holds a claim on one's memory by virtue of its timeless embrace of eternal youth and endless summers—what the artist Joseph Cornell referred to as the "centuries of June." *Accident* moves in a world that is privileged, stillborn, insular, and sodden with alcohol; it is also a world of great beauty and sudden death, power and weakness, splendor and decay. The film represents an idyll, a high-water mark in the careers of Harold Pinter, who wrote the screenplay based on Nicholas Mosley's novel; of Joseph Losey, who brought Pinter and Mosley's vision to the screen; of the actors Dirk Bogarde, Stanley Baker, Jacqueline Sassard, Michael York, Vivien Merchant, Delphine Seyrig, Alexander Knox, and Freddie Jones, all of whom have seldom been seen to better advantage; of John Dankworth, whose cool, sparse score epitomized the trancedout self-assurance of 1960s British high society; and of Gerry Fisher, the brilliant cameraman whose later credits include *Mr. Klein* (1975), *Fedora* (1978), *Wise Blood* (1979) and numerous other films, but who never surpassed the work he did on *Accident*, his first film as director of photography.

Shot "on location at Cobham, Oxford, London and Syon House, and Twickenham Studios [from July through] September 1966" (Milne, 189), *Accident* is a film of stasis and movement, celebrity and obscurity, clarity and internal chaos. It is also a film of supreme illusion. As Losey himself has observed,

> all those summer scenes were shot in icy cold weather, and a lot of it was rain . . . we would often prepare a shot for some hours and then get forty-five seconds to shoot it; and if it wasn't right on the first take, there wasn't time to do another; and by the time there seemed to be enough exposure to get another take, the sun had moved so completely that all the lights had to be changed. So it took us days and days to get that stuff. (Milne 113)

And yet this tedious process of perfectionism is precisely what lends the film its undeniable air of supreme, arrogant, delicious visual authority. Everything takes forever. The set-ups take forever, and the light is so fleeting that one can only count on a few minutes of precisely the right sunlight before the moment ineluctably slips away.

But it is in the essence of this process—capturing the same "forty-five seconds" of perfect light over and over again on successive days—that Losey found the inexorably unchanging visual universe ideal for Pinter's protagonists. More from Losey:

> The overall texture of summer sunshine was very important, and very hard to get . . . the texture of sunlight, I think, is probably one of the most important [visual aspects of *Accident*], not just sunlight, but sunlight coming and going, clouds moving, obscuring the sun and then revealing it, and the different ways things look when they're in the sun and when they're not, when they're in darkness or not. (Milne, 112)

The world of *Accident* is above all a world of light, and without light; of nights redolent with heat and torpor, and days of interminable beauty. Picnicking on the lawn, boating on the river, or ensconced in his rooms at Oxford, Stephen (Bogarde) is the sun-blessed intellectual who prefers to squander his days, and his talents, in pursuit of the ineffable—the dream of the eternal and immutable present. The world of *Accident* is summer, and the summer of *Accident* is the world entire for Stephen, Charley (Stanley Baker), Anna (Sassard), William (York), Rosalind (Merchant), and Francesca (Delphine Seyrig). One cannot imagine them existing in another universe. Like inverted vampires, they must live in the sun in order to exist. When they venture out at night, the results (as seen in the opening moments of the film) are usually disastrous.

It is altogether fitting that the two textual authors of *Accident* are present within the work, visually entombed in the world they have helped to bring about. Nicholas Mosley, author of the novel, is seen briefly as an Oxford don; Pinter appears as Mr. Bell, a mid-level executive at the television network Stephen so assiduously courts. For *Accident* is about celebrity, and the creation of images to support the myth of celebrity, and the jettisoning of outmoded visual constructs that no longer appeal to the public, or serve to propagate the myth of interchangeable celebrity. Freddie Jones, the "Frantic Man at [the] TV studio" is beside himself because he can feel his hold on the visual slipping away; Bell (Pinter), seated behind him in the sleekly impersonal space of the studio exudes confidence, and sports a feral grin. Charley is a televisual celebrity. He discusses books and cultural trends, wears the proper glasses to give him a more forbiddingly "intellectual" look, and holds Stephen in contempt because Stephen is unable to command a similar position.

Yet when Stephen tells Charley that he has "a meeting with *your* producer" during a particularly alcoholic and nasty supper at home, Charley is unnerved. Charley is disposable, just as Freddie Jones has been proven disposable, and perhaps, with some grooming, even Stephen can be tapped to replace him. Both men despise William as a shallow undergraduate whose chief attribute is his desirable girlfriend, Anna. During supper,

William becomes hopelessly drunk as Charley and Stephen exchange taunts over the dinner table, brutally competing for the ownership of televisual space, of Anna, of a claim on William's naive admiration. And yet both Stephen and Charley lack one essential element which William possesses in shameless abundance: youth. William is blond, conventionally handsome, athletic, and can easily best Stephen in physical contests (as he proves several times throughout the film). Both Charley and Stephen wish to possess William's youth, and with it his strength, so that they may in turn possess Anna, who admires the older men for their magisterial command of the academic world they all share. When William dies (at the beginning of the film; his presence is seen only in flashbacks) he takes his youth with him, but he also takes the abstract ideas of hope and possibility, of the future (any future) with him to his grave. Eternally dead, William is also eternally young, possessed of a future which, though removed, still radiates promise.

Eternally alive, Charley and Stephen are also members of the society of the living dead; all hope, all sense of promise, has been removed from their lives. They search for external validation (appearances on television, the possession of Anne) as proofs of their continued existence, but all these empty pursuits accentuate is the bankruptcy of their stillborn non-existence. Stephen and Charley have hit the glass ceiling of academe; they are afraid of scandal, afraid of reproof from the aging but implacable provost, afraid of their aging bodies, afraid of their inner vacuity. Their relationships are lies or competitions; Stephen is unfaithful to his wife Rosalind in the most casual manner, as if infidelity within marriage is both inevitable and ineffably boring. When Stephen meets Francesca in a shabby London restaurant, and then returns to her flat, their thoughts are heard on the film's soundtrack, but they have no need to actually *speak* to each other. Whatever they might say would be utterly banal (as indeed it is), so why bother? Stephen and Charley both inhabit a world they no longer believe in. They simply go through the motions, and repeat the required phrases, cite the appropriate texts. If, as F. Scott Fitzgerald observed, "action is character," by their assiduous non-action both Stephen and Charley *have* no character. All they possess is artifice, and even that is running out.

For both Losey and Pinter, collaboration was initially extremely difficult. Pinter's screenplay for Losey's *The Servant* (1963) was their first work together. On that film, Losey noted that Pinter had

> already written a screenplay which I thought was 75 percent bad and unproduceable, but had a number of scenes which were not changed as they reached the screen. I gave him a very long list of rewrites which enraged him, and we had an almost disastrous first session. He said he was not accustomed to being worked with this way—neither was I, for that matter—but he came to see me the next day, I tore up the notes, and we started through the script. (Milne, 152)

By the time of *Accident*, the writer and director were working together much more smoothly.

> With Harold now [in 1967], it's a question of detailed discussion of intent; then he usually writes a first draft, which I comment on, and which he then rewrites; and there may or may not be small rewrites during the course of shooting—more often than not there aren't. I may ask for additions, there may be tiny things within a scene—[and] he's very often around during shooting . . . (Milne, 152–153)

Pinter was indeed "around" during the lengthy production of *Accident*.

Casting was also difficult. Bogarde and Baker had both worked with Losey before, but were perceived by the public as widely divergent cinematic types—Bogarde the repressed intellectual of *The Servant*, Baker the rough-and-tumble man of action in Losey's peculiar and atmospheric prison drama *The Criminal* (1960). The casting of Baker as an Oxford don, successful novelist, and television personality surprised many of Losey's intimates, yet in retrospect Baker was the perfect choice to play against Bogarde's mild-mannered, yet intensely pressurized, persona. Losey commented after *Accident* opened that "I thought the combination of Dirk and Stanley was a very good one, and it was one which was ultimately financeable, although with great difficulty. Also because I knew from several pictures, in each of which the performances are quite different, that Baker could do it. I always go with actors on feel, not on what they have done" (Milne, 165). Baker was, of course, delighted for a chance to play slightly against type (the thick eyeglasses helped, to a degree, in the transformation of his iconic presence), but what Losey was banking on was Baker's hyperaggressive sexuality spilling over into Bogarde's performance area, providing Bogarde with a presence of raw physicality to respond to (something James Fox couldn't provide in *The Servant*). In this film, precisely because he has so many confrontations with Baker, Bogarde discards his usual mask of passive acquiescence on a number of memorable occasions (the dinner table scene being one), to create a new and more charged persona, seething with frustration and barely controlled violence.

As Losey noted, the visual look of the film achieved by Gerry Fisher was the result of a good deal of patience and hard labor; it is also worth noting that Fisher was not his first choice as director of photography. "I couldn't get Douglas Slocombe," Losey told an interviewer,

> who was my first choice . . . I couldn't get Chris Challis. Gerry Fisher had been my [camera] operator on *Modesty Blaise* [1966], and I liked the way he worked. I gave him three days to decide whether he wanted to try as a lighting cameraman, whether he could, and told him if he said he could, I would accept him. In somewhat less than three days he said he could, and did, and he's done a brilliant job. (Milne 159)

So both in front of the camera and behind the camera, *Accident* was itself the product of a series of fortuitous acts of random chance and suggestion—but perhaps none so magically transcendent as the circumstances surrounding the scene between Stephen and Francesca.

Losey had decided that the scene between Stephen and Francesca, shot for the most part in a dingy restaurant (whose decor is dominated by a sign reading "Eat Your Meals Here and

Keep the Wife as a Pet") should be silent, with their thoughts heard on a voice-over soundtrack, while the actors' lips never move on the screen. Losey recalled that

> this happened partly because Delphine Seyrig was enormously busy and expensive and I got her to play the role on the basis of spending two days shooting in England. She came over on a Friday, we read and rehearsed, we shot the restaurant on Sunday, and the scene in the flat on Monday . . . she was gone before we saw the rushes on Tuesday. (Milne, 115, 117)

When "laying in" the voice over the silent shots, Losey discovered that although both actors had been instructed not to speak, they were making the tiniest, involuntary lip movements anyway, giving the viewer the suggestion that the characters are about to speak, but are too embarrassed to do so; or alternatively, and less poetically, that the scene is unintentionally "out-of-synch" (Milne, 117). Although these slight stirrings of the actors' lips are somewhat unnerving, and certainly unplanned, they do impart to the audience a sense of tension, failed communication, and unspoken desire, which is precisely the territory *Accident* surveys.

As one might expect, Pinter's use of dialogue in *Accident* is spare and minimal. In the opening minutes of the film, there is no dialogue at all, just the natural sounds of the English countryside at night, almost immediately punctuated by "a sudden screech, grind, smash and splintering" as the car carrying William and Anna accidentally crashes (Pinter, 219). Stephen investigates. His first line of dialogue is a single word, as he stares down into the wreckage of the car at William's lifeless body. "William?" he asks (Pinter, 221). As Anna emerges from the wreckage, Stephen suddenly screams, "Don't! You're standing on his face!" (Pinter, 222). As if fixed in a dream, Anna and Stephen stand next to the car, staring at each other, until Stephen scoops Anna up and deposits her by the side of the road. Through the next few scenes, as Stephen escorts Anna back to his house, there is very little said at all, and all of the dialogue belongs to Stephen. Anna remains mute, expressionless, stunned by the tragedy that has befallen her. Only when the police arrive to investigate the car crash does Pinter's dialogue take on the "normal" cadences of speech, and even here, the interrogation sequence is surreal, phantasmal.

As the film progresses, Pinter cuts from a mini-flashback of "Anna's shoe, standing, digging into William's face" (Pinter, 228) to Stephen's rooms at Oxford, where Stephen and William (we are now further in the past) exchange mildly confrontational ripostes under the pretext of a tutorial session. The real object of discussion is Anna, "Anna von Graz und Leoben" (Pinter, 229). Stephen is clearly taken with Anna, William is smitten with Anna, Stephen's wife Rosalind (in a domestic scene following this one; Pinter, 232–233) is clearly threatened by Anna, and Charley pursues Anna with arrogant and transparent lust. A long weekend at Stephen's house brings all these contradictory passions to a boil, and transforms the serene British countryside into a metaphoric and physical battlefield, as in the tennis game between Charley, Anna, William, and Stephen (described in Pinter, 245) and the brutal game of medicine ball between William and Stephen and an assorted group of jaded, male aristocrats which proceeds entirely without dialogue (as does the tennis game) (Pinter, 270–372).

Within the world of *Accident*, all is a contest. Manners merely cover up the savagery that lurks underneath the manicured surface. Within the context of this world of endless trials and rematches, William's death comes almost as a relief, because only death can take him out of play, out of jeopardy. By the conclusion of the film, in which Anna dumps Charley after their brief relationship (much to Stephen's ill-concealed delight), we have come to feel as trapped within Losey and Pinter's world as the protagonists of *Accident* are. And at the very end of the film, as Stephen gathers up his children, Ted and Clarissa, and takes them back into the house under a dazzling sun, there is no sound at all except for a replay of the car crash that initiated the film (Pinter, 284), directly indicating that the only escape from this hell of class privilege is death, and an ignominious death at that. None of the characters in the film derive any satisfaction out of their existence, with the possible exception of Anna (when she escapes from Charley's possessive clutches [Pinter

281–282]). Yet all of Pinter and Losey's characters will continue to play out their parts, silhouetted against a serene, bucolic landscape—a landscape of surface beauty and internal, ceaseless corruption.

Losey's visual style as he brings Mosley and Pinter's world to the screen is a study in contrasts. In some sequences, particularly the dreamy boat ride during which Stephen covets Anna while William poles along the canal, Losey changes camera positions with alacrity, framing Anna's legs, Stephen's crossed arms, William's pole refracted on the surface of the water, the figure of a swan unfurling its feathers with nonchalant ease. Supplemented by Dankworth's jazz-inspired score for wind and harp, the sequence effortlessly captures the rarefied atmosphere of academe at play. In opposition to this, during the kitchen sequence directly after Stephen's meeting with Francesca, Losey's camera runs for nearly six minutes without a break. In this lengthy scene, Stephen makes himself some scrambled eggs, while Charley reads a "confidential" letter that his estranged wife, Laura, has written to Stephen asking Stephen's help in patching up their troubled marriage.

The exteriors of the film are flooded with sunlight, but the interiors are drab and almost colorless, an effect that Losey admitted he was striving for. In an interview with Tom Milne, Losey noted that "on the interiors of the house, and also the colleges, the effort was primarily to remove colour, or at least colour that would be at all obtrusive; and at the same time to get cluttered interiors that were not purposeless, giving an overall sense of disorder" (Milne, 112). Stephen's isolated country house is a tangle of narrow stairs and warren-like rooms, offering neither comfort or any sense of real domesticity. Enormous amounts of alcohol are consumed throughout the film, ostensibly to blot out the emptiness of the characters' lives, but to no avail. As with Stephen's brief fling with Francesca ("a real lost night, which instead of relieving frustration, makes it worse," as Losey observed [Milne, 117]), the endless scotch and lager consumed by Stephen, William, and Charley will bring them no solace.

Significantly, Anna and Rosalind refrain from over-indulgence. Rosalind has a compelling reason for not drinking; she is expecting (with a good deal of stoic apprehension) the birth of their third child. Anna doesn't drink to excess because she wants to remain in control. Although superficially the film seems to center on three men lusting after Anna, in actuality the narrative of *Accident* is a demonstration of Anna's dominance of the social milieu the members of the group inhabit. When Charley orders Anna to "get the letter" that his wife has written Stephen, during the previously described sequence in Stephen's kitchen, Anna makes no response of any kind, forcing Charley to retrieve the letter himself. Although Anna offers to cook Stephen's eggs for him in the same scene, she is not the endlessly domestic drudge Rosalind has allowed herself to become. One might forcefully argue that *Accident*, in its own primitive 1960s fashion, is to some degree a feminist statement. Just as the protagonist of Chantal Akerman's *Night and Day* (1991) abruptly and wordlessly leaves both her lovers behind in that film's final moments, so Anna decides at the conclusion of *Accident* that she has extracted all that she cares to from either Stephen or Charley, and leaves Oxford for her home in Austria. This she does with the same sort of cool detachment that the character of Julie displays in Akerman's film; Charley's entreaties are powerless to hold her, and Stephen understands implicitly that "there's nothing to keep her here" (Pinter, 282).

The only clear "loser" in *Accident* is William, the young aristocrat who was "made to be . . . slaughtered" (Pinter, 237), as Stephen notes in his rooms near the start of the film. During the brutal game of medicine ball at Lord Codrington's house between William, Stephen, and the other guests, Stephen reminds William of his mortality and his class. "Isn't it true that all aristocrats want to die?" asks Stephen. "I don't," William promptly responds (Pinter, 270). But both references are far too ominous to be taken lightly. William is doomed precisely because he is too beautiful, too rich, too much in love with Anna, too dependent upon others for the knowledge he alone must gain through practical experience. Losey frames William throughout the film in a series of Christ-like close-ups, underscoring his imminent martyrdom, and yet for all of that, the viewer finds it hard to work up much sympathy for William. He is simply too naive.

Rosalind keeps her eyes shut to that which she does not wish to know, and Charley and Stephen behave like rapacious animals, satisfying their appetites of the moment without any regard for possible future consequences. Even just after the car accident, which had rendered Anna momentarily passive and semi-catatonic, Stephen disposes of the policemen and their routine inquiries, and can't restrain himself from raping Anna (Pinter, 274–277) in the bedroom of his home—while William's body is presumably on its way to the morgue. Stephen and Charley are absolute monsters, and they know it. They accept their living damnation with a certain amount of panache and style, even if that doesn't for a moment excuse their actions. Stephen's children are innocent bystanders in all of this, barely aware of what is going on around them, and both the children and Rosalind have been neatly packed away to "Granny's . . . for three weeks" (Pinter, 244) by the time matters have come to a head. Rosalind has implicitly agreed to live with the horrific situation she has helped to create through her indifference, and has given up any hope of real communication with anyone. If it is impossible to feel sympathetic for any of the film's protagonists then, Anna emerges as the narrative's victor by default, simply for having the presence of mind to flee from an impossible situation.

The sexual ethos of the 1960s is everywhere apparent in *Accident*; blatant infidelity is routinely condoned, no one seems to use any sort of contraceptives, and the issue of sexually transmitted diseases is never broached (at the time, of course, the existence of AIDS was unknown). For all their moral squalor, Losey finds the twilight world inhabited by Pinter and Mosley's characters both sensuous and sinisterly seductive. The endless days of leisure at Oxford must, of course, give way to a harsher reality in time, but in the static world of *Accident*, that day of reckoning exists in the dim and distant future, if at all. There is the sense throughout the film that one can play a seemingly endless series of highly dangerous games and still get away with it, because the safety nets of wealth, tenure, and class are firmly in place, and will scoop up anyone unlucky enough to make a potentially fatal misstep.

Near the end of the film, after Stephen's rape of Anna and the morning after William's death, Stephen receives word by telephone of the birth of his third child. Already, Stephen has begun to move Anna out of his life ("right . . . your handbag" [Pinter, 277]) so that Rosalind and the children can return. In his own view of events, Stephen has "scored" over Charley—he has taken Anna against her will, and it seems he will get away with it. As the dawn breaks over the university, Stephen helps Anna over the Oxford dormitory wall ("no one must see you" [Pinter, 278]), implicitly demanding Anna's silence in exchange for his silence about the still-murky details of the fatal road accident. To all of this Anna acquiesces. Stephen has too much power. During a final sequence in Stephen's rooms at Oxford, Charley, superficially shocked by William's death, still has the arrogance to believe that Anna will stay with him. Stephen knows better. In the exchanges of power which form the narrative of Accident, Anna has been a victim and a participant at the same time, the kind of moral (or amoral) multivalency that infuriates those who wish for clear-cut solutions to the vicissitudes of existence.

But where, then, is the real location of power in Accident? At what point does the narrative focus become fixed? At what juncture are we able to clearly discern the motives and values of the characters we've just spent 105 minutes with, as the final end credits for the film appear on the screen? I would submit that the struggle for power that informs the narrative of Accident implicates every one of the film's protagonists, even William, who is clearly seen as "too good" to survive in a world comprised of lies, subterfuge, and elaborate deceptions. The world of Accident is a world of fatal and continual moral compromise, in which every character is guilty of some sort of manipulation and/or vanity, and no one is entirely free of blame. Most critical analysis of Accident has focused on William, Charley, and Stephen and their ostensible mid-life crises as the central focal points of the text; I would submit that the central focus of the film is instead the visual and tactile world its denizens inhabit, a domain of summer sun and shade, drab interiors, freshly cut lawns, and genteelly shabby university libraries. As I read it, Pinter, Losey, and Mosley are saying that this environment of endless power and prestige has fatally compromised all of the participants in Accident. Anna may escape, but she will not escape unscathed. She will carry the humiliation and anger of her rape by Stephen with her for the rest of her life, to say nothing of the trauma of William's death, while Stephen and Charley will embark upon yet another round of senseless infidelities, as Rosalind and Laura look the other way. Life will go on. New students will arrive to be schooled by Charley and Stephen, but they will find to their dismay that the lessons they have to learn are very harsh indeed.

If the world of *Accident* is alluring and romantic in a decadent, excessive fashion, something like a fantasy of Lautreamont or Rimbaud, it is also a domain of endless, circular pain (witness the repeated car crash) and disappointment. Losey and Pinter have contrived to make this world real and immediate to us, but even as we are seduced by the luxurious aimlessness of *Accident*, the film's final frames serve as a warning. This picture-perfect world is a gigantic and alluring deception, and we would be well advised not to be taken in. Even for a few hours, to live in the suffocatingly perfect world of *Accident* is a trial. Imagine, then, what it must be like to live there for an eternity.

THE POST-COLONIALIST WORK
OF THE SANKOFA COLLECTIVE

In direct opposition to the work of empiricist Losey is the work being carried on by the member of the Sankofa Collective in London, which serves as the center of film- and video-making by some of the leading members of the Black British Cinema, particularly Maureen Blackwood. In late 1994, I conducted an interview with Blackwood at the offices of the Sankofa Collective in London. Blackwood offered me this account of Sankofa's genesis, culled from the Sankofa Papers, a series of loosely collated working documents that recount the history of the collective and the various films made by its members, past and present:

> Sankofa is a proverbial term from the language of the Akan people of Ghana. The symbol used to represent Sankofa is that of a bird turning back its head to look at its tail. This image signifies going back into the past and discovering knowledge that will be of benefit to people in the future. The current directors of the Sankofa Film and Video are Maureen

Blackwood, Robert Crusz, and Nadine Marsh-Edwards. Sankofa Film and Video was set up in 1983 by Martina Attile, Maureen Blackwood, Robert Crusz, Isaac Julien, and Nadine Marsh-Edwards to produce work which explores the diverse images available within black experiences, outside the realms of the exotic, the victim and the threat. Sankofa has gained world wide recognition for a range of innovative and challenging films which have won numerous awards. The company has secured financing from Channel Four Television, the British Film Institute, British Screen, and Sony (UK), amongst others. Apart from developing projects internally, Sankofa has, from the outset, been committed to providing support for aspiring writers and directors, often trying to secure funds on their behalf. (Sankofa Papers)

As Barbara Kruger notes, the Sankofa Film and Video Collective was just one of a number of independent film/video/audio production collectives that blossomed in the UK in the early 1980s as a result of the national Workshop Declaration of 1981, which gave "support to non-profit media production units. These workshops [functioned] as community focal points for education and training[,] and help[ed] produce media projects which could not be made through commercial channels" (143). This "racially sensitive cultural policy" (Kruger's words, 143) thus gave rise to Sankofa, the Black Audio Film Collective, and other radical film and video production collectives.

As Maureen noted, however, the matter of funding was never an easy battle, in the '80s or the '90s. When we spoke, Maureen had just finished *Home Away from Home*, an eleven-minute film shot in 35mm color in cooperation with Channel Four Television and British Screen Finance. Produced by Johann Insanally, the film was written and directed by Maureen Blackwood. Shot entirely without sync-sound dialogue, the film relies on the power of its visuals to carry the viewer along. *Home Away from Home* is described by Blackwood in the Sankofa Papers as being:

. . . a bittersweet film which uses minimal dialogue throughout[;] instead the "natural" sounds of the various locations, heightened and layered, form the soundtrack, which together with the body language and facial expressions of the actors tells the story. Miriam lives with her four children in a cramped suburban house near her workplace, Heathrow Airport. The constant passage of aircraft overhead only serves to remind Miriam of just how far removed from her rural African roots she is, or just how little her own children know of that side of themselves, especially her eldest daughter Fumi, with whom Miriam seems constantly at odds. A sequence of events lead Miriam to build a mud hut in her back garden, a magical space which takes her out of, and away from, the loneliness which crowds her suburban existence. Happiness is short lived, however, as Miriam's outraged neighbours bear down on her. (Sankofa Papers)

Maureen was justifiably pleased with the success of this modest short film, but seemed wearied by the continual struggle that is endemic to producing films of any length (feature or short) in Britain today. "I mean, who *are* we in Europe?" she asked me rhetorically. "Why do we stay here? Europe is swinging to the right, and the BNP (a British neo-nazi, ultra-rightish group) is gaining more power everyday." Maureen spoke about a trip to Milan where "a rather pathetic young boy gave me a fascist salute—and all I could do was laugh. I thought, 'come over here to Britain, dear—I'll show you a real one.'" The specter of racism in London did indeed seem everywhere apparent, as it does in major cities like Los Angeles and New York. Sankofa was continuing to function in the face of this fierce antagonism, but the toll of ineluctable racism was clearly apparent in the sadness of Maureen's voice.

"We're a 90s collective surviving on equipment from the '80s," she said in our interview.

We teach the fundamentals of filmmaking here, to people who might not get the opportunity otherwise. How to shoot film, how to shoot video, how to edit, access to equipment, how to write scripts—we keep it simple. We're a resource to the Black British Community. Channel Four and British Screen are our main distribution outlets—without them, God knows what we'd do. Black people have different stories to tell than whites do, and that's what we're about here. Whites also have stories they tell amongst themselves, but the work we do here is showing black people how to tell the stories that matter to them.

And yet, the cultural climate in Britain was clearly less hospitable than it had once been. As far as Maureen was concerned, Britain had never really left the Thatcher/Reagan era. "It is a struggle, it really is. We try to keep up and move along, move ahead. But as you can see, our offices are hardly what you'd call posh. We can only survive here because the British Film Institute pays the rent on our offices and production facilities. It's very fragile, very tenuous. This support is absolutely essential to our work." She paused to stir her tea reflectively. "We're struggling here."

I suggested that perhaps the best way out was "up," into feature filmmaking that reached a wider audience. Two major black British filmmakers have, in fact, made this jump. Isaac Julien made his move with *Young Soul Rebels* in 1991 (produced in association with the Sankofa Collective, Channel Four, Le Sept, and Kinowellt). *Young Soul Rebels* has been described as an "ambitious drama about the clash of cultures in Britain [that] centers around two English friends [who] run [a] pirate radio station in London's East End, and find themselves caught up in an investigation between law and order [,] rich and poor" (Scheuer, 1217). The ninety-four-minute film (which won the Critics Week Prize in Cannes in 1991) opened to generally excellent reviews and good business, and Julien was tabbed as a young director to watch. However, after the success of *Young Soul Rebels*, Julien left the Sankofa Collective (although producer Nadine Marsh-Edwards stayed on with the group).

Ngozi Onwurah was another young black director who made the jump to feature films. Her *Welcome II the Terrordome* was featured on the cover of *Time Out*, London's influential entertainment guide, in an article on the new wave of young British filmmakers—a group that the magazine dubbed "The

Brit Pack." Both Julien and Onwurah were veterans of the independent Black British Cinema. Julien, of course, was one of the founding members of the Sankofa group, and one of its most prolific directors: his films with Sankofa include *Territories* (1984), *This Is Not an AIDS Advertisement* (1987), and *Looking for Langston* (1988); he also co-directed *The Passion of Remembrance* with Maureen Blackwood in 1986. Onwurah, though not associated with Sankofa directly, was very much "on the scene" during this era of early black British independent cinema, creating her own short films (*Coffee Colored Children* [1988], *The Body Beautiful* [1991], and *And Still I Rise* [1993]) before directing the feature film *Welcome II the Terrordome* in 1993–1994 (the film was released in 1995). So what about this strategy of feature film production as a possible solution, I asked?

"Well, if Ngozi wants to do action pictures, so OK, why not?" Maureen responded. "There are many stories to tell. Making the jump to features is a possibility, but there are trade-offs. It's incredibly expensive, it uses up your energy for several years, and I'm not sure I want to do that. I think it's important that we do what we do, addressing cultural themes and encouraging younger filmmakers. We want to try to provide access to tools for the next generation of artists." Robert Crusz is an excellent example of someone who worked his way up through the ranks of Sankofa: starting as a production assistant on *Looking for Langston* in 1988, he moved up to the director's chair for the 1992 Sankofa production *Inbetween*, which he also wrote and produced. Still, through the interview I got the feeling the entire enterprise of film production was becoming ever more difficult on an independent scale in England, as it certainly is in the United States. Between 1988 and 1992, production at Sankofa came to a standstill, and it was only after the Sankofa board of directors reconsolidated the collective's sense of Sankofa's mission as a force for independent cinema that *Inbetween* appeared in 1992. To date, Sankofa has produced ten films directly: *Territories* (1984), *The Passion of Remembrance* (1986), *This Is Not an Aids Advertisement* (1987), *Looking for Langston* (1988), *Dreaming Rivers* (1988), *Perfect Image?* (1988), *Young Soul Rebels* (1991), *Inbetween* (1992), *A Family Called Abrew* (1992), and *Home Away From Home* (1993).

Production values vary widely on Sankofa films. *The Passion of Remembrance* (1986), directed by Blackwood and Julien and produced by Martina Attile, mixes electronically and photographically manipulated newsreels and "found footage" with spoken commentary delivered directly on camera and brief sequences of staged narrative. At eighty minutes, it is the longest of the Sankofa films, and the diversity and audacious intensity of its fictive/factual mix is reminiscent of Godard's Dziga Vertov political films, or one of Valie Export's "collage narratives." Of *The Passion of Remembrance*, Blackwood and Julien wrote:

> This film gives a mosaic impression of the different dimensions of a black experience lived and imagined by a new generation of filmmakers in the UK. In its particularly eclectic style, the film poses some important questions within the drama. What emotions remain in the silences left by the unfinished business of the 60s and 70s—the continuing business of sex and gender? What other forms of representations of young black people are possible outside those traditionally constructed—"sports, entertainment, that's all we're good for." What happens when the dancing stops.
>
> In the Speakers Drama, the black woman and black man meet and engage momentarily in an anonymous landscape for the first time or the last. They talk of how each other's past has shaped the present. The complexities of sharing dialogue fraught with tension—and longing. Maggie's Drama explores the personal histories of the Baptiste life and identities—suggest a totality and diversity of the Black experience—a UK experience. It signals historical instances, instances in which memories of generations overlap, sometimes igniting as they fuse with present realities.
>
> Intertwined with these two segments of the film is Maggie Baptiste's video document of images of an England fractured through the decades. It shows images of protest and celebration—vibrant and dangerous. The Struggle is defined to meet the demands of sexuality and gender—demands that have always been there. (Sankofa Papers)

But creating work as a member of a politically committed collective has its drawbacks. As Julien noted in a 1988 interview with Lynne Jackson and Jean Rasenberger on *The Passion of Remembrance*,

> you must give up individual decision-making privileges once you start to work in a collective . . . everyone chose different spaces and areas of knowledge that they wanted to work on for the project. Then we all came together again . . . rewriting and unwriting through a collective process . . . Maureen directed the Speakers landscape and I handled Maggie's Drama. In the editing process, collective decisions were made through the second rough cut. (Jackson and Rasenberger, 23)

Reading between the lines, the tension that would disrupt the group later that same year (1986) is readily apparent. Blackwood's voice is notably absent from this interview, and it seems clear that Julien regrets surrendering even a degree of his artistic autonomy.

In contrast, Blackwood's *Perfect Image?*, made two years later in 1988, is a much slicker film in its visual presentation, with fewer ragged edges, but it is a film in which "seamless" technique subdues the work's often powerful message. It is also a "non-collective" work, made during the year of greatest internal tension within the group, as Blackwood, Attile, and Julien all went their separate artistic ways (while ostensibly remaining within the Sankofa group) producing three "solo" films. However, *Perfect Image?*'s visual surface is so alluringly professional that the film remains one of the most "prized" Sankofa films, and was judged Winner, Best Film, Black Filmmakers' Hall of Fame, 1990; and Winner, Best European Short Film, Créteil et du Val De Marne Films De Femmes Festival, 1989. Blackwood describes the film as an

> . . . exploration of "self" through multiple eyes. Using two actresses who constantly change persona, the film throws up questions about self worth in a variety of ways. A Chorus of women takes us through the action, sometimes mis-

chievous, sometimes sympathetic. They add another layer of "wordsound" to this short film. Using a mainly jazz soundtrack, *Perfect Image?* draws on the art of personal testament and the ritual of insult to ask questions relating to how black women see themselves/each other and the pitfalls that await those who internalize the search for that *Perfect Image?* (Sankofa Papers)

In contrast to *The Passion of Remembrance*, *Perfect Image?* might well be an advertisement, so mainstream is its visual style. Cool dollies through an art gallery at the beginning of the film frame an aesthetic discourse on the self as potential other, and the self as a purely visual signifier; yet ironically, the polished sheen of the film's images reflexively critiques the very issues the film explores. The images of *Perfect Image?* are professional and polished, but the raw visceral energy offered by the whirlwind of disparate images harvested in *The Passion of Remembrance* is missing. Yet *Perfect Image?* succeeded in its informing ambition: it broke through on the festival circuit and helped solidify the public visibility of the Sankofa group.

Territories, in contrast, is a good example of the rough and tumble energy and imagistic ferocity of Sankofa's earlier films, and it created a series of shockwaves in the British filmmaking community when first released. Directed by Isaac Julien from a screenplay by Julien, Kobena Mercer, Paul Gilroy, and Michelle Cliff, the 1984 thirty-minute documentary was a groundbreaking and audacious film in every respect. Julien wrote of the film:

> *Territories* is a kaleidoscope of sound and image which challenges conventional modes of documentary in its focus on the representation of Black peoples and more significantly, the social context which limits that representation. From 1976 to 1984. From West London to Northern Ireland. The film traces not only geographical spaces but also those of Race, Class and Sexuality—spaces in which there is a continuous battle for representation, for control. The film embodies a critique of traditional ways of looking at Black Cultures and adds a crucial historical dimension to the populist view. The film forces the spectator to look

again, not in recognition of the reggae beat, the steel bands, the riots etc., but beyond that currency of symbols towards the forces that perpetuate and maintain their misrecognition. (Sankofa Papers)

But the tensions within the Sankofa collective were by this time coming to a head. Although Julien and Blackwood continued to function as a team, producing several films and tapes over the next four years, Julien wanted "to concentrate more on Queer work, that wasn't an area that Sankofa was particularly interested in . . . it's like the members of a pop group—they join up, do some work together, and then split off to go solo and do some independent work of their own. There was more to it, of course, but basically we were going in different directions" (Dixon interview, November 15, 1994). While Maureen Blackwood declined to address the circumstances that led to Julien's departure from the Sankofa collective, David Lawson of Normal Films told me in a telephone interview that Julien had been "dismissed—yes, I think that's the right word for it" from the Sankofa group (Dixon interview, November 15, 1994). Julien himself told me that there were other reasons behind the split that he didn't want to go into publicly, and I respect that. Nevertheless, it seems to me that whatever personal motivations may have been behind Julien's break with Sankofa, the principal point of rupture was ideological, exacerbated by differences of personal direction.

While Blackwood remained interested in issues of race, identity, and cultural heritage and examinations of the political power structure in the UK, Julien was moving into the intensely personal area of queer identity issues with *This Is Not an AIDS Advertisement*, a 1987 videotape dedicated to the memory of Mark Ashton and Lina Palmier. Julien's own description of the video is both modest and moving:

This short video tape combines mourning and celebration. Linking politics to the visual excitement of a rich video-art format, it uses images of sexuality to celebrate gay love and gay desire in the age of the New Puritanism. It constructs desirable representations of gay men at a time when others equate them with notions of illness and disease. The first half contains poetic images of death, sensuality and loss. The second half is more assertive and celebratory. Accompanied by a funkheavy soundtrack, the rap directs the viewer to "Feel no guilt in your desire" as pictures of male beauty move across the screen. (Sankofa Papers)

This film was followed by the more ambitious *Looking for Langston*, a forty-five-minute black and white film shot in 16mm, a film which, in Julien's words:

> . . . uses the life and work of Langston Hughes during the jazz/blues infused Harlem Renaissance of the 1930's and 1940's as one central motif for the representation of the black gay artist. The poetry of Essex Hemphill, the poetry and words set to blues music by Langston Hughes and other texts weave through the stylized dramatic sequences and archive material in a film which celebrates gay desire and laments the attitudes against those desires felt and expressed by contemporary society. (Sankofa Papers)

Looking for Langston remains one of the most critically successful films of the Sankofa group, and was honored at the Berlin International Film Festival, the Barcelona Festival, the Copenhagen Gay and Lesbian Film Festival, and the 2eme festival images Caraibes, in Martinique, all in 1989 to 1990. This film, Julien's last for Sankofa (with the exception of Sankofa's co-production with Channel Four of *Young Soul Rebels* in 1991), clearly showed the direction Julien was interested in pursuing in his work. It was during this same year that Maureen Blackwood directed *Perfect Image?* (1988), and fellow Sankofa Collective member Martina Attile created the thirty-minute, 16mm color film *Dreaming Rivers*, a project altogether different from both *Perfect Image?* and *Looking for Langston*.

Attile's film, which in her own words "illustrates the spirit of modern families touched by the experience of migration" (Sankofa Papers), focuses on

> Miss T., a dark-skinned woman from the Caribbean, [who] lives alone in a one-room flat. Her children and husband

have left their family home in search of new dreams, and Miss T. is left to indulge herself in her little pleasures and reflect upon her new found freedom. When Miss T. dies her family and friends gather at her wake. The tapestry of words that interweave the drama remain voices that convey the fragments of a life lived, but only partially remembered. (Sankofa Papers)

Winner of the Film Ducat at the 1988 Mannheim Festival, *Dreaming Rivers* is a hypnotic and hallucinogenic vision of the disruption of a life by the exigencies of modern existence, and a moving and technically accomplished piece of work. Yet for all this external affirmation, nothing could disguise the fact that Attile, Julien, and Blackwood were headed into very different aesthetic and ideological territories. 1988 was thus a watershed year for the collective, one which marked the moving away from the formative years of collaborative enterprise, into a group loosely supporting the activities of several widely different film and video artists.

Robert Crusz's 1992 documentary *Inbetween*, shot on location in Sri Lanka, was the next true Sankofa production after a hiatus of nearly four years. (*Young Soul Rebels* in 1991 was more of a personal project for writer/director Isaac Julien.) The internal tensions resulting in Julien's departure had clearly had an impact upon the group. When Blackwood herself returned to the director's chair in 1992 with *A Family Called Abrew*, a forty-minute color film shot in 16mm, it was obvious that priorities within the Sankofa Collective had shifted. *A Family Called Abrew*, while diverting and technically accomplished, is far more traditional in content and structure than the early Sankofa works. Although it received several awards at film festivals internationally, and won a major prize in the "Biography" section of the 1993 Black Independent Film Festival, *A Family Called Abrew* is never more than a gently nostalgic valentine for the now-lost world of "Black British people active in the worlds of boxing and music hall[s] during the 1900s" in the UK (Sankofa Papers). As Blackwood writes in her notes on the film:

The worlds of entertainment and sport have traditionally been seen as the two most viable routes to financial success

open to Black people the world over, with the achievements of African-Americans taking centre stage . . . By
turns warm and poignant [,] the film uses oral testimonies,
archive footage, and a sound track which features music
from the period, to chart achievements in these fields
which emanated from members of one extraordinary family [the Abrews]. (Sankofa Papers)

A Family Called Abrew never really questions the supposed "objectivity" of the so-called documentary format, and in
its surprising conventionality fails to address the larger issues
that Territories and The Passion of Remembrance so effectively
and audaciously explored. Significantly, the raw visual and aural
mix presented in Territories and The Passion of Remembrance
distanced many potential viewers, who consciously or unconsciously longed for the safety of conventional filmic suture, a
zone of protection distinctly not afforded by these intentionally
disturbing films. Neither Territories nor The Passion of Remembrance garnered the mainstream festival awards of the more
superficially accomplished later works. But the whirlwind
image and sound mix of the first Sankofa films stays in the
mind, precisely because of their crude energy, long after the
impact of the later, "slicker" Sankofa films has faded from
memory.
    Thus, the Sankofa Collective, and other collective
film/video organizations like it, whether they share the same
political, social, racial, and/or ideological concerns or operate
merely as commercial production entities, face a crisis of identity as they enter the 1990s. The "short film," or the film of odd
length (rather than thirty, sixty, ninety minutes, and so on) has
been so marginalized by current distribution practice as to be
almost invisible. Feature filmmaking is one way out, but the
costs and risks, as Blackwood pointed out, are enormous, and
directors are faced with the issue of becoming commodities
themselves, in order to effectively exploit their works within
the perimeters of mainstream cinema. Sankofa's early films, as
critic Barbara Kruger noted, were effective because they sought
to "break down the conventions of what is [an] 'appropriate'
Black visual production" (144). The current Sankofa films, how-

ever, seem more compromised than the early work by a desire to "fit in" with the world of film festivals, symposiums, and television distribution. What Sankofa attempts in the future is therefore very much an open question. But the legacy of the early Sankofa films remains, as does the need for revisualizing the black British identity (particularly in late 1990s Britain).

THE COLONIAL VISION OF EDGAR WALLACE

In direct contrast to the work of the Sankofa Collective, and seemingly at odds with Joseph Losey's work (but actually, I would argue, very much a part of it), is the literary project of the British colonial writer Edgar Wallace. Wallace's books have been translated into several hundred films, nearly all of which take considerable liberties with their source texts, yet which nevertheless bear the stamp of Wallace's unrelenting embrace of colonialist desire. In Wallace's case, one's examination of his texts is a difficult matter: if it is possible to find of interest the works of an author while simultaneously deploring many of that author's inherently held cultural prejudices, then it is possible to appreciate, on its own scale, the writings of Edgar Wallace (1875–1932), the phenomenally successful British colonial author whose work is all but forgotten today. And yet Wallace has much to tell the contemporary reader about the construction of the British Empire, and the inherent inequities that comprise that Empire's self-perpetuating social fabric.

H. G. Wells, Rudyard Kipling, Charles Dickens, and other Victorian/colonial authors somehow endure in the public consciousness, but Wallace has been all but obliterated from memory. He does, however, still command the attention of a few readers, and even has a scholarly society dedicated to the study of his works; his life and works are the subject of an excellent critical biography by Margaret Lane, *Edgar Wallace: The Biography of a Phenomenon*. This act of erasure, as I will argue, is not entirely surprising, for Wallace's fictive voice represents one of the last unexamined sites of British colonial discourse, sweeping across an astounding output of work as a novelist, short story writer, newspaper essayist, dramatic critic, playwright, and even as the director of some of the films made from his various texts. Thus, for many, Wallace is better forgotten than examined, as a literary relic of an age of social inequity and exploitation best left to gather dust on the shelves of the various libraries and bookshops where one can still find his mostly out-of-print texts.

But a closer scrutiny of Wallace's work reveals a series of structures that one can find of both great interest and usefulness in our present sphere of textual and social discourse. The works of Edgar Wallace represent nothing less than a blueprint for the hegemonic structure of British colonialism, and thus colonialism as practiced by other nations and societies. The narrative structures of his works offer as well a catalogue of the assumptions and unspoken rules and values governing colonial discourse, which is precisely why Wallace was such a popular writer during his lifetime, and why his work is unknown today.

A study of these texts can tell us much about an era that constructed and maintained one of the most spectacularly exploitational regimes in the history of Western social discourse, and as such, the works of Edgar Wallace deserve contemporary critical attention. And yet, even within these sites of colonialist despair, there is another voice speaking out in the best of Wallace's fiction, a surprisingly disruptive voice, which also should hold a claim on our attention. While Wallace understood "the rules of the game" of British colonial discourse all too well, we should remember that he was born an illegitimate child in the poorest of circumstances, and worked his way up from the bottom rungs of the social ladder using only his imagination, and his prodigious capacity for work, as his tools of empowerment. Thus it is that in many of his works, characters and events appear that seem to question the very colonialist structure Wallace so avidly upholds elsewhere in his writings; partly this is a function of his need to produce so much material to support his lifestyle and his family, but there is also an undeniable air of social criticism in much of Wallace's work, a sort of subversive criticism of the values and prejudices that he eventually was able to manipulate on his behalf.

There are at least two strands in Wallace's fiction: Wallace the colonial exploitationist, a racist and homophobe whose public pronouncements in these areas (as well as in other contested sites of social discourse of the era) were entirely in tune with the "othering" project inherent within British colonialism; and Wallace the surreptitious social critic, within whose texts one finds surprising endorsements of feminist self-determinism and racial equality, condemnations of socially inequitable structures, and a clear vision of his own limitations as a writer and as a person of circumscribed social/political self-construction. As Jonathan Dollimore notes, "what culture 'should' repress it actually begins to produce, and it produces it in the very act of repression" (187). In producing these sites of rupture, then, Wallace was acting as the manufacturing agent of texts grounded in an oppositional social discourse, however unintentionally.

During his life, despite a spectacular series of social and financial reversals that would easily have dissuaded a less resolute person from continuing work as a writer, Wallace was a phenomenon, a popular writer whose combined works sold more than fifty million copies in various editions. The public at large adored and embraced him; his works sold many millions of copies in England, the United States, and even Germany, where his work remains popular today in inexpensive paperback translations. (It is worth noting that Hitler found Wallace's novels subversive texts rather than escapist entertainment, as most critics have described his fiction. Hitler thus banned Wallace's writings entirely during the reign of the Third Reich, and Wallace joined the long list of forbidden authors who were clandestinely read as acts of cultural resistance in Nazi Germany; see Glover, 144). As Wallace's daughter Penelope notes, Wallace was the author of "173 novels translated into 28 languages, [as well as] 23 plays, 65 sketches [and an astounding] 957 short stories" (Penelope Wallace, n.p.); in addition Wallace wrote numerous reviews and articles for a number of London's most influential newspapers (particularly *The Daily Mail*), and served as a foreign correspondent on assignment in what was then the Belgian Congo in 1906 to 1907. Wallace also distinguished himself with his daring coverage of the Boer War, filing numerous dispatches from the battlefront, and served for a time as editor of the Johannesburg *Rand Daily Mail*. More than 165 films have been produced from Wallace's works, and one of his last assignments was the original scenario for *King Kong* (1933), which Wallace wrote at white-hot speed shortly before his death from pneumonia and other complications in Hollywood in 1932, while under contract to RKO studios.

Yet of all of Wallace's many novels, only a few remain in print today in England and the United States, and Wallace's work as a whole has been unfortunately slotted within the generic realm of "detective thrillers," when in fact Wallace wrote in a variety of narrative and/or fictive voices, producing science fiction, historical surveys, tales of feminist self-empowerment, social criticism, autobiography, as well as a number of crime and detective novels. In all of Wallace's best work, what carries the reader forward through the text is not the complicated solution to some self-imposed mystery, but rather the voice of the author as he creates his narrative, a voice which fairly compels the reader to continue through the text. There is, as it turns out, a very good reason for this. Edgar Wallace dictated most his work, either to a secretary (usually Robert Curtis) or into a Dictaphone using wax cylinders, and then left the actual typing of the manuscript to Curtis, who would then send it to Wallace's publishers.

Wallace's best works are the novels he dictated within the space of two or three days, completing an average text of seventy thousand words within the space of seventy-two largely uninterrupted hours. These novels constitute the bulk of his work. Other narratives, conceived and delivered as "serials" and composed a chapter at a time, are easily recognizable as lacking both the passion and fabulistic sweep of his more speedily composed texts. Nearly all of Wallace's novels originally appeared as serials, but to create his most exceptional fictive or factual narratives, he would shut himself up in his study with a Dictaphone, an endless supply of cigarettes and fresh pots of tea brought in from the kitchen by a servant at regular intervals, and dictate the complete book using only a bare outline of fifteen hundred words, in addition to a hastily composed list of character names, places, and a few scraps of additional material to be inserted into the narrative as authentic talismans of the material world.

Thus engrossed, Wallace would dictate his text around the clock until he was finished, and then retire to his bed to recuperate while Curtis finished the typing. Once he had completed his dictation, in fact, Wallace scrupulously avoided reviewing the typed transcript of his work; as soon as the typing was completed, off it went to Hodder and Stoughton, Ward Lock and Co., or one of Wallace's other publishers, and the author was free to contemplate his next assignment.

The subjects of his work were far more varied than is generally supposed. This wide range of subject matter, together with Wallace's compelling narrative voice, makes his current anonymity all the more difficult to fathom. For far from simply repeating a single formula without variation in his novels (as with Mickey Spillane, Ian Fleming, Horatio Alger, Sue Grafton, Dean Koontz, Stephen King or many other commercial authors), Wallace's work reveals a wide range of interests, theories, and deftly rendered characterizations, which linger long in the memory of the reader.

The best of Wallace's texts address an impressive scope of concerns, including feminist self-determination and self-actualization (*Barbara on Her Own* [1926; the dates given here are for first editions], in which Barbara Storr, a young shop clerk is propelled into a management position at a huge department store, and concomitantly to personal and professional success, despite numerous obstacles placed in her path); critiques of Victorian society (*Chick* [1923], concerning the affairs of Charles Beane, a young "commoner" who inherits a Peerage, and then works to bring about social change from within the system); science-fiction (the remarkable *The Day of Uniting* [1926], in which the British government conspires to keep from the public the fact that a huge asteroid is on a collision course with the Earth by staging a national Day of Uniting celebration, designed to bring all classes and races together under the umbrella of the Colonial Empire for one final gathering, before the entire world is destroyed); internal voyages of self-discovery (*The Books of Bart* [1923], in which Bartholomew Foreman, a young and rather impractical man, gradually awakens to a deeper understanding of the then-prevalent governing mechanisms of social intercourse, and effects a series of improvements in both his own life and the lives of those around him); psychological thrillers (*The Man Who Knew* [1919], whose protagonist, Frank Merrill, is revealed only on the last page of the text to be a schizophrenic, pathological liar); popular history (*This England* [1927], a series of essays on then-contemporary British life, and *The Black Avons* [1925], a four-volume history of the British monarchy from the Tudor dynasty onward); and even autobiography (*People* [1926], a remarkably self-reflexive text which many regard as Wallace's finest work).

Other Wallace texts of interest include the picaresque comic novel *The Brigand* (1927), in which social climber Anthony Newton, at length unable to obtain suitable employment because of an uncertain economy and a lack of "skills" despite a long career in the military, decides instead to become a career scoundrel. He derives his living from a canny exploitation of those who, in turn, would seek to defraud others, including a gallery of official public figures whose actions should be, but are certainly not, above reproach. The novel's voice is so unlike the rest of Wallace that one expects it to be the production of a twentieth-century Henry Fielding rather than an author nominally known as a writer of mysteries.

There is *Four Square Jane* (1929), chronicling the adventures of a working-class feminist Robin Hood figure, who redistributes the wealth of the ruling classes back to the poor who created much of this social capital in the first place; *The Lone House Mystery* (1929), the central protagonist of which, Joseph John Field, is a black British subject continually exposed to racist exploitation by the empiric authorities, a disempowerment Wallace chronicles with unsparing detail; *The Square Emerald* (also known as *The Girl from Scotland Yard*, 1926), which concerns itself with the career of Leslie Maughan, a woman fighting for gender equity while working as an operative of Scotland Yard (Maughan manages to solve the problems set for her within the narrative entirely without patriarchal intervention, it should be noted, and she emerges as a remarkably convincing embodiment of early twentieth-century feminist empowerment); *Captains of Souls* (1923), a compelling tale of the supernatural in the tradition of James's *The Turn of the Screw*; *Elegant Edward* (1928), in which an inept con man continually outsmarts himself through his own arrogance and greed throughout the length of the novel; and numerous other texts that deviate from the standard impression that one has of Wallace as being solely a writer of generic thrillers.

I feel I should now turn to some of the reasons why Wallace's work has been so thoroughly marginalized by contemporary readers and critics. Reading through his texts, one is struck both by the vitality of Wallace's imagination and his compelling skill as a narrativist; why, then, is his present reputation confined to a small coterie of admirers? I would suggest that one reason Wallace has been largely forgotten (along with a great many other deserving artists) is because he was a *popular* writer, whose works appealed to the public at large. Near the end of his life, the demand for Wallace's novels was so great that out of every four books purchased in England in the late 1920s, one was by Edgar Wallace. Such fantastic commercial success cannot help but inspire jealousy, and Wallace during his lifetime had to continually battle the most pernicious slander of all: that he employed "ghosts" to help him create his fiction. In fact, every word that Wallace signed his name to was created by him, primarily through dictation, and he was a master of "manuscript management," able to keep numerous projects moving at one time with the aid of his faithful secretarial staff, much as Erle Stanley Gardner did in his last years (dictating, at one point, three Perry Mason novels in rapid serial progression to a battery of stenographers).

This prolific output inevitably inspired a considerable amount of jealousy, particularly among those writers who were then competing for the public's approbation. Dorothy L. Sayers, Arnold Bennett, and George Orwell led the main critical attack against Wallace's work, with Bennett arguing that "Wallace has a very grave defect . . . he is content with society as it is. He parades no subversive opinions. He is 'correct'" (as cited in Glover, 153). This opinion cannot be entirely supported by a careful examination of Wallace's work. Wallace continually criticized Victorian society in his works, in matters both minor and major, as well as found fault with the gender roles assigned to men and women within that society. In addition, at his best Wallace was often roused to a passionate advocacy for the concerns of the disenfranchised, both women and men, as they fought against a monolithic power structure which sought to deny them effective agency.

In *The Man Who Bought London* (1915), Kerry King, an American millionaire, realizes an ambitious scheme to restructure the fabric of London's business district to the betterment of both workers and members of the general public; he appoints Elsie Marion, a young woman with enormous business acumen but little professional experience, as the agential force to execute this radical transformation of the metropolitan landscape. In his efforts, King is opposed chiefly by one Hermann Zeberlieff, a ruthlessly opportunistic opponent who engages an unceasing attack on King's social project. In the exceedingly bizarre conclusion of the narrative, Zeberlieff is revealed to be King's wife, who has been posing as a man for several decades to get ahead in the business world (which is seen by the narrative to be—quite correctly—hostile to successful women). This elaborate ruse is reminiscent of director Maggie Greenwald's film *The Ballad of Little Jo* (1993), which documents the life of Josephine Monaghan, a woman who passed as a man in the American West during the 1900s to avoid the harassment and gender inequities of the period directed against women (see Foster 1995, 156–158). It demonstrates that Wallace was aware of the existence of these unreasonable prejudices, and deeply sympathetic (as the last pages of *The Man Who Bought London* make clear) concerning the circumstances that would force the adoption of such an extreme plan of action.

While Orwell felt that Wallace displayed an almost messianic attitude towards the British constabulary (Glover, 153), in fact the figures of authority in Wallace's works are often seen to be arrogant, self-absorbed, and entirely incorrect in their apprehension of the events within the narrative. Thus it is that the detective Saul Arthur Mann in *The Man Who Knew* is paraded throughout the text of that novel as an infallible authority on human nature whom all the other characters defer to; as previously noted, it is not until the final paragraphs of the work that Wallace reveals that Mann has been entirely mistaken in all his judgments concerning Frank Merrill, the central figure of the novel. His supposed authority is thus both counterfeit and factually bankrupt. Throughout the novel, Mann steadfastly refuses to divulge the source of any portion of the vast source of knowledge he is supposed to possess. As the novel nears its conclusion, we are aware that this strategy is yet another of Wallace's "fronts," and an echo of the entire British colonialist strategy; Mann's false authority is solely the result of self-presentation as an oracular commentator on the fabric of the colonial criminal mentality.

Another reason for Wallace's relative obscurity is the fact that he wrote so much, and wrote it so rapidly. Wallace's prolificity became, much to his chagrin (but to Hodder and Stoughton's delight, who did everything to exploit Wallace's speed and facility, thus turning the writer into an exploited commodity in his own right), something of a public joke. Yet Wallace kept up the torrential pace of his output to support his lavish lifestyle—which included heavy losses to his bookmakers, for the sport of racing and betting on horses was Wallace's sole recreation.

This leads us to another problem in an accurate assessment of Wallace's works, both as cultural talismans and acts of literary text production. It must be admitted that much of what Wallace wrote *was* frankly second rate, churned out to keep his head above water financially. Wallace's technique of dictating his best novels in seventy-two–hour bursts also works against the enhancement of his literary reputation. This method of instantaneous text production goes against the time-honored grain of methodical craftspersonship, and a number of contemporary writers who lacked Wallace's facility were frankly jealous of his abilities in this regard. Yet both his publishers (Ward Lock and Hodder and Stoughton were his two chief representatives in this area) as well as those closest to him (his typist Robert Curtis and others) agreed that it was precisely these rapidly dictated novels, historical surveys, and romances that constitute the bulk of Wallace's best work. Swept up in the increasing pace of Wallace's most compelling narratives, the reader experiences her or himself in a trance, propelled forward through the text through the sheer force of Wallace's fictive voice.

Not surprisingly, these dictated texts have an intensity of address and a spontaneity of construction mirroring the gift of a superb storyteller at work; it can be argued that when one reads Wallace's finest texts, the page upon which his words are printed becomes an opaque or transparent medium designed solely as a matrix to convey the author's *voice* to the reader. The listener/reader is thus transported into Wallace's world directly through the speech of its author, and the actual text evaporates as the novel sweeps forward in an inexorable wave, enfolding both the characters within the text and the author of the tale being told.

There are other reasons why Wallace's works have failed, thus far, to receive the attention they deserve. Wallace's close associates were so unremittingly and continually involved in the creation of one text after another (in fact, Hodder and Stoughton gave Wallace an open-ended contract, guaranteeing to publish as many books as he could write, as fast as he could create them), that no one, including Wallace himself, had time to reflect upon past literary production. Wallace could not afford the luxury of even a brief respite from his writing schedule to evaluate his works; the demand for fresh product was always pressing upon him.

Thus, Wallace began to see himself (particularly after his success as a colonialist author was firmly established) as a sort of writing machine, and (partially as a device to fend off adverse criticism in advance) professed to find little of literary value in his works himself, when in fact it is well documented that he continually sought the advice and opinions of those around him as he worked. To complicate matters further, Wallace was paradoxically hypersensitive to the slightest criticism, and so those around him often learned to withhold their opinions rather than injure the writer's pride. Still, Robert Curtis and some of Wallace's other associates (including Isabel Thorne, a magazine editor who helped Wallace launch the ultra-colonialist *Sanders* stories, which arguably catapulted the author to his initial prominence) would often offer their opinions on an ongoing project. Wallace was also capable of destroying work that others considered not up to par: on at least one occasion, Wallace threw a large portion of a nearly completed novel into the fireplace after an editor whom he had submitted it to (Willie Blackwood) found it wanting (Lane, 296–297).

In the matter of revisions, Wallace generally followed a course charted by his biographer, Margaret Lane: initial refusal, then consideration of the requested alterations, then actualization of the proposed emendations, and finally agreement that the changes were all to the better. This was particularly true of his plays, which Wallace considered the most difficult writing he did; his best works as a playwright went through numerous revisions before they were presented on the stage.

The novels, however, went out to the publishers without change after Wallace dictated them; Curtis would comb through the manuscript for errors of fact and incorrect character identifications, but other than this cursory examination of the manuscript to be submitted, no other changes were countenanced. As a consequence, it has been left to contemporary literary scholarship to judge the best of Wallace on its own terms, and the best of his work in this respect, as I have argued, is very good indeed. But as most of the novels are out of print, unless one searches for them in second-hand book shops and university libraries (where many of these books can still be found), how is one to judge the quality, or the lack thereof, of Wallace's various textual productions?

FILMIC TRANSLATIONS OF EDGAR WALLACE

Another critical factor contributing to Wallace's canonical erasure is the extremely poor quality of most of the films made from Wallace's works: with the exception of *King Kong* (1933) and, arguably, Walter Forde's near A-level 1939 adaptation of Wallace's 1905 novel *The Four Just Men*, filmic adaptations of Wallace's texts fall into two groups. The first group of films begins with a series of silent British films made during Wallace's lifetime, including several directed by Wallace himself. The 1929 silent version of *Red Aces*, directed by Wallace, is typical of this series; it is a straightforward filming of one of Wallace's better detective thrillers, shot at the Beaconsfield Studios in the summer of that year, featuring Muriel Angelus, H. Cronin Wilson, Nigel Bruce, and others in what is a careful but unimaginative rendering of the original text.

These silent films were followed by an equally indifferent series of early sound films, made both in England and America, including Howard Bretherton's *The Return of the Terror* (1934), Walter Forde's *The Phantom Strikes* (1939), William Nigh's

Mystery Liner (1934), T. Hayes Hunter's *White Face* (1933) and *The Calendar* (1931, which despite its inherent staginess features lively performances from Herbert Marshall and Edna Best), and other modest productions that presented Wallace's texts as photographed stage plays, rather than as fully realized visual constructs. Wallace himself directed one talking picture, *The Squeaker* (1930), based on his novel of the same name during this period; it, too, is a static and unimaginative rendering of the source text.

These sound films continued into the 1940s with such projects as Columbia's *The Green Archer* (1940). This fifteen-chapter serial (seemingly an appropriate format for Wallace), so altered Wallace's text that only the names of the protagonists remained, with all of the author's original narrative structure replaced by an alternative (and rather weakly structured) plot line. None of these films adequately presented Wallace's vision, for all its inherent defects, on the screen.

More distressing still is the second group of films ostensibly based on Wallace's novels, made after a long hiatus in the 1960s, as German/British co-productions. Directed by Alfred Vohrer and a series of equally indifferent auteurs, these cheaply produced travesties update Wallace's works to a phantom zone of 1960s London, as haphazardly recreated on sound stages in Berlin, with liberal deviations from the original texts and enormous doses of sadism and violence added, which appear nowhere in the novels themselves.

Thus, Wallace's *The Dark Eyes of London* becomes *Dead Eyes of London* (dir. Alfred Vohrer, 1961), a brutally sadistic film with shoddy production values that wastes the talents of Klaus Kinski, among others, in an unpleasantly misogynist splatter film which elides the more thoughtful (and motivational) sections of its source text. Other German Wallace films made during the 1960s, including *Der Hexer* (dir. Vohrer, 1965), *Zimmer 13* (dir. Harold Reinl, 1964), *Das Phantom Von Soho* (dir. Franz Josef Gottlieb, 1967), and *Der Bucklige von Soho* (dir. Vohrer, 1966), pursued a similar strategy of sadism, general unfaithfulness to the original novels, and rock-bottom production values, which were further undermined by atrocious dubbing into English when the films were released in the United States and Britain.

A total of thirty-six 1960s versions of Wallace's films were made in Germany, Italy, and the UK during this second wave of production. While the films were phenomenally successful in terms of commercial audience response, the shabby violence, unconvincing sets, indifferent acting, and relentlessly *grand guignol* structures of these films permanently damaged Wallace's reputation as a writer, relegating him to second-rung cult obscurity, if he is remembered at all (see Schneider, particularly 59–64, for more on the production and reception of these films).

It should also be noted that in both cycles of Wallace films, but particularly in the second group, it is the author's more sensational texts that dominate the series of adaptations. This in itself is an editorial decision of major importance. Wallace's most restrained and deeply felt works—I would nominate *The Nine Bears* (1910), *The Fourth Plague* (1913), *The Man Who Bought London* (1915), *Those Folk of Bulboro* (1918), *Captains of Souls* (1923), *The Black Avons* (1925, a four volume historical work), *Barbara on Her Own* (1926), *The Day of Uniting* (1926), *Four Square Jane* (1929), *Planetoid 127* (1929), *The Calendar* (1930), *The Devil Man* (1931, a heavily fictionalized biography of Charles Peace), *On the Spot* (1931, a brutally efficient crime drama, which had the distinction of being produced on the stage with Charles Laughton in the starring role), and even the action thriller *When the Gangs Came to London* (1932)—have either never been produced as films, or produced as small-scale early talking or silent adaptations which cannot hope to have an impact upon the contemporary public.

In the choice, then, of those texts of Wallace's which have been brought to the screen, those novels by the writer that fall strictly within the crime genre have been favored to the virtual exclusion of the rest of his work. And, for the most part, those novels of Wallace that have been brought to the screen have been altered—often altogether mutilated in their execution—so that what finally emerges bears little relationship to Wallace's original conception.

This brings us to the central problem facing a more discursive understanding of Wallace's work: the author's resolutely colonialist discourse, which is present, in one form or another, in all of his works. There can be little argument that his protagonists are all white, for the most part young (played off against a gallery of older, sympathetic characters), but also that, like Kipling, Wells, and other empire-builders, Wallace's work is both racist and homophobic, often explicitly so. Furthermore, I wish to make it clear that Wallace's work is entirely intertwined with the politics of racial and social marginalization, and entirely a part of the overall British colonialist project; it is, for me, his mapping of this contested terrain of colonial exploitation which makes his work such an instructive site of critical discourse.

As recounted by Margaret Lane, when Wallace was assigned to cover the exploitation of native African labor and resources in the Congo in February 1907, he wrote an article for the *Congo Balolo Mission Record* in which he stated that "frankly, I do not regard the native as my brother or my sister, nor even as my first cousin; nor as a poor relation. I do not love the native—nor do I hate him. To me he is just a part of the scenery, a picturesque object with uses" (as cited in Lane, 213–214), once of many instances (in both his newspaper reportage and his fiction) of Wallace's shockingly vicious and callous racism, which is all too often present in his work and mirrors the attitude of many of his contemporaries.

Yet in another article, written about the Congo rubber trade during the same period, Wallace describes scenes of

> oppression and neglect . . . unimagined cruelties . . . already the Congo is to me a dreadful nightmare, a bad dream of death and suffering . . . when every law of man and nature is revolted, and the very laws of life are outraged. . . . In another place, and in other columns than these, I shall take upon myself the journalist's privilege of prejudging posterity's verdict. (as cited in Lane 213–214)

He seemingly contradicts his earlier pronouncements.

Wallace's colonialist experiences in Africa gave birth to perhaps his most famous, and certainly his most infamous texts, the *Sanders* series, beginning with *Sanders of the River* in 1911, and continuing on through a series of volumes chronicling the adventures of Mr. Commissioner Sanders, a British colonial officer posted in Africa at the turn of the century. As David Glover points out, there is considerable irony in Wallace being sent as a correspondent to Africa to expose the evils of colonial exploitation (most vividly recounted in E. D. Morel's 1906 text *Red Rubber*), and then turning the material from this expedition into colonialist literary capital to create "stories with . . . firm district commissioners, gullible missionaries, child-like natives and wily Arabs" (Glover, 147). Commissioner Sanders is treated as a deity in these stories, and sadly (but perhaps inevitably, given the realities of British film production during this period, and its insistence on perpetuating exploitational dreams of a vanishing empire) *Sanders of the River* (dir. Zoltan Korda, 1935), remains the one truly A-level production of any of Wallace's works, produced by Alexander Korda's prestigious London Films Company, with Paul Robeson and Leslie Banks in the leading roles.

In the matter of Wallace's homophobia, a trait he shared with many other colonialist writers, artists and political figures, perhaps no one piece is more eye-opening than his essay "The Canker in Our Midst," which appeared in the *London Mail* in 1926. As described by Margaret Lane, the article "was a blustering, intolerant, kick-the-blighters-down-stairs [essay] (313)," which managed to offend even a number of Wallace's colonial contemporaries, among them the noted theatrical personality Gerald du Maurier. When du Maurier and Wallace subsequently met for lunch to discuss the production of Wallace's play *The Ringer*, du Maurier had every intention of upbraiding Wallace for the piece. However, he eventually succumbed to the author's persuasive charm, and agreed to work with Wallace on his new theatrical project.

Du Maurier's opinion of "The Canker in Our Midst" remained unchanged. According to Lane, he felt that "the article [was shocking] in its brutality; it had been dictated—so it seemed to him—by the kind of mentality which makes lynching possible" (313–314). And yet du Maurier, many of whose associates were either gay or lesbian, ultimately agreed to work with Wallace on a string of productions, despite his grave personal reservations concerning Wallace's obvious prejudices in this matter.

There is certainly the figure of du Maurier the shrewd businessperson figuring in this, but perhaps du Maurier, as did others, recognized in Wallace an undercurrent of social criticism implicit in the precise mapping of the terrain of the inherently inequitable British social system, and thus assisted in bringing aspects of Wallace's work into sharper focus. The association with Gerald du Maurier was one of the more felicitous alliances of Wallace's later career, and allowed him to venture, as a playwright, beyond the commercially proven boundaries of the thrillers, which were demanded from him at increasingly regular intervals by his publishers and readers.

As disturbing as Wallace's jingoistic colonial racism and homophobia rightly are to contemporary readers, within the context of work written by his contemporaries and predecessors, one is confronted by the distressing yet undeniable fact that such deplorable and unenlightened attitudes were then common social currency—which does not make this any the more excusable, but does demonstrate a shared cultural deficiency common to nearly all British writers of the period. Kipling, Conrad, James, and others embraced the British colonial empire with equal fervency; in the early part of the twentieth century we are confronted by the anti-Semitism of Hemingway (the figure of Robert Cohn in *The Sun Also Rises*), Pound, Fitzgerald, T. S. Eliot and others, who consciously or unconsciously perpetuated the racist and homophobic attitudes of their milieu.

Were Wallace marginalized for the defects of his humanist vision in these matters, one would find his exclusion from the literary canon altogether justified. Yet the critical attack on Wallace, mounted by Dorothy L. Sayers, Q. D. Leavis, George Orwell, Arnold Bennett, and others was primarily an elitist cultural colonialist project of its own. It was centered around the creation of a series of rules governing canonical inclusion or expulsion, and concerned with Wallace's structural approach to his fiction and his undeniable popularity, rather than with his racial and/or sexual orientational prejudice.

Wallace's popularity was seen by these critics to exist at the supposed expense of "better" fiction. Nor were these criticisms confined to those who critiqued literature for a living. The political theorist and activist Leon Trotsky (who picked up a

novel by Wallace in 1935 while recuperating in his sickbed)
derided the author as "mediocre, contemptible, and crude
[. . . without a] shade of perception, talent or imagination" (as
cited in Glover, 143). Mystery writer and marketplace competi-
tor Dorothy Sayers found Wallace's work lacking "that quiet
enjoyment of the logical which we look for in our detective fiction"—thus neatly ignoring the rest of Wallace's considerable
output as a writer—although she admitted that Wallace's fiction
was "strong in dramatic incident and atmosphere" (as cited in
Glover, 150). On the other side of the critical coin, Gertrude
Stein enthusiastically stated (in her typically breathless style)
that Wallace "writes awfully well he has the gift of writing as
Walter Scott had it" (as cited in Glover, 144).

Q. D. Leavis, however, writing in 1932 (Glover, 144),
deplored the fact that Wallace's novels were so popular with the
public. Because of Wallace's success with the average reader,
Leavis argued, the public ignored works that might better their
intellectual faculties. This is the same elitist line of reasoning
that led Orwell to charge that Wallace accepted the status quo
without reservation in his fiction, thus consciously or unconsciously upholding the existing order of things—a charge that is
only partially true.

Orwell saw Wallace's fictive universe as being composed
solely of the empowered and the marginalized, a world where
luck played a role out of all proportion to all other mitigating
societal factors, and the institutions of government, church, and
racial boundaries were transgressed at both individual and societal peril. Yet a careful examination of Wallace's work reveals
that his tales are in nearly every instance documents of successful societal rupture, in which the carnivalesque triumphs
over the gossamer fabric of social institutionality. Agency is
power in the world of Wallace, and the true agency is often
entrusted in his fictive universe to those who have appropriated
it in direct defiance of the ruling order.

But perhaps the least remarked aspect of all of Wallace's
work is the manner in which he marginalizes not only the
Africans of the *Sanders* stories, or even the British non-natives
who populate the periphery of much of his work set in Victorian
colonial London (these characters thus constituting, in the

words of Mas'ud Zavarzadeh, the denizens of that fictive world which is "denarrated" within Wallace), but rather the ways in which even those members of the empire whom one might suppose would be enfranchised are continually relegated to the domain of the unseen, the subservient, the non-voiced and non-faced within Wallace's Orientalist world.

In *Dark Eyes of London*, Jake the executioner mimics Sanders the colonial empire-builder and civil servant, ready to commit murder in the name of the state at the slightest provocation. Both men act as agencies of erasure of all who would transgress against the established order of things. Both do the bidding of the agencies of power whom they respectively serve. Jake's master, John Dearborn, who masquerades as the proprietor of a home for the blind, is as corrupt as the Victorian empire supported by Sanders, and both systemic structures depend entirely upon the willingness of their subjects to destroy all those who would oppose them without hesitation or compunction.

Captain Jack Bryce (whose real name, we are told, is John Richard Plantagenet) was unable to find a job after being "demobbed" from the British Army. He is summarily hired in the opening pages of Wallace's *The Iron Grip* (1930) specifically to use strong-arm tactics on those who threaten (financially, socially, or physically) the clients of the law firm of Hemmer and Hemmer, and who cannot be "reached" through the more conventional agencies of writs, trials and summonses. James Hemmer, head of the firm, nods with approval as Bryce dangles various miscreants out of windows to exact repayment of gambling debts, or silences any opposition to the firm's activities with brute physical strength in one instance after another. Bryce's sole function as an agent of Hemmer and Hemmer is to enforce through violence the privileges of the upper class who constitute the bulk of the law firm's clientele.

Neither Hemmer nor Bryce has any problem with this arrangement; of the ten chapters in this volume, more than two-thirds conclude with Bryce either threatening or executing physical violence to serve the needs of his paternalistic employer. Thus the world which Wallace describes in his texts is one which is inherently precarious, and in need of continual reinforcement through violence and obedience; Wallace realizes that the British colonial system would collapse entirely were it not maintained by these ritual sacrifices and tests of servitude.

There is yet another troubling aspect of Wallace's fiction, beyond his glorification of violence and summary execution to support the existing class structure of colonial Britain. Wallace withholds useful agency to all save the protagonists of his novels, who are usually in their early twenties or thirties and overwhelmingly white. This quality of Wallace's fictive constructs is another function of the peculiar narrowness of his vision as a writer; even the avuncular uncles and long-suffering mothers who dot the borders of Wallace's fictive frame lack any real power, beyond the bestowal of dowries or the bequeathal of fortunes through death.

Wallace's vision functions as a mirror of the age he lived in and chronicled, an era in which the British empire was engaged in a process of spectacular collapse and iridescent decay, and in this respect, Wallace's fictive voice serves as one of the more remarkable totemic agencies of this peculiar false-zenith in recent European history. It is beyond the scope of this text to delve more deeply into the matrix of contradictory and often opaque power structures embraced by Wallace as both an author and a citizen (and personality) of early twentieth-century Britain; yet it is nevertheless important to call critical attention to Wallace's work as an author whose particular gifts as a storyteller fulfilled the implicit and often unspoken dreams and ambitions of his colonial-subject readers.

Wallace's work is certainly not a major literary legacy, marred as it is by the ruthless manipulation of power that constitutes the primacy of its fictive discourse, but neither is it to be dismissed. A careful examination of his fiction leads the reader to a better understanding of the British colonial imagination, or the lack thereof; it is also to be noted that none of the films based on his works can be in any manner construed as faithful to his vision, for better or worse, and this fact in itself calls for a closer examination of the texts upon which these visual constructs are based. Wallace's narrative drive is that of every great storyteller: he seeks to keep his reader enthralled from first page to last with nonstop incident and an ability to withhold from the reader numerous "facts" within the narrative which might lead the reader to guess the outcome of his texts (crime fiction or not), which would detract from the overall enjoyment of the text.

Yet we must not be blind to the enormity of Wallace's shortcomings as a fictionalist, shortcomings that have little to do with the artificial distinctions between "high" and "low" art, which have long since been abandoned by most critics as being wholly subjective and thus generally useless as a critical mechanism. The genuine defects in Wallace's work, which neither he nor his most uncritical adherents were aware of, have little to do with his skill as a writer or as a narrational strategist. Rather, the limitations (and thus, for the critical, the fascinations) of Wallace as a writer are precisely those blind spots upon which the unsteady, repressive, and unjust foundation of the British "empire" was constructed; when we read Wallace carefully, we will find that we are reading the blueprint and historical record of this inequitable, racist, Orientalist, and homophobic society itself.

THE DANZIGER BROTHERS:
THE BRITISH MIDDLE CLASS

In the late 1950s and early 1960s, there was still a market, and a social need, for the British B feature, whose birth had been brought about by the government-enforced quota system. Rather than the single film system which dominates international theatrical cinema distribution today, most theatres throughout the world presented a double bill for their audiences (except in special "road show" or "premier" engagements such as *Ben-Hur* [1959] or *2001* [1968]). Often these B films were more interesting or more culturally relevant than their A counterparts, and from such mesmeric Italian dystopian sci-fi films as *Planets Against Us* (1961) to the tawdry studio-bound ersatz neo-realism of the British film *Beat Girl* (1962), these commercially viable, seemingly compromised films often spoke to their viewers in a more direct manner than the glossier big-budget films that were the ostensible attraction.

Thus it was that Edward J. and Harry Lee Danziger, who were "the sons of an American theatrical impresario [who had been] the partner of the Dublin-born composer of operettas, Victor Herbert [. . .] came to Britain around 1950 after making films in the [United] States" (Grantham, 1). The brothers decided that the British quota system, which decreed that a certain percentage of all films run on British cinema screens must be of British origin, offered them a superb opportunity to churn out a steady stream of second-string features and low-cost television series for a guaranteed market. Of the Danzigers' work in the United States, Peter Pitt notes that:

> Eddie, the elder of the two, had studied law, and while in the US Army had been associated with the War Crimes Tribunal at Nuremberg. Harry had studied music at the New York Academy, and had at one time been a librarian to an orchestra in the States and had also played trumpet in a band on board a ship that sailed from New York to South America. After the war, the Danzigers had a sound studio in New York that specialised in the dubbing of films from Europe, and in 1946 they produced a feature film, *Jigsaw*, starring Franchot Tone. They were associated with a few other films, including *Babes in Bagdad* (1952) starring Paulette Goddard, which was made in Spain, before they began production in England.
>
> Various studios, including Shepperton, Riverside, and MGM, had been used by them to shoot their feature and television films—*Devil Girl from Mars*, directed by David McDonald, and *Satellite in the Sky*, directed by Paul Dickson, were two of their early productions over here. But with the amount of production planned for the future, the Danziger brothers decided that they needed a studio of their own. They bid for Beaconsfield Studios, which were being sold by the Government, but the Ministry of Works turned down the offer in favour of Group 3 Productions who were moving out of Southall. Discussions then took place for a lease on Twickenham: that also fell through. It was then that the decision was made to build a new studio. (15)

Rather than fighting for bookings in the United States, the Danziger brothers, cost-conscious to a fault as they were, could be assured of theatrical exhibition in the United Kingdom, in part because of the British quota system then in effect and in part because the Danzigers' films were made so economically that they could be counted on to generate a profit even in the most modest distribution circumstances. By 1956, the Danziger brothers had opened their New Elstree Studios on Elstree Road, Elstree, Hertfordshire, which consisted of six sound stages dedicated to the production of low-budget films and teleseries (Warren, 92). The budgets for these features were astonishingly low, running between £15,000 to £17,500 at the most (Pitt, 15). As Edward Danziger boasted to screenwriter Mark Grantham, "We make the cheapest TV series and films in the world. Nobody makes 'em cheaper" (Grantham, 1–2).

Nevertheless, each of these productions featured a prominent credit title crediting "the Danzigers" as producers, along with the signatures of both Harry Lee and Edward J. Danziger as part of the company logo. This intense personal involvement and identification with their modest films is yet another singular aspect of the New Elstree set-up; although their films are modest and unpretentious, it seems obvious that, in some perverse and not altogether fathomable manner, the brothers Danziger were proud of their films. Certainly the studio was a well-built, well-run production facility. Pitt comments:

> The completed studio had six stages ranging from 1,500–6,000 square feet, and the site covered seven and a half acres. During its heyday more than 200 technicians and craftsmen were employed. Many well known artistes and technicians at one time worked for the Danzigers. One teenager who was employed as an assistant in the cutting rooms was Terence Nelhams, later to achieve fame as a pop singer and actor under the name of Adam Faith. (15)

As Warren points out, the Danziger brothers occasionally ventured into near-A territory with such films as *Satellite in the Sky* (1956), a CinemaScope film starring Kieron Moore, Lois Maxwell (later known as Ms. Moneypenny in the James Bond films), Sir Donald Wolfit, and Bryan Forbes (later a consummate director of such classic British films as *The Wrong Box* [1966]). This eighty-five–minute film was considerably longer than the typical Danziger feature, which usually clocked in at slightly under one hour, but the complicated sets and involved scenario made the film a relatively high-risk venture for the studio.

More typical of Danziger films were such B features as *Feet of Clay* (1960), *Man Accused* (1959), *High Jump* (1958), *Sentenced for Life* (1959), *Spider's Web* (1960), *An Honourable Murder* (1960), and *A Date at Midnight* (1959), to name just a few of many feature films made at the studio between 1956 and December, 1961, when New Elstree closed its doors for good. The studio was sold for use as a warehouse in 1965 (Pitt, 16). In addition to these B films, New Elstree also saw the production of such teleseries as *The Vise*, *The Man from Interpol*, *The Cheaters*, *Richard the Lionheart*, and the internationally successful thriller series *Mark Saber* (aka *Saber of London*), which ran in both Britain and the Untied States for several years in the late 1950s and early 1960s. Saber, played by Donald Gray, was a London-based detective who routinely became embroiled in robbery, blackmail, and murder; all of Saber's cases were neatly solved within the compass of a half-hour format.

Much of the series' popularity apparently derived from the fact that star Donald Gray, "a handsome, British leading man who had lost an arm in an accident" conducted his investigations despite his handicap, which was never directly mentioned, yet was prominently displayed throughout the series. Gray, as Saber, would "take out a pack of cigarettes, flick one up to his lips and light it, all with one hand" (Grantham, 2); he would navigate about the streets of London in his sports car, seemingly without the slightest bit of difficulty. As with other Danzigers' series, the shooting schedule of *Mark Saber* episodes was brutally short: two episodes were completed every five days (Pitt, 15).

The story of Grantham's early years as a screenwriter, and his apprenticeship with the Danzigers, is typical of the experience of others who had dealings with the owners of New Elstree Studios. Mark Grantham broke into writing screenplays for the Danzigers in 1958 with a half-hour script for *Mark Saber*; he followed this with scenarios for many of the Danzigers' teleseries, as well as screenplays for more than twenty B features, each shot at New Elstree in "under two weeks" (2). As Grantham recalls, "location work was limited to establishing shots of houses and cars whizzing hither and thither to jizz up the studio-bound sludge" (2). A no-nonsense journeyman craftsperson, Grantham seemingly had little respect or affection for the work he did for the Danzigers. More affectionate in his recollections is writer Ken Taylor, who wrote me that:

> I had a short association with the Danziger brothers in the early 1950s. They introduced me to the mid-Atlantic market which was then coming to birth with a series under the title *The Vise*—"the story of a man who was caught in a vise—a dilemma of his own making." I was engaged on a salary of £10 per week plus expenses with the promise that they would purchase the screen rights in anything I wrote which proved acceptable. After two or three of my 25-minute dramas had been filmed I was informed by Eddie that as a salaried employee everything I wrote with the exception of my personal correspondence was owned by them. Through the Screenwriters' solicitor, Arnold (later Lord) Goodman, I sued and a year or so later reached a settlement of (I believe) £60 out of court! Eddie informed me at that time he would ensure that I never worked for television again—something I remembered in 1964 when I received the Screenwriters' award for the best original teleplay and the Producers' and Directors' writer of the year award. (Letter to the author, February 13, 1997)

Taylor also noted that Brian Clemens, who created *The Avengers* teleseries (along with numerous other projects), first began his working career with the Danzigers: "Brian was introduced to screenwriting by the brothers and worked for them for several years. [They] launched him on a career from which he never looked back" (letter to the author, February 13, 1997). Indeed, by 1956 Brian Clemens was the Danzigers' chief screenwriter, and in the spring, 1956, issue of *Sight and Sound*, Clemens wrote a letter to the editor of that journal stating the Danzigers would be branching out into major productions in the next few years (Pitt, 16). But, as we will see, except for a few A films, work at New Elstree was confined to program pictures and teleseries. Nevertheless, the torrid pace of production proved a fertile training ground for young talent.

In the "high cultural" atmosphere of British television in the 1950s, working for the commercially minded Danzigers offered many writers, directors, and actors a valuable training ground for their skills, as well as a crash course in the economic realities of the business. As Grantham recalls, when the Danzigers invited him down to New Elstree to inspect their facilities and begin work on the *Mark Saber* series, Grantham was expected to pay his own way: "I had a taste of the deft way the Danzigers pared their cheese when they invited me to lunch in the studio canteen. I paid my own bill" (2). And Ken Taylor adds,

> There must be a lot of people in this business who first got their name on a TV screen through the enterprise of Harry and Eddie. At that time we had only BBC TV drama, which consisted mainly of TV versions of West-End stage plays. The first time I saw the words "Commercial Break" was at the screening where I was introduced to the boys. (Letter to the author, February 13, 1997)

Taylor also told me that writers were expected to crank out a thirty-minute television script in a week's time; apparently Brian Clemens was able to do this, but Taylor invariably took two weeks or longer to write an episode, much to the Danziger brother's displeasure (telephone interview with the author, March 2, 1997).

It is in their one-hour "Quota Quickies" that the Danzigers lay their most effective claim to a small place in British cultural and cinematic history. The bulk of these films were directed by David McDonald, Max Varnel, Godfrey Grayson, and Ernest Morris (Pitt, 15), and still hold up well today. Because of their economy of means and expression, and their compact running time, the Danzigers' films have recently been screened (in 1997) on the Showtime and Movie Channel television cable networks—absolute proof that the films are as commercial today as when they were first produced. But in addition to their escapist entertainment value, the Danzigers' films offer a fascinating microcosm of British social values in the 1950s, as seen through the lens of American commercialism. Thus, the Danzigers' tele-films and modest program pictures can correctly be seen as early examples of inverse-colonialism in the production of imagistic commerce; the vision that Harry and Edward Danziger presented on the screen was simultaneously rooted in the British colonial past, and yet aware of the newly encroaching forces of social change which were shortly to rip the fabric of this social system asunder.

Man Accused (scripted by Mark Grantham) stars the ultra-colonialist actor/icon Ronald Howard (in real life, the son of British leading man Leslie Howard), who at one time played the character of Sherlock Holmes in a British teleseries actually produced at the Poste Parisien studios in France for reasons of economy. Howard plays the role of Canadian Robert Jensen, who sweeps Kathy Riddle (Carol Marsh) off her feet in a whirl-wind romance, despite the objections of her longtime friends and her ex-fiancé, Derek Arnold. Kathy lives in isolated splendor in a huge mansion house, doted on by her genial and uncomprehending father, Sir Thomas Riddle, who has no misgivings about Kathy's new romance. Director Montgomery Tully and lighting cameraman Jimmy Wilson stage the early scenes of the film in a nostalgic glow of sunlight, with bouquets of flowers that seem to dominate the rooms of Sir Thomas's mansion. At an engagement party for Robert and Kathy, Tully's camera sweeps among the guests as if it is a participant in the proceedings, which seem simultaneously lavish and decadent.

Yet there is something more than a little ominous in Tully's Ophulsian mise en scène in these early sequences. The lighting is too lush, and highly concentrated in key lights, making Sir Thomas Riddle's mansion more a museum of the British colonial past than a human habitation. Into this snug domain of privilege and power comes Henry Curran, an insurance investigator, who has been invited by the family solicitor, Beckett, to attend Kathy and Bob's engagement party. Shortly thereafter, Kathy is informed by Henry Curran that Bob is, in fact, an international jewel thief on the run from the police, who was last seen in a police line-up in Rio de Janeiro. While Curran unfolds his story in the library to an astonished Kathy, a drunken Derek lets the veneer of his barely concealed contempt for Jensen slip in a brief but undignified brawl in the adjacent ballroom.

Thus, no sooner has Kathy's safe and well-appointed world been introduced than it is under siege from a supposed impostor who is her fiancé, the ill will of her ex-fiancé and the rest of the household staff, and the unannounced "investigator" who spins lurid tales of suicide, murder, and scandal which Kathy finds hard to reconcile with Robert Jensen's mild-mannered demeanor. Shortly after this, Sir Thomas Riddle's family jewels are stolen; Curran shifts suspicion to Bob. In the end of the narrative, however, it is Curran who is revealed to be an impostor, a fabulously successful jewel thief who has managed to temporarily undermine Kathy's faith in Bob, as well as Bob's social standing within the community. At the conclusion of the film, Kathy and Bob are happily reunited and again set firmly on the heterotopic path of wedlock; Sir Thomas's jewel collection is restored. Curran, the interloper who threatened the security and sanctity of the colonial domain of the Riddle household (and who keeps rooms in a rather shabby, lower-class boarding house throughout the film, in sharp contrast to Kathy's life of wealth and material comforts) comes to an untimely end. Yet the threat of Curran, as outsider, remains the controlling force throughout much of *Man Accused*'s running time; as in much British escapist fiction, the figure of the disruptive "other" is one of the motivating elements of the film's narrative construction.

Of even greater interest is *High Jump*, which stars Richard Wyler and Lisa Daniely in a tale of a circus acrobat who loses his nerve during a high-wire performance. He is subsequently reduced to being a TV repairman in a run-down shop in East London, while he attempts to assuage his pain with alcohol. The film opens up with near-documentary footage of a series of grotesque clowns during a circus performance; the lighting is harsh and stunningly bright, making the working-class entertainment of the shabby circus seem simultaneously unappealing and garish. The film's main titles are slammed over this newsreel material seemingly without care or concern; as the clowns douse each other with water, or parade around the center of the one-ring big top on stilts, the pageant we witness seems both degrading and dehumanizing to both audience and performer. Once again, the reliable Jimmy Wilson serves as Director of Photography, with Brian Clemens and Eldon Howard providing the film's script, and Godfrey Grayson the direction.

As the opening credits fade out, the camera swings up to observe an aerial act in progress. All seems well, until one "catcher" misses his connection, and his partner plunges to earth. Several spectators react with justifiable horror, but we are never shown the result of the accident. Instead, Grayson fades out on the scene, and then fades back into a publicity still of one of the aerialists, Bill Ryan (Richard Wyler) staring mockingly at the audience at the height of his fame as a circus performer. The camera tracks back to reveal the alcoholic wreck of an apartment, with chairs overturned, cigarette butts overflowing in ashtrays, and the figure of Bill passed out on his bed in a stupor. At length, Bill rouses himself and reports to the TV shop where he now works; Kitty, a young secretary, hopes for a relationship with Bill, but Bill is almost immediately attracted to the dubious Jackie Field (Lisa Daniely), a customer whose television is always in need of repair. While Kitty is presented as obedient, wholesome, blond, and modestly dressed throughout the film, Jackie Field accessorizes her wardrobe with costume jewelry, a trench coat, perfume, and a dangerously ripe French accent.

As the film progresses, we realize that Jackie Field has a hidden motive; aware of Bill Ryan's prowess as an aerialist, she wants to recruit him for a dangerous robbery that requires a "high jump" between two buildings. The job goes awry, with predictably disastrous results, but Ryan manages to escape serious consequences by cooperating with the police in the aftermath of the aborted heist. *High Jump* presents the viewer with a world that is at once drab, rife with temptation, and hermetically sealed, as if offering no real escape to either its protagonists or its audience. Jackie Field's "luxury flat" is nothing more than a trap for the unsuspecting Ryan; Kitty, the one sympathetic character in the film, toils thanklessly at her job in the TV repair shop in the midst of poverty and squalor. The "high jump" that Bill Ryan is asked to make is in fact a leap from the seedy gentility of his dead-end existence into the realm of criminal wealth, but even this leap is an illusion. As Ryan discovers, the mastermind of the robbery is Jackie Field's putative lover; they intend to double-cross Ryan the moment that the loot is in their possession. Brutality in the film is rampant, both psychic and physical. Ryan callously stands up Kitty for numerous dates throughout the film, without any apology for his behavior; during the robbery itself, two guards are senselessly shot down for the pure thrill of killing. *High Jump* presents a world devoid of hope, the desire for ambition, or the possibility of advancement; indeed, the only aspect of the production that rings false is the obligatory happy ending, which, while meeting the demands of conventional narrative closure, undermines the *noirish* despair of the rest of the film.

Feet of Clay (1960), another Danziger second feature of the period, deals with the murder of a social worker whose activities are really a front for a group of recidivist criminals. Boasting a superb "cool jazz" score by Bill Lesage, scripted by Mark Grantham, and shot by Jimmy Wilson, this brief but effective thriller was directed by Frank Marshall. As with *High Jump*, the stark sets and claustrophobic interiors add to the no-apologies intensity of the film, which effortlessly conveys the shabby gentility of the working-class milieu of the period. Angela Richmond, "the angel of the police courts," is found shot dead in an alleyway of a London slum as the film opens; the rest of the narrative unravels the circumstances of her existence. Far from being a benefactor to newly paroled criminals, Angela in fact runs a "hotel" whose sole purpose is to force the men and women put in her charge back into a life of crime. Angela Richmond's social status as a legitimate probation officer further adds to her veneer of respectability, but as *Feet of Clay* makes abundantly clear, Angela Richmond and her associates are utterly unscrupulous in their exploitation of the unfortunate women and men put into her custody. The hotel itself is a drab, cheerless domain, whose staff enforce their regime with blunt displays of brute force. In this instance, it is not so much the narrative of the film that is of interest, but rather the situation into which *Feet of Clay*'s protagonists are placed. As the surface of Angela Richmond's respectable existence inexorably erodes before us, we see the vision of an empire in collapse, a system of government in which even legitimate authority has been compromised. *Feet of Clay*'s brief sixty-minute running time is admirably suited to the world the film depicts; indeed, one could barely stand to endure being trapped in Angela Richmond's hotel much longer.

Although the Danzigers' feature films successfully played in theatres throughout Great Britain, audiences were often less than enthusiastic about the vision they presented. "An insult to audiences" complained one viewer in a letter to *Films and Filming* in 1961, singling out the Danziger film *The Middle Course* for particular abuse. Another correspondent to the journal described the Danzigers' films as being comprised of "cliché-ridden situations set against cardboard backgrounds" (Pitt, 16). But perhaps the view of daily existence presented in the Danzigers' films was hitting a little too close to home. The vision that the Danziger brothers conveyed of British society was one of a twilight world in inevitable slow-motion collapse. Far from being escapist entertainment, the gritty social realism and shabby location filming that marked the typical Danziger quota film reflected the world in which many of the audience members of the period found themselves on a daily basis.

Harry Danziger himself noted that the Danziger brothers' films often received an unusual amount of criticism from both the members of the press as well as the general public, when he told Tony Gruner of *Kinematograph Weekly* that "we have to take the sort of critical beating that should be reserved for producers whose films cost ten or twelve times as much as ours" (as cited in Pitt, 16). By this time, the Danzigers were beginning to tire of the press' constant criticism of their films, and *Mark Saber* was no longer running as an international television series. The Danzigers' final foray into television was the series *Richard the Lionheart*, which starred Dermot Walsh in the title role. But Harry and Edward Danziger had failed to allow for the extra time such a relatively ambitious series, involving period costumes, sword fights, and detailed post-production work, demanded (Pitt, 16). At the same time, a final set of features was being produced by New Elstree Studios, but the market for these B features was rapidly disappearing. Thirty-nine episodes of *Richard the Lionheart* were shot, but the Danzigers realized that they were no longer able to compete with television series produced in the United States, and announced in December, 1961, that the New Elstree facility would close once the series had been completed (Pitt, 16). The Danzigers spent more time on their hotel properties, particularly the Mayfair Hotel, and several staff members from the studio were absorbed into the brothers' hotel operations. But above all, the Danzigers were pragmatic, cost-conscious producers, and they were aware that it was no longer feasible to continue producing films for an increasingly spectacle-driven market; smaller films had lost their ability to attract a sufficient audience. As the studios closed, Harry Danziger told an interviewer, "Eddie and I have been in show business all our lives. We are not saying goodbye for all time to films and television but it will be a long *au revoir* until conditions alter in favour of the independent producer" (Pitt, 16).

Ironically, this was at the same time that Hammer Studios at Bray, best known for their Gothic escapist horror films, were involved in an expansion of their production activities, with maximum budgets of £300,000 considered for their more ambitious projects. Hammer, too, would eventually fall by the commercial wayside in the late 1980s as a result of the Hollywood blockbuster syndrome; increasingly explicit horror films from the United States (beginning with George Romero's ultra-low-budget *Night of the Living Dead* [1968]) were also a factor in Hammer's demise. The plight of the Danzigers was similar, directly related to economic considerations and changing audience expectations. But unlike Hammer's films, the productions of the Danziger brothers were rooted in the everyday realities of quotidian existence, rather than the escapist realm of supernatural horror. Perhaps it was the gritty realism of the Danzigers' most representative films which, paradoxically, afforded them their greatest initial commercial success, and eventually led to their decision to cease production. At their best, the films of the Danziger brothers, and their early teleseries *The Vise* and *Mark Saber*, held up a mirror to a particular side of post-colonial British existence, and presented this fatalistic, unadorned vision to receptive audiences in theatres and on television. If the films of the Danziger brothers are marginalized now, it is not so much because of their inherently compromised circumstances of production, but, rather, I would argue, because of their uncompromisingly realistic portrayal of ordinary men and women in the struggle to survive in post–World War II Britain. This vision, at once repellent and yet seductive, informs the best of the Danzigers' films, which were not the larger scale epics they hoped someday to produce (the proposed *Ali Baba* series), or even the occasional A film (such as 1956's *Satellite in the Sky* or their 1962 production of *The Tell-Tale Heart*, based on Poe's short story), but rather the cheaply transcendent crime dramas that formed the backbone of the studio's output, and held the attention of viewers throughout the world for a brief, if eventful, half decade.

CHAPTER THREE

The Limits of Cinematic Spectacle: Considerations on the Horror Film

THE BODY IN TORTURE

His whole frame at once—within the space of a single minute, or even less, shrunk—crumbled—absolutely *rotted* away beneath my hands. Upon the bed, before the whole company, there lay a nearly liquid mass of loathsome—of detestable putrescence.

—Poe, *The Facts of M. Valdemar's Case*

Operating at the margins of figurative literary discourse, Poe's Gothic tales presented to his audience, in the words of Elaine Scarry, a world composed of "physical pain [that] is so . . . real that it seems to confer [this] quality of 'incontestable reality'" upon the reader (27). Poe's macabre texts deal with "the conversion of real pain into the fiction of power" (27), and revel in a celebration of the Bakhtinian grotesque. His embrace of the corporeal unreality of torture forms, as Scarry notes, the "language" of his work. In her discussion of *The Pit and the Pendulum*, Scarry states that "whatever its political naiveté or its melodramatic intentions, Poe's 'The Pit and the Pendulum' discovers in its final moments the single distilled form of torture that in many ways represents all forms of torture, the wall collapsing in on the human center to crush it alive" (45).

Cinematic horror, too, operates at the margins of corporeal signification, in an ineluctable process that raises the stakes of graphic specificity with each successive wave of new horror films. Many cinema theorists/historians point to George Romero's *Night of the Living Dead* (1968) as some sort of jumping off point in terms of violent simulacric representationalism, yet from director J. Searle Dawley's 1910 version of *Frankenstein* for producer Thomas Edison and Alice Guy's 1913 version of *The Pit and the Pendulum*, cinema practice has been aggressively engaged in the pursuit of more spectacular significations of torture and physical subjugation. What is suggested in the 1961 *Pit and the Pendulum* by Roger Corman is insistently foregrounded in the 1991 Stuart Gordon version: torture, in all its manifestations, is the centerpiece of Gordon's interpretation. For Poe, and for Gordon, "torture . . . is itself a language, an objectification, an acting out. Real pain, agonizing pain, is inflicted on a person; but torture, which contains specific acts of inflicting pain, is also itself a demonstration and magnification of the felt-experience of pain" (Scarry, 27), this "demonstration and magnification" being seemingly intensified by the cinematic reception/production apparatus.

Using Poe's literary vision as a starting point, I wish to demonstrate how this embrace of the mechanics of fleshly destruction, detailed with such clinical relish in Poe, has found its counterpart in the modern-day horror film, more than in the horror film of any other era. For today, the visions that Poe gave to his readers are no longer implied at the margins of the page, frame, or narrative discourse: they are foregrounded with inexorable insistence, presented with a vital brutality that drives us deeper into the spectacle, or out of the theatre altogether. This figurative shift, which has been solidified in the 1980s and 1990s with such films as *Dr. Giggles* (1993), *Ghost in the Machine* (1994), *Night Shift* (1992) and many others, is my subject/object here.

Near the conclusion of Roger Corman's version of *The Pit and the Pendulum*, Nicholas Medina's mind snaps, and he imprisons his wife, Elizabeth, in an iron maiden in the torture chamber of his late father, Sebastian Medina. There follows a memorably staged sequence in which Nicholas tortures one of his guests, the hapless Francis Barnard, with Sebastian's "favorite" device for inflicting pain upon the human body: a gigantic metal pendulum, graced with a razor sharp edge, gradually lowered in unceasing arcs over the bound and gagged corpus of the victim. Poe writes: "The vibration of the pendulum was at right angles to my length. I saw that the crescent was designed to cross the region of my heart. It would fray the serge of my robe—it would return and repeat its operation—again—and again" (Mossman, 753).

What is most horrific in the operation of this instrument of torture is its combination of mechanical inexorability and phantom human agency. The pendulum removes the torturer from direct contact with the victim, and yet the agency of this removal forges a bond between the two. When the victim is removed from the instrument of torture, the bond is broken. As Barnard is freed from his bonds beneath the pendulum at the last possible moment and conducted from the chamber, the camera sweeps across the interior of the torture chamber to force us to gaze upon that which we have forgotten. In the final shot of the film, we see the blood-stained eyes, doubly-framed within an ever-contracting rectangular iris, of Elizabeth Medina, sealed behind the mask of the iron maiden, gazing in mute horror at the audience, returning *our* gaze of agonized spectatorship. The last words spoken in the film—"no one will ever enter this room again"—underscore the mute agony of Elizabeth's fate, and our fate as well.

In contrast, Gordon's version presents as its central figure Torquemada, a depraved sensualist solely in love with the act of inflicting pain, who achieves corporeal reintegration with another only through the act of torture. The film devotes most of its running time to increasingly specific and degrading acts of mutilation and subjugation, with most of the torture being inflicted upon the feminine corpus. What Corman and his predecessors had suggested, Gordon (who has also "adapted" H. P. Lovecraft's "Herbert West: Reanimator" for the screen) presents with brutal insistence, withholding nothing, reveling in the specifics of fleshly destruction concomitant with the process of torture. What compels our attention in the Corman version is the distance, and the connection, between the objectified and objectifier. Elizabeth Medina's final imploring look at us from the confines of the iron maiden suggests, through the power of the gaze, this distanciational contract between torturer and victim, as seen through the mediational agency of the cinematograph (see Vernet and Willemen for further discussions of the function of the reciprocal gaze in cinema).

Gordon, along with other contemporary practitioners of graphic specificity (what Barthes has termed "a monotonous inventory of parts" [113]) in the current wave of Gothic cinema, functions within this zone of gaze reciprocity also, by urging the viewer to avoid the returned look of the victim during an act of torture so specifically detailed as to force us to avert our eyes in any event. The spectacle of the victim in pain in contemporary graphic horror films becomes a Medusic construct to be viewed at the risk of one's becoming a potential victim of torture oneself.

Lucio Fulci's 1984 film *The Tell-Tale Heart*, for example, uses Poe's short story as a jumping off point for a bizarre mixture of Samuel Beckett's *Krapp's Last Tape* conflated with large doses of *grand guignol* butchery, as the reclusive writer Mr. Miles (Patrick Magee) recounts to a tape recorder an endless succession of torments visited upon him through the agency of a malign and seemingly supernatural black feline. Shut up alone in a country house that no one visits, Miles has entombed himself in the manner of many of Poe's protagonists; he is already one of the living dead. Miles's reminiscences are intercut with a series of disconnected and violent interludes that have nothing to do with the exterior narrative of the piece; rather, they serve as further proof of the random nature of violence within the sphere of human endeavor. Fulci's narrative voice here is at one with Poe. Miles's recitations are the cry of a man who has inflicted the unendurable torture of catatonic internment upon himself. Miles has enacted Kristeva's mimetic structure of self-destruction, and in so doing, has become one with his tormentor. Miles's agony and pain are framed within his ceaselessly spoken and ceaselessly recorded words as one buried alive is framed within the compass of a coffin.

Near the end of Fulci's document of aural/visual surveillance, the black cat knocks over a conveniently placed candle, thus starting a fire that both destroys the audio tapes and burns Miles to death in an excruciatingly graphic sequence that takes many minutes to unreel. The cat's penultimate act seems utterly random, as random as the scenes of disassociational violence that punctuate Miles's tortured memoir throughout the film. Thus, it matters little what circumstances have brought the victim and the active agency of the victim's destruction together within the frame (narrative or cinematic) of torture. The very absence of motivation is the hallmark, the seal of authenticity of torment in Poe, as in Fulci's walking dream state manifest within this film.

The narrator in Poe's text of *The Tell-Tale Heart*, who kills his employer for no apparent reason, admits that for his crime of murder, "object there was none. Passion there was none. I loved the old man. He had never wronged me." And yet, there is something that drives Poe's protagonist to commit murder: "I think it was his eye! Yes, it was this!" (Mossman, 799). Poe's obsessed narrator imagines himself the subject of constant surveillance, an inhabitant of a world where "inspection functions ceaselessly. The gaze is alert everywhere" (Foucault 1979, 195). The panopticonic eye of "the old man" projects the gaze of torture onto the hapless narrator, who must then do anything to rid himself of the gaze which he feels seeks to control him. Yet even through the agency of murder, Poe's malefactor obtains no release from surveillance; the incessant "heartbeat" of the dead man replaces the accusing gaze of control, and leads Poe's narrator to confess his crime to the police. The crime itself is of no importance, nor is the eventual self-incrimination of its perpetrator. Torture, in Poe and in Fulci, is the centerpiece of *The Tell-Tale Heart*; the aural and optical torture of the self by the self, the Gorgonesque embrace of the gaze of punishment.

Often, remakes of Poe films from the 1960s carry more visual authority that their original counterparts, precisely because they can freely depict activities that hitherto had to be suggested or implied. Larry Brand's 1989 version of *The Mask of the Red Death* restages a number of the visual conceits of Roger Corman's 1964 version with considerably less pretension, and is far more direct in dealing with the themes of incest, death, and corporeal destruction (all present, by strong implication, in Poe's original narrative). In addition, deviant versions of Poe can also present the viewer with an alternative vision of the writer's vision. Brian Desmond Hurst's 1934 version of *The Tell-Tale Heart*, though not graphically specific, is an early example of manifestly queer cinema, in which Poe's narrative becomes a metaphor for the paranoid secrecy exacted from homosexuals during the era, who justly felt themselves constantly under watch in a hostile and uncomprehending environment of compulsory heterosexuality. The flesh in this film is subject to the torture of the look; the flesh in later films will become subject to the torture of the knife.

Clive Barker's 1987 *Hellraiser*, for example, imposes upon the viewer an unceasing series of harrowing tableaux involving the mutilation of the flesh by a variety of natural/supernatural agencies. The climactic sequence of the film presents the spectacle of complete corporeal disintegration. The body of the male protagonist is literally shredded to pieces before the viewer's gaze, through the agency of a multitude of minute grappling hooks, deeply anchored in the flesh of the victim. The victim's last words, "Jesus wept," structurally signify Barker's vision of the fragmented and crucified body of Christ. This time, however, there will be no redemption or resurrection. As Bynum notes, "displaying the bloody fragments of the executed was a way of underlining their eternal damnation," (280) and it is this display of unceasing agony that we witness here.

While subsequent films in the *Hellraiser* series have failed to live up to the promise of the first, Barker, as director/scenarist of the original *Hellraiser*, is onto something here. Central to the conceit of the film is a little black box—the "torture box"—that contains all the pain and suffering imaginable in this, or any, world. Freed from the confines of the box, the denizens of Barker's netherworld inflict torture for the sake of torture upon the living, as they themselves (particularly the Pin-Head character) are the victims of constant pain. Barker's torture box represents the closed confines of the torture chamber, the body sealed inside itself during the act of torture, the bond forged between torturer and victim, the black box of the cinema apparatus, the grey box of passive television reception. At the end of numerous sequences in *Hellraiser*, we are tortured with scenes in which the body, unable to support further pain, collapses against itself, imploding in a maelstrom of final terminal release.

In this so different from the spectacle of M. Valdemar's corporeal collapse presented at the beginning of this chapter—indeed, does it present any significatory contradiction at all? Poe's vision in his tales of the macabre depended precisely upon the graphic visualization of the complete and illimitable corruption of the body. In *The Mask of the Red Death*, "Darkness and Decay and the Red Death [hold] illimitable dominion over all" (Mossman, 744); in *The Murders in the Rue Morgue*, the dread Ourang-Outang dispatches his victims with unrelenting violence ("with one determined sweep of his muscular arm he nearly severed her head from her body" [683]); in *The Black Cat*, the walled-up body of the narrator's victim confronts the reader/spectator with a clinically detailed vision of human ephemerality ("the corpse, already greatly decayed and clotted with gore, stood erect before the eyes of the spectators" [845]); and in *The Cask of Amontillado*, the screams of Montresor's "friend" Fortunato as he is interred within the catacombs of Montresor's cellar alive are unflinchingly detailed ("a succession of loud and shrill screams, bursting suddenly from the throat of the chained form, seemed to thrust me violently back" [1095]). In the presence of these vivid descriptions/imagistic word-constructs, it might well be argued that no degree of visual, cinematic specificity can ever attain the effect that Poe achieves in these passages. Cinematic violence, no matter how clinically depicted, is a *construct*, designed to replicate our imagined *vision* of the "reality" of torture and/or mutilation. Yet it never partakes of actual torture in and of itself (with the exception of "documentaries" composed of actual scenes of death, such as the *Faces of Death* series). Staged cinematic violence is a working out, a *playing with* the specularity of dismemberment. It is this that disturbs us, because the elaborate play acting inflicted upon the viewer urges us to identify, as Carol Clover persuasively argues, with both victim and torturer either simultaneously or concurrently, in a state of constant oscillatory flux (Clover, 229–230).

What the spectacle of the corruption of the human corpus in Poe offers the reader/viewer is, in Kristeva's phrase, "something to be scared of" (33–54). For Kristeva, abjection is a central figuration in the domain of horror. Kristeva sees the configuration of victim, torturer, pain, and suffering, and the human loathing of/longing for these conditions as a journey through the human landscape of powerlessness/domination by the self/other. The result of this confluence of forces is described by Kristeva as "the laughter of the Apocalypse," recalling the final moments of Poe's *The Pit and the Pendulum*, as the narrator, at length exhausted, giddy, and ready to accept his doom, falls "fainting, into the abyss" (Mossman, 757) prepared by his tormentors, only to be rescued at the last moment. In the face of pain and disfigurement, is not laughter (Kristeva, 56–89) the only logical/illogical response? Confronted by the painstakingly staged visions of controlled mutilation afforded us through the agency of current cinematic practice, what can we do but surrender, laughing, in the face of our publicly schematized extinction, a spectacle which will be enacted in the most ceremonial, protracted, and agonizing fashion our torturers/narrators can devise? A spectacle, moreover, which we have purchased entry to as a form of amusement and/or escapism? This is the spectacle of torture as carnival, as holiday, as bloodless bloodsport, a sensation that transcends all other forms of ritual body display.

The healthy body in the horror film *exists* to be corrupted, destroyed, transmogrified into a metanarrative structure signifying the immutability and illimitable dominion of death, pain, corporeal disintegration. Thus, horror films function most persuasively as Gothic fictions in their embrace of the *mise en abyme*, or the structure of the abyss. Torture, dismemberment, and the dominion of the grave are the true territory of the contemporary horror film's domain. The narrative structure adopted by postmodern horror films, that of a headlong plunge into a world that is alien, inviting, evil, and all-encompassing, diegetically enunciates this vertiginous state, as did Poe in his Gothic tales. Robert Stam, writing on Rosa von Praunheim's *Ein Virus Kennt Keine Moral* (*A Virus Knows No Morals*) calls it a "brilliant example of a 'carnivalesque' approach to the unlikely topic of AIDS." He notes that one of the film's set pieces features a group of "transvestites staging a contemporary version of Poe's (vestigially carnivalesque) *Mask of the Red Death* (172). This dance of death, whether through the agency of torture, disease, or mesmeric spell (as in *The Case of M. Valdemar*) holds the spectator in scopic thrall, even as one acknowledges that the images presented in graphic horror films retain a margin of audience safety, allowing us to engage in the play of torture, dismemberment, and sadomasochistic oscillation between the figure under torture and the ground it seems to occupy, without true physical risk.

"Torture is the realm of the pure signifier, or even better: torture is the *democracy* of the pure signifier," as Ñacuñán Sáez notes in "Torture: A Discourse on Practice." The victim, through his body, enunciates her/his all-encompassing guilt: "Yes, I am guilty. Of anything. I am guilty of anything, everybody is guilty of everything" (133). For all of the abstraction we have been bringing into play here, the reality, the actual agony of torture, mutilation, and dismemberment in the service of exacting a tale—any tale, at any price—renders the torturer/narrator at one with her/his victim, a co-fabulator of fictions designed to satisfy the whims of one's self/tormentor. Thus, all horror tales can be seen, in a sense, as captivity narratives, or dialogues of enslavement. Just as Poe's protagonists wall up their enemies (real or imagined), within catacombs, within the walls of houses, so the victim of torture is walled up with her-or himself as the sole bearer of the stigmata of torture—a prisoner within what Bynum has termed "the closed body" (272), now doubly sealed against itself under the sign of punctuated, ruptured skin of the corpus-in-pain.

As we witness these spectacles of action/character, we run a fearful risk. If we fall under the shadow of the cinema image of torture, we "shall endure the pain" of it (Lacan, 44). The tale being told in the horror film signifies the inevitability of torture through the agency of its narrative construction: we have only to ask, where will the shadow fall on us? As victim? As perpetrator? Or perhaps, as an admixture, a congruence of these two artificial polarities? For are we not one with the agency of our pain, even if we have only experienced the invasion of body as part of a potentially healing surgical procedure, a rite of purification which the body must endure if it is to continue to exist? Whatever the reason for any invasive procedure, we still bear the scars of entry. Torture constitutes a double invasion of the body, piercing the flesh for no purpose other than to cause pain, force a confession, or to silence the body, at last, altogether.

Because of this, women and men in horror films are sites of activity, situations rather than characters. As the level of graphic specificity continues to rise in the horror film, it is not so much the text of the film that matters, but rather the certainty of fleshly mutilation, torture, dismemberment, violent death, and cruelty. Suspense and mood have, for the most part, been dispensed with. It is the transgressions upon the flesh, upon the person(s) under torture that mesmerize the audience. No longer is it enough to suggest these actions; they must be shown in clinical detail. This new requirement of specificity is an integral part of the horror film; simply put, the contemporary horror film must "horrify" the spectator. The old legends of Dracula, Frankenstein, the Wolfman, and the Mummy no longer suffice, no longer hold audiences enthralled. Horror films have always operated on the margins of cinematic discourse, trafficking in precisely those images and situations we seek to avoid in our actual corporeal existence. They are a safe ticket to a dangerous zone, a zone of uncertainty and imminent danger.

No longer are these dark visions primarily a public commodity, unspooled in a dark room filled with strangers (the conventional movie theatre). Now these visions are played out in the sphere of domestic commerce, on home TVs, using individual VCRs and/or Sega/Nintendo CD game players. In the 1980s, with prosthetic special effects, it was thought that the limits of graphic, simulacric representationalism had been reached, as displayed in such films as *The Howling* (1981) and John Carpenter's remake of *The Thing* (1982). Current developments in digital effects demonstrate what should have been obvious all along: this was just another plateau to be transcended. With digital imaging, films are now made out of nothing at all, just magnetic impulses entered into computers and then downloaded from discs to create a chroma-key blue-screen world of endless/transfiguration and corporeal unreality.

Extras are cloned, artificial polar bears pitch Coca-Cola in a synthetic landscape, blood and flesh become steel and chrome in *Terminator II* (1991). With the new interactive CD films, we enter an entirely new area of one-on-one participation, in which we can become either victim or tormentor, role-playing our way to a complete disavowal of our physical existence. When "playing" these "games," we become solely the sum of the impulses we transmit to the CD controlled device. Violently graphic horror films teach us to revel in the Bakhtinian grotesque, to embrace the destruction of the flesh in this age of AIDS as an inevitable ritual to be sought out and metacorporeally incorporated into our consciousness.

Contemporary horror films, then, proceed on the assumption that violence, degradation, and ritual torture are inescapable facets of contemporary existence; whether we seek them or not, the agencies of destruction will find us out, and inflict lingering damage upon our persons with inevitable delight. The destruction of the body in the horror film of the 1990s is the act that cleanses the body of disease, removes it from the realm of death through erasure, transgressively reinscribes the sign of mutilation upon the flesh, in the manner of Christ, as an agency of figurative redemption, or at least surcease from suffering, the death to be longed for.

All of these films traffic in the rupture of societal discourse, the abrogation of the tyrannical rule of normative social values through the agency of the torture box. "Under the general demand for slackening and for appeasement, we can hear the mutterings of the desire for a return of terror, for the realization of the fantasy to seize reality. The answer is: let us wage a war on totality; let us be witnesses to the unpresentable . . ." (Lyotard, 82). Let us witness these spectacles of the unspeakable, seek release in the destruction of the flesh, the self-signification of pain and self-obliteration. Poe's narrators seek a return to the liberating freedom of violence, embracing their torment, seeking to penetrate the "closed" body. Within the sphere of the torturer/tortured, we may experience the totality of the subject/object relation as a unified field.

"Fantasy may itself be a kind of transgressive reinscription, one presupposing a radical impurity in all identity, not excluding the transgressor" (Dollimore, 324). The fantasy of torture, the torture of the flesh and of the mind through the flesh, inscribes the body and psyche of the torturer upon the victim, and creates a fantasy of corporeal reintegration in which that which is born separate becomes momentarily transmogrified into an artificial whole. When we talk about torture, when we speak of the victims of the rack, the pendulum that slices into bound flesh, those who are walled up within tombs while yet alive, we invoke the flesh that bears witness to this mortification, the cry of "the body in pain."

THE FILMS OF REGINALD LeBORG

As another exemplar of the instinct towards Gothicism on the screen, it is constructive to consider the case of Reginald LeBorg, a Hollywood director who specialized in horror and suspense films for cinema-goers of an earlier, less graphically specific era. LeBorg flourished in the '40s and '50s, creating in his lifetime a body of compromised yet ultimately transcendent works that directly question the patriarchal phallocentric narrative order embraced by most filmic practitioners during this period. And yet, much of this work was accomplished in a state of intense personal psychomachy. On the one hand, LeBorg embraced imagistic and thematic structures that liberated the feminine; yet in person, LeBorg often denigrated and dismissed his own films, and seemed unaware of his own preoccupation with feminist narrative structures and/or codes of representation.

Still, if one examines LeBorg's filmography, and more importantly, LeBorg's films themselves (as we will see, access to these works is a key problem in any evaluation of LeBorg's oeuvre), mixed in with a number of undistinguished program pictures one finds a compelling and disturbing (or disruptive) vision of feminine power and a disdain for the dominant patriarchal discourse of traditional Hollywood practice. In this section of the text, I will focus on three films of LeBorg's that challenge classical cinematic narrative patterning: *Weird Woman* (1944), *Destiny* (1944), and *Jungle Woman* (1944).

Weird Woman, based on a novella by Fritz Leiber, centers on a professor of sociology, Norman Reed, who marries a young "white priestess" while on a field trip in the South Seas. Returning to the university where he teaches, Reed is caught up in a series of scandals arranged by Ilona Carr, a vengeful ex-girlfriend. Norman's wife, Paula, is blamed for these events, and branded a "white witch" by the college community. Eventually, through the agency of a sympathetic Dean of Women, Norman and Paula are exonerated of any blame, and allowed to return to their "normal" lives.

The female characters in *Weird Woman* dominate the narrative entirely; Norman Reed's sense of control is seen from the outset of the film as illusory and distressingly superficial. Ilona Carr, Paula Reed, and Grace Gunnison (the Dean of Women) form a triangular inversion of the usual patriarchal narrative structure, in which a group of men fight to possess a young woman. Here, LeBorg gives us Paula as mythic nurturer and redemptive figure, Ilona as vengeful destructive harpy, and Grace as the first of a series of psychopolitical "seers" who have both the natural instinct and social acumen to intervene in worldly affairs. LeBorg will explore this same theme in *Jungle Woman*, but in *Weird Woman* he brilliantly articulates the trappings of the masculine domain that exude authority, yet fail to possess any genuine degree of control.

Norman Reed's critical writings seek to deprivilege the mythic and feminine, which Paula embraces. Paula has previously rejected (before she and Norman meet) conventional academic pursuits in favor of a return to the natural order of things. Paula's father, a university professor like Norman Reed, had been grooming his daughter for the academic life when Paula impulsively abandoned her graduate studies to partake of tribal culture. In fact, Norman had at one time been a student of Paula's father; but Paula has rejected (or de-emphasized) the primacy of her father's teachings, while Norman still upholds the academic tradition imparted to him by Paula's father.

Norman thinks that he has "acquired" Paula as a trophy of his field trip; in fact, it is Paula who, through prayer and magic, saves Norman from ritual execution and a subsequent illness in her island domain, and guides him safely back to academe and the United States. Paula has been treated as a near deity by the members of her adoptive tribe, and is a figure of great power within the tribal hierarchy. Yet she gives up all her own social power to return with Norman to Monroe College. This initial acquiescence is just the first act in a series of self-denials that parallel Norman's fall from official favor. Though Norman seeks to deny it, his position within academe is not secured by his critical work (which seeks to discount nature in favor of rational empiricism), but rather through Paula's protection and guidance, a fact immediately recognized by both Grace and Ilona.

Women, in this film, have the power to see, to heal, and to control; they allow men to maintain their illusions as to their dominance solely as a function of their own unquestioned supremacy in all affairs. Evelyn Ankers, the actress who played Ilona, was traditionally cast by LeBorg's home studio, Universal, as the desired object in their more conventional Gothic narratives; here, LeBorg employs Ankers as an agent of destruction. Even when women's powers are subverted or misdirected (as when Ilona manipulates Evelyn Sawtelle or the student Margaret in her campaign to destroy Norman), it is the power of the matriarchy that controls the power and destiny of all the characters in *Weird Woman*. The power of Ilona is such that her hold over the narrative ends only with her destruction.

Yet Ilona, it might well be argued, is ultimately marginalized by the film, along with Paula, because her femininity within the dominant narrative discourse in itself constitutes sufficient "Otherness." As Noel Carroll points out:

> A politically minded critic, however, might . . . [argue] . . . that horror exists because it is always in the service of the status quo; that is, horror is invariably an agent of the established order. It continues to be produced because horror is in the interest of the established order. This supposes that the creations of the horror genre are always politically repressive, thereby directly contradicting the (equally incorrect) view, discussed earlier, that horror fictions are always emancipatory (i.e., politically subversive). (196)

The feminine "threat" to the existing order posed by the narrative dominance of Ilona, Grace, and Paula, is consciously foregrounded by LeBorg's staging. Throughout the film, the actions of Norman Reed (and, in a tragic subplot, Millard Sawtelle, an aging professor who plagiarizes a student manuscript, and then commits suicide to escape detection) are weak, indecisive and inconsequential to the thrust of the plot.

In *Weird Woman*, there is no male authority worth applying to; whether or not Norman Reed survives is up to Grace, who instinctively pits herself against Ilona. Paula, marginalized because of her "uncertain" racial/social origin, attempts to control events through her connection with the elements (her role as a priestess), but Norman forces her to abandon this, and thus her power to protect him. As a consequence of this, Paula's emotional balance is threatened. The male social construct within the film will certainly not assist her efforts to regain control of her destiny.

Because of this pathology, the world of *Weird Woman* emerges as the location of a series of forbidding contests. The obligatory happy ending tacked on to the end of the film (lasting all of thirty seconds, and contained entirely within one shot) reinforces the artificiality of the generic narrative closure forced by Universal upon LeBorg. Life at Monroe College is seen as a contest between the feminine and the masculine, for both students and teachers (at one point in the film Norman Reed is falsely accused by a young woman student of sexual harassment, at Ilona Carr's instigation), and 1940s "mainstream" Caucasian society against other cultural influences. If one structured the level of cross-cultural and sexual awareness displayed in the film, adapting a popular model often used in the classroom, one might schematicize the world of Monroe College as a series of assimilatory levels; the characters in the film would be conscious of only the primary level of interpretational analysis.

One third of LeBorg's *Destiny* was originally shot as a section of a four-part film directed by Julien Duvivier, released in 1943 under the title *Flesh and Fantasy*. Conventional wisdom has it that Universal felt that the ultimately excised story made *Flesh and Fantasy* too long, and that the decision to edit the film down to three interlocking narratives was strictly a question of pacing. Conveniently supporting this version of events is the fact that LeBorg's reworking of the footage (for this is what *Destiny* became), received little or no critical attention when initially released. A viewing of the film—indeed, of both films—casts much doubt on this account of the events surrounding the production of *Destiny*.

Flesh and Fantasy is a conventionally poetic and labored patriarchal romance fantasy; each of its sections is dominated by a series of male protagonists. In one sequence, Betty Field desires a more "beautiful" face so that she can capture the "love" of Robert Cummings; Field wears a mask to disguise her features as she courts Cummings, and magically, when the mask is removed, her own face has taken on the superficially more acceptable configurations of the mask's contours. The sequence is perhaps one of the most nakedly overt confirmations of the feminine role positioning in 1940s classical film narrative. To obtain a man, a woman must conform to certain iconic standards of conventional beauty. (We will see LeBorg explore this theme later in *Jungle Woman*.) Edward G. Robinson and Charles Boyer also dominate their respective sections of the film; in each of the three stories, the artificial primacy of the masculine is celebrated.

The excised section given to LeBorg centered around Gloria Jean as Jane, a young blind woman who lives on her father's farm (Clem, played by Frank Craven). Jane, though blind, is another of LeBorg's seers. She also controls the forces of nature. She can summon the wind or birds, and bring sunshine or rain. As with Paula in *Weird Woman*, Jane is a feminine figure in touch with nature, a woman who privileges the superiority of the natural over the synthetic society of men. Cliff (Alan Curtis), an ex-con framed for bank robbery and fleeing the police, chances upon Jane and Clem's farm and asks to stay on. In Duvivier's much darker original version, Cliff murders Jane's father and strangles Jane after pursuing her through the woods surrounding the farm; in LeBorg's revision, these events are presented as a nightmare of societal rupture that Cliff seeks to prevent from coming true. By the end of LeBorg's film, Jane has reintegrated Cliff into both the natural and social structures Cliff sought to evade.

I argue that Universal eliminated Gloria Jean's section of the film because the sequence's primacy of the feminine clashed with the dominant patriarchal narrative employed by the rest of the film. Through all of 1943, Duvivier's twenty minutes of footage languished in Universal's vaults. In 1944, never willing to let anything go to waste, Universal screened the existing twenty minutes. Universal had Roy Chanslor and Ernest Pascal (Pascal had worked on the script of *Flesh and Fantasy* with Samuel Hoffenstine; this script was, in turn, based on stories by Oscar Wilde and Laslo Vadnay) create a new script incorporating this footage, and asked LeBorg to direct an additional forty-five minutes of film to be grafted on to Duvivier's original material. Significantly, Duvivier, when apprised of the project, told LeBorg that he would absolutely refuse to accept co-direction credit. Still, LeBorg accepted the project, hoping that he could do something with the material. Although LeBorg later disowned the film, he finally received sole directorial credit. It is a remarkably effective and coherent film, even though the studio had designed it solely as a way to utilize some expensive out-takes.

Jane, not Cliff, is the protagonist in LeBorg's revision of Duvivier's film, and the narrative and imagistic structure of the revision clearly privileges the domain of the feminine over the masculine desire for traditional societal trappings of power. Wild hawks, a medieval heraldic device signifying feminine power, perch on Jane's shoulders. Though blind, Jane sees much more clearly than those around her gifted with conventional sight. Both LeBorg and Duvivier continually frame Jane in scenes of pastoral beauty; she seems most at home outdoors. Cliff, on the other hand, is a creature of the city and the penitentiary, marginalized by society, distrustful of the feminine and the natural. Jane's victory over nature, and over Cliff's desire for the purely physical, forms the fabric of the film's thematic structure, a structure directly at odds with the other phallocentric segments of the film.

LeBorg's first revisionary work can be seen in the opening reels of *Destiny*, detailing Cliff's discharge from prison and his reversion to the criminal milieu that initially disgraced him in the eyes of society. LeBorg and Duvivier both had a hand in the sequences in which Jane integrates Cliff into life on the farm.

Duvivier alone directed the harrowing dream sequence in which Cliff, overcome by a need to displace the power of the feminine, as well as the patriarchy which seeks to simultaneously define and suppress him, murders Jane's father, and then attempts to rape Jane. At her silent command, Jane's dog intervenes and attacks Cliff, allowing her to escape through the front door of the house. Bruised and shaken, Jane seems at a loss, unable to control either her own emotions or the forces of nature she has so easily commanded throughout the film. Within a few moments, however, Jane summons up a dust storm to blind her would-be attacker, and flees through the woods.

Cliff attempts to follow, but is thwarted in his pursuit by the same trees that shelter Jane, which are now seemingly alive. Cliff stumbles and falls. The trees trap him with their branches. As Jane continues to run from Cliff, the revised dream sequence ends and Cliff wakes up, understandably shaken. LeBorg now directs the rest of the film. Cliff tells Jane of his dream, and says that he must leave—he is afraid that the events he has dreamed will actually come to pass. Moments later, Jane's father is accidentally wounded by a shotgun. Though it may mean his capture, Cliff takes Clem to town, and the hospital. Recognized by the police, Cliff is taken into custody on the false charge of bank robbery. Jane, however, has retained her control of both natural and societal events. LeBorg shows us a brief shot of Jane during Cliff's interrogation by the police, and a moment later, as if by magic, the man who framed Cliff entirely exonerates him. It is, in the natural order of things, a miracle, much like the final scene in Roberto Rossellini's 1953 film *Viaggio in Italia*. Jane and Cliff return to the farm; Jane's father will recover; Jane and Cliff will marry. All of this has been accomplished through Jane's power alone. Although she uses the forces of nature (and ultimately, the emotions of men) as agencies of her dominion, Jane has given life to Cliff, and returned him to harmony with nature. Thus, Jane can be seen as a *femme vivante*, a figure opposed to traditional 1940s psychic iconography. The *femme vivante* is the giver of life, the bearer of hope, the locus of reason, the giver rather than the bearer of the gaze. The dark vision afforded of the feminine in most 1940s Hollywood films (the *femme fatale*) is here transmuted into something life affirming:

the woman as myth-bearer, controller of nature, seer, mystic. It seems significant to me that the most positivist sections of *Destiny* are those directed by LeBorg, depicting Jane's oneness with nature, the simplicity and beauty of country life, and Jane's miraculous intervention on Cliff's behalf.

Duvivier's sections focus on Cliff's attempted rape of Jane, his murder of her father, and Jane's escape through the woods. Although Duvivier also directed some of the pastoral sequences, it is easy to see where Duvivier's work ends and LeBorg's begins; Duvivier's imagery, both literally and figuratively, is darker in every respect. Cliff's demeanor seems irredeemably evil and psychotic in Duvivier's footage; LeBorg envisages him as confused, but not beyond reclamation. With *Destiny*, LeBorg took the fragments of a feminist narrative and expanded upon them to his own ends, even though the film was never seen by the studio as more than a clever way to utilize Duvivier's existing material.

Gloria Jean's Jane emerges as a figure of power and ability, able to rescue those she loves from danger and instruct those who have strayed from the path of moral virtue; she is a seer who places real value in warnings and signs, a ruler of the womb-like world of the farm and the forest that surrounds it. In contrast, Cliff dwells in the rationally ordered universe of American urban society, a society represented by the prison and the city (and in *Weird Woman* by the university). Nature is seen as a redemptive feminine agency, and the feminine divinity of Jane (as of Paula) is shown to be more in tune with the forces of natural law. In an early sequence of *Destiny*, just after Cliff arrives at the farm, an older woman (who very much conforms to the iconographic profile of a conventional witch) tells Cliff that Jane can control the powers of nature—the animals, the wind, the elements. Cliff scoffs at this, but later acknowledges the truth of the woman's words. Almost alone in the films of the 1940s, *Destiny* offers a compelling vision of an alternative feminist universe.

Jungle Woman is another film in which the feminine instinct is paralleled with the natural order, but the film addresses other issues, particularly racial marginalization. The plot of *Jungle Woman* is both simple and preposterous. Paula, the Ape Woman (Acquanetta), who at one time had been a gorilla before a series of operations gave her a temporary human aspect, attempts to recuperate at the private sanitarium of a Dr. Fletcher (J. Carrol Naish). She falls in love with Bob Whitney (Richard Davis), who is about to marry Dr. Fletcher's daughter Joan (Lois Collier). Paula, the Ape Woman, is denied the love of Bob Whitney because she is seen by the film's narrative as a "freak of nature"; the final elimination of her disruptive presence underscores the ultimate victory of the dominant order the movie celebrates. *Jungle Woman* might well be subtitled *The Gaze of Acquanetta*. As with Paula in *Weird Woman* and Jane in *Destiny*, Paula, the Ape Woman in *Jungle Woman*, controls those around her with her gaze alone. In scene after scene, it is Paula who really controls the "wild animals" Fred Mason seeks to dominate with his guns, whips, and chairs. Marc Vernet aptly describes the power of this all-controlling gaze:

> The look here is impersonal, unreachable: here again, it is an unbearable look. It is that look that condemns without appeal, that crushes whomever it is addressed to: it is the look of murderous folly, a devouring look, the look of the Law, the look of Death. . . . a look that is unanswerable, impersonal, and to which there is no court of appeal. (Vernet 59)

Thus, it is through her gaze, and the medium of her visual power, that Acquanetta emerges as the central "giver of the look" in *Jungle Woman*. Reason, rational discourse, the "power" of the patriarchy—all of these forces are seen as contrary to the power of the natural order. Norman Reed's critical writings are of no use to him in *Weird Woman*; Cliff in *Destiny* also finally realizes the futility of relying on force. One must be in communion with nature to control it, rather than attempt to force one's self upon the natural order through the use of intrusive (and inappropriate) methodologies. The most effective sections of *Jungle Woman* rely entirely on Acquanetta's luminous visage, as she silently hypnotizes the "untamed" circus animals to do her bidding.

As Paula, the Ape Woman, Acquanetta, too, is seen as "untamed" by the film's narrative, and thus able to communicate on a nonverbal, purely visual plane with her fellow denizens of the jungle. In this film of looks, it is appropriate that the text of the work derives most of its power from visuals, accompanied by natural sounds; for the most part it is bereft of dialogue. The structure of the film is a series of narrative flashbacks from various different personal viewpoints. Once the flashbacks have been introduced, the respective narrator's voice drops out of the remembered images. Words in the film tell little about the characters. It is through Acquanetta/Paula the Ape Woman's gaze that we will know, and yet still not comprehend, her connection to Rousseauian naturalism, and her uneasy alliance with the world of women and men.

In the absence of the look, or when the look fails, only force is applicable. Having tried every other means at his disposal to civilize Paula, the Ape Woman, Dr. Fletcher finally kills her with a hypodermic injection after a fierce struggle on the grounds of the sanitarium. Significantly, the murder of Paula is shown twice; once at the very beginning of the film, and once at the end. The image of female subjugation that thus frames the text of the film is not to be taken lightly; Paula, and the forces of feminist naturalism she represents, are here forcibly suppressed by the patriarchy which has tried, unsuccessfully, to bend Paula to its will. Implicit in the film's subtext is the notion that Paula is more suitably matched with the slow-witted caretaker employed by Dr. Fletcher than the iconographically perfect Bob Whitney. Being less than human, Paula's desires are seen as being of lesser importance. Linda LeMoncheck notes this differentiation of desire in her study, *Dehumanizing Women*:

> My claim is that, if we believe objects and animals have rights to well-being and freedom different from those of persons, it is because they are not believed to value the kind of well-being and freedom that persons do. So, for example, since an object is not believed capable of feeling pain, it is not believed capable of valuing freedom from physical discomfort and so be thought to deserve protection from such discomfort by having a claim or right against it. (19)

Paula's tragic death results, in part, from her attempts to rise above her animist origins. The outrageous racism of the film is underlined by the visual conceit that, since the operation that originally changed Paula from simian to human form has been only partially successful, Paula must emerge as a person of non-Caucasian racial heritage.

But Acquanetta's marginalization within the text of the film is ascribed solely to her desires and her feminist attempts at self-expression and self-determination. Like Paula in *Weird Woman*, and Jane in *Destiny*, Paula, the Ape Woman (the appellation itself being a conflation of feminine nature with bestial impulse) is more firmly in control of the world around her than any of the male protagonists in the three films. As with Ilona, Paula's dominion is ended only by her murder. Clearly, she cannot be allowed to publicly subvert Bob Mason's wholly artificial dominion over the animals in his circus. Nor may she express her desire for Bob Whitney, who is seen by the film as the property of Joan, Dr. Fletcher's daughter. Of the three films discussed here, *Jungle Woman* is easily the most tragic, in that it combines sexual and racial marginalization in a single ferocious instance, and then (doubly, with Paula's twin death) expunges it from the narrative.

It can be argued that Reginald LeBorg was simply assigned the direction of these three films (and indeed he was), and that the thematic and imagistic structures discussed in this text have been artificially introduced by the application of an external critical apparatus. The physical cheapness of the production of all three films has led a number of critics to ignore the films altogether. The phantom availability of the texts also works against a deeper appreciation of the films, ensuring that past critical reviews of the works will subsume the authority of the films themselves, "becoming," in a sense, the work under discussion. The films have also been appropriated by cultists, and ridiculed (without insight or critical precision) both for their "rud'ly stamp'd" origins, and their admittedly bizarre narrative structures.

But none of these objections ultimately has any validity, or even usefulness, in an understanding of the films themselves, or of LeBorg's career as a whole. The films received inferior pro-

duction values because they dealt with themes of marginalization and societal rupture, and did not conform to conventional
sexual role modeling or patriarchal narrative form. Those who
ridicule the films seek to dismiss and deprivilege them, and fans
in general are hesitant to deconstruct texts of any sort for fear
that the process will remove them from an adolescent stage of
textual comprehension, the rapture of childhood. The physical
difficulty of locating the films remains a problem, yet this
should also not be allowed to interfere with any analysis of the
films. Finally, though LeBorg was indeed a contract director,
assigned to most of the projects he completed during his long
career, there is little doubt in my mind that LeBorg picked up on
the themes presented in these films and effectively foregrounded them, as evidenced by the concerns of a number of
other films that LeBorg directed.

Space does not permit a detailed analysis of LeBorg's other
feminist films, but even a brief consideration of his other works
reveals that the director more often than not anchored his narrative within the concerns of his female protagonists, de-center-
ing the males in his films, and undermining or questioning their
fugitive authority. Minor cases might be made for such films as
She's For Me (1943), *Susie Steps Out* (1946), or *Honeymoon
Ahead* (1945). More importantly, LeBorg directed *San Diego, I
Love You* (1944) with Louise Allbritton as Virginia McCooley, a
young woman striving to keep her family together in the face of
her father's impracticality (as perfectly personified by Edward
Everett Horton). This film, incidentally, was very much a personal project, and one that LeBorg had a considerable hand in
developing for the screen. *Little Iodine* (1946), based on Jimmy
Hatlo's comic strip, privileges the authority of a disruptive
young girl who creates havoc wherever she goes, while seeking
to reunite her feuding mother and father—the feminine counterpart of Dennis the Menace. *G. I. Jane* (1951) is a story of feminine difference within the military, as the title implies, and
another example of a subversive text masquerading as a light
comedy. *Models, Inc.* (1952) deals with the objectification of the
feminine, in a narrative structured around a modeling agency
that operates as a front for prostitution, thus mirroring imagistic debasement with physical degradation.

The Dalton Girls (1957) can correctly be seen as a forerunner of Ridley Scott's *Thelma and Louise* (1991). Holly, Rose, Marigold, and Columbine Dalton, daughters of a deceased Dalton Gang member, turn to crime after Holly (Merry Anders) is forced to kill a man who attempts to rape her. Knowing that her story will not be believed because of her ancestry, Holly bands together with her sisters to form a new Dalton Gang. The four women commit a number of successful robberies, but are ultimately tracked down by a vigilante group at the conclusion of the film. LeBorg clearly sides with the Dalton women, and views their choice of an outlaw existence as their only chance for freedom, dignity, and independence. Although the male ruling group represented by the conventional forces of law triumphs with the closure of the narrative, LeBorg suggests that this ending is both arbitrary and false, dictated by patriarchal narrative requirements more than anything else. Along with Roger Corman's early feminist westerns, *The Oklahoma Woman* (1955) and *Gunslinger* (1956), LeBorg's *The Dalton Girls* is an overlooked addition to the director's canon, certainly worth revival and further study.

There is also *The Eyes of Annie Jones* (1964), an earlier version of *The Eyes of Laura Mars* (1978). The film centers around Francesca Annis as the seer Annie Jones (comparable to Jane in *Destiny*), and deals with Annie's attempts to locate Carol Wheeler (Myrtle Reed), the sister of David Wheeler (Richard Conte). Made quickly and cheaply in England, the film nevertheless exudes an air of drab authority (set, as it is, almost entirely in Annie's flat). LeBorg's interest resides almost entirely in Annie's visionary ability and its consequences and de-centers Conte, the nominal star of the piece.

Among his unfinished projects, LeBorg left the screenplay for a film to be titled *Madame Prime Minister* (shades of Margaret Thatcher!), "dealing with life 100 years from now when women rule the world." Though LeBorg instinctively fought against the representational strategies of the feminine as employed and defined by Hollywood cinematic practice in the 1940s, in the end, the overwhelming power of the imagistic construct then favored by the studio hierarchy ensured that his approach would, itself, be marginalized.

LeBorg's vision may also be seen as a co-efficient of wartime propaganda response efforts, and in this light, perhaps the self-sufficiency displayed by LeBorg's feminine protagonists can be seen as emblematic of the social and political agenda of the era. Yet Reginald LeBorg never really got the opportunity to do the work he was so obviously capable of. His disdain for the commercial Hollywood system remained intact up to his death in 1989, and throughout his career, he made little secret of his disaffection for the more odious requirements of genre narrative structure. During the late 1940s, LeBorg fought for great control over his work, and more independence to produce projects be believed in, but he lacked the political acumen to work within the studio structure tactfully. Because of this, LeBorg was ultimately marginalized himself.

LeBorg's keen apprehension of classical literature, art, and music was out of step with the merciless mercantilism of such producers as Oliver Drake and Will Cowan, and LeBorg was thus forced to compromise in all his work. LeBorg made the films that the system allowed him to, often, as in *Destiny* and *Jungle Woman*, forced to work from existing scraps of other projects to shape his vision. But the best of LeBorg's work is beyond physical compromise and a testament to his fierce intransigence as a force of rupture within the confines of an impersonal and unsympathetic community. *Weird Woman*, *Destiny*, and *Jungle Woman* are the works of a man who was, in many respects, ahead of his time, and whose concerns were in opposition to established codes of gender behaviorism. It may be true that, at last, the tale told in LeBorg's films can be extricated from the mechanism that informed their creation, and that LeBorg's vision, though compromised, may be seen for the disruptive and illuminating force that it represented.

THE FEMINIST HORROR FILM

As a further consideration of the spectacle of horror film, I would like to suggest that the women who direct contemporary horror films bring a substantially different vision to their work than that of their male counterparts. I wish to argue that in their creation of a considerable number of Gothic films, women have seized a certain degree of control over the discourse of the horror movie. By choosing forms of representation in their horror films that deviate from the patriarchal models of the Gothic narrative, these filmmakers have given us a fresh and exhilarating vision of the uncanny that undercuts and questions much that has been created by men in the domain of the horror film. To cite Susan Wolstenholme,

> The Gothic structure of looking and being-looked-at offers certain "covers" for the coding of women within the text, because its plot often revolves around the issues of seeing and hiding (12).

The text of the horror film seems ripe for reinterpretation. It is the "internal coherence" of the text of the horror film that needs to be questioned, which, in the words of Georges Bataille, resides in "our horror of nature:"

> What then is the essential meaning of our horror of nature? Not wanting to depend on anything, abandoning the place of our carnal birth, revolting intimately against the fact of *dying*, generally mistrusting the body, that is, having a deep mistrust of what is accidental, natural, perishable—this appears to be *for each one of us* the sense of the movement that leads us *to represent **man*** [my emphasis] independently of filth, of the sexual functions and of death. (91)

Note the gender specificity encoded by Bataille. It is precisely this unquestioned specificity that needs to be addressed and explored, and it is in the work of the feminist horror film that many of Bataille's most pressing concerns are concretely and compellingly played out. Such filmmakers as Alice Guy (who, as we will see, offers one of the earliest configurations of alternative feminist film practice in a number of genres), along with contemporary figures including Kathryn Bigelow, Stephanie Rothman, Kristine Peterson, Katt Shea, Amy Jones, and others have given us a new vision of the horror film, one which throws all previously existing generic structures in this area into question.

This process is still an evolving one, over hotly contested ground, as the horror film can correctly be seen as a nexus of desire and disgust, fear and pleasure, sexuality unleashed and repressed—a very hot zone indeed. If there is any one criticism that might be offered at the outlet, it is that these new films do not go far enough into previously explored terrain, and fail to overturn as many conventions as they might. Yet several of the horror films directed by this group of cinéastes are genuinely revolutionary, although, perhaps predictably, they often fail to attain the distribution (and hence the success) of the misogynist constructs that flood the screen in rapid succession which are scripted and directed by men.

Kathryn Bigelow's often-overlooked vampire film *Near Dark* (1987) is a good starting point for a consideration of these new models of the graphic horror film. Bigelow's other films, particularly *Blue Steel* (1990) and *Point Break* (1991), have received a good deal of critical attention, but *Near Dark* and Bigelow's interesting first feature *The Loveless* (co-directed with Monty Montgomery in 1981) have been abandoned to the near oblivion of the video rental shelf. *Near Dark*, as Bigelow notes, is a generic hybrid, a "vampire western"; it enables Bigelow, in her words, "to invest the genre [of the horror film] with new material, seeing where the edges of the envelope are, so to speak" (Tasker, 157).

Near Dark chronicles the vagrant existence of Caleb (Adrian Pasdar), who is taken in by a group of country-western vampires who roam the southwest in a customized trailer in search of liquid sustenance. Though the vampire group is nominally headed by the rapacious Jesse (Lance Henrikson) and his sidekick Diamondback (Jenette Goldstein), there are schisms within the group, most notably configured within the character of Mae (Jenny Wright), who "adopts" Caleb and sponsors him to the reluctant members of the "family." Of all the characters in the film, it is Mae who is arguably the most fully realized, feeding Caleb with her own blood when he is afraid to make his first "kill" and thus initiate himself into the group of vampiric outlaws, and fighting for his possession as a totemic love object over the strenuous dissent of Jesse and Diamondback.

What has particularly disturbed a number of critics in all of Bigelow's work is, paradoxically, her brilliance as an action director, and more specifically, a director of scenes of unremittingly inexorable choreographed violence. Similar objections were raised when Ida Lupino directed *The Hitch-Hiker* in 1953, and the press book for that film stressed Lupino's "femininity," even as she directed scenes of murder and cruelty with genuine flair and originality. In *Near Dark*, the arguable highlight of the film from a purely plastic/kinetic point of view occurs as the group attacks a group of rednecks in an isolated tavern late at night, effortlessly slaughtering patrons and employees alike as though the entire process constituted some sort of monstrous game, which is, of course, exactly what it is: the dance of death between the predator and victim.

As Alain Silver and James Ursini note,

> *Near Dark* is a redneck version of the vampire legend. The film showcases a clan of violent "good old boys," including two women and a lecherous dwarf, who terrorize country bars, listen to hard rock, guzzle liquor, steal cars, curse profusely, and survive shootouts right out of *Bonnie and Clyde*. This vampiric Hole in the Wall Gang is on a crime spree through the Midwest, showing no mercy in their violent depredations.
>
> At one of their stops a disaffected young man, Caleb, falls for Mae, the youngest vampire, and is vampirized or, as the others refer to it, "turned" by her. In spite of the objections of the clan, Mae takes him under her wing, feeding him from her own blood as she would a baby until he is able to make his own kills. As he sucks from her open veins, Mae becomes both his mother and his lover. (197–198)

With the possible exception of Caleb's penultimate nurturing of Mae into a non-vampiric state (and Mae's initial adoption of Caleb into the gang), this sort of spectacle is, apparently, supposed to be alien to women: a neat irony inasmuch as women are far more likely than men to be the victims of violent assault in real life. For several years, Bigelow was married to one of Hollywood's most adept action directors, James Cameron, and their relationship must have found some common ground in a shared admiration for kinetic cinema. Cameron's *Aliens* (1986) and *Terminator II* display a similar panache in their construction of scenes of violent spectacle, although Bigelow seems more involved in her use of camerawork. She dives and darts through her action sequences with a continually moving camera, where as Cameron often seems content to set up a scene and observe it from a clinical distance.

Caleb's passion for Mae is reciprocated by her with reluctance (because Mae knows all too well how difficult a vampire's existence is), but for this one time, at least, one gets a sense of mutual response and desire on both sides of the relationship, rather than Caleb simply wishing to possess Mae, or Mae fixating on Caleb. Lance Henrikson's Jesse figures in as a sort of balancing force within the nuclear structure of the vampire family; resourceful, mordant and world-weary, he plots the next raid, arranges for motel rooms so the group can sleep during the day, insists that every member of the pack pull her or his own weight. Jenette Goldstein's Diamondback is seen as a goal-oriented survivalist within the narrative of *Near Dark*, a feminist foot-soldier of the blood brotherhood (a role she would reprise, to a degree, in her portrayal of Vasquez, the paramilitary trooper in Cameron's *Aliens*). All of these elements are woven together into a trancelike fabric of sleep, slaughter, and survival, an endlessly evolving tapering of thirst and fulfillment underscored by Tangerine Dream's hypnotic, droning electronic music track buried deeply into the aural/visual mix of the film.

What makes *Near Dark* so successful is Bigelow's participation in the world she creates—she, and we, become one with the marauding outsiders. Fellow director Kristine Peterson, creator of *Body Chemistry* (1990), in a telephone conversation with me in late 1991, instantly singled out *Near Dark* as Bigelow's most interesting and personal work, and I agree with her assessment. *Blue Steel* and *Point Break* are accomplished pieces of action filmmaking, particularly the latter, but they never achieve the claustrophobic intensity of *Near Dark*, or that film's embrace of a parallel world of "difference." Bigelow has continued her work in this area with more big-budget films in the 1990s, most notably the interesting if flawed Dystopian mindtransference film, *Strange Days* (1995).

Kristine Peterson's early work for producer Roger Corman encompassed several forgettable exploitation films, as well as assistant director (AD) work on *Night Flyers* (1987), a narrative concerning demonic possession in outer space, and AD work on *Nightmare on Elm Street Part Five* (1990) and *Bill and Ted's Excellent Adventure* (1989). With *Body Chemistry* (1990), Peterson finally got a chance to display her considerable talents as an action director. Not surprisingly, one of the directors she admires most is Kathryn Bigelow. While *Body Chemistry* is more an "erotic thriller" than a straight horror film, Peterson manages, through the sheer force of her visual involvement with the material, to raise it above the level of the standard Corman/Concorde project. The relationship between researcher Tom Redding (Marc Singer) and his nemesis Claire Archer (Lisa Pescia) is effectively charted in a series of bold, confrontational set-ups, and Peterson plunges into the schizoid intensity of their illicit relationship in a hopped-up visual style reminiscent of Bigelow's work, but one which, through sheer intensity of engagement, becomes entirely her own.

Peterson's comments on her working situation in Hollywood, in an unpublished interview with Gwendolyn Audrey Foster, tell us much about the ways in which Hollywood seeks to perpetuate existing modes of gender roles in contemporary horror films and/or action thrillers.

> One of the trends in Hollywood right now, especially for cable television, and I've been told this by two producers, women producers, "We're looking for films that feature women in jeopardy." The reason they are looking for these films is not so much that they want to make films about or for women in situations of jeopardy, but because they want to make men feel good. And how do you make men feel good? What's their fantasy? Their fantasy is to be the savior. This is the attitude in Hollywood. "We want to make men heroes." How can you do that? Have them save something. Who can you have them save? Women are the most obvious choice. I think it would be great to have the reverse sometimes, but in this set-up we have always something bad happening to a woman. She gets abducted,

raped, something horrible. The hero goes off to save her.

I'm just amazed at how insensitive some directors are about this, but I'm not in a position to save the world. The scripts have been so unimaginative for women. In order for a woman to be a savior, they have to rape her and then have her save herself. Unless it's a child.

She can also save a child. She can't save a man, because they can't be portrayed as vulnerable. It's a cultural thing. It's kind of sad. But that's what's happening. You do try to minimize what you can as best you can, but you can't bite the hand that feeds you, can you?

But, as Peterson's own work indicates, one must do *exactly* this—transgress upon existing limits—in order to push beyond conventional genre boundaries. Peterson's vision is considerably bleaker; at the conclusion of *Body Chemistry*, Claire murders Tom and successfully passes off the crime as an act of self-defense against a relentless stalker, when in fact it is Claire who has been obsessively infatuated with Tom. In this, the film can be seen as something of a reworking of Adrian Lyne's *Fatal Attraction* (1987), in which Glenn Close obsessively shadows Michael Douglas after an adulterous one-night stand. Peterson's Tom, too, is married, and Claire's obsession begins after a brief and violent sexual encounter. The rage and anger floating barely beneath the surface of Claire's persona in *Body Chemistry* makes this a horror film of repression and transfigured desire/lust in which Claire seemingly seeks to be objectified by Tom, yet all the while retains her true status as initiator and controlling agency of their sexual liaisons.

Katt Shea, another Corman alumnus, directed *Stripped to Kill I* (1987) and *Stripped to Kill 2* (1989) for Concorde before going on to more mainstream work with *Poison Ivy* (1992), which was, despite generally excellent reviews, a commercial disappointment. Shea shares Bigelow's and Peterson's interest in the action genre, but adds a moody flavor of her own to the many confrontational tableaux of *Poison Ivy*. In *Poison Ivy* orphan Drew Barrymore moves in with Sara Gilbert and her well-to-do mother and father (Tom Skerrit and Cheryl Ladd), creating a tangle of sexual desire within the familial domain.

Befriending each member of the family in turn while systematically seeking their destruction, Ivy's situation within the narrative of *Poison Ivy* reminds one of Pasolini's *Teorema* (1968), in which Terence Stamp insinuates himself into an Italian household with similarly apocalyptic results. In her refigurement of the object-of-desire as Ivy, Shea creates an androgynous figure of sexual tension, a locus for the fears and desires of the family she nearly destroys. Since the release of this "American family horror movie," Katt Shea has not had a chance to direct another film—due perhaps in part to the unflattering vision of the familial unit the film displays, and the concomitant lack of commercial success congruent with this vision. Yet certainly we will hear more from Shea; *Poison Ivy* is simply too accomplished for its auteur to be forced to languish in semi-oblivion. In 1996, Katt Shea directed a Showtime TV movie for Corman's Concorde-New Horizon's company, *Last Exit to Earth*.

Stephanie Rothman, director of the horror films *Blood Bath* (1966) and *The Velvet Vampire* (1971), as well as *It's a Bikini World* (1967) and *Terminal Island* (1979), is another Corman alumnus who initiated the first wave of feminist horror films in the 1960s. Yet by the end of the 1970s she was both bored and frustrated by the severe limitations forced on her by typical Hollywood practice. Rothman's first horror film, *Blood Bath*, a vampire slasher film, had a decidedly compromised genesis: Rothman was brought onto the project halfway through shooting. The finished film has a phantasmal, uncertain air about it (not surprisingly given the production circumstances), but Rothman demonstrated that she could take over a project in difficulty and bring in *something* usable, and so, for a time, her career prospered. But as the '60s turned into the '70s, Rothman failed to obtain the opportunities she deserved.

In a 1979 interview with Ally Acker, Rothman stated that "a great deal of the problem women have today is that they don't demand change. If you don't complain, no one knows you have a complaint. What roles women will play in the future depends on what women expect and want to happen to them. It isn't up to men . . ." (47). By this time, Rothman had made the horror film *The Velvet Vampire*, again under Roger Corman's aegis, and again under tight constraints of budget and casting. As Silver and Ursini note in their discussion of Rothman's *The Velvet Vampire*, the film is

> interesting both because the antagonist has no compunctions about the practice of her vampirism and also because it parodies certain aspects of the *genre*—ranging from simple homages such as an art exhibit in the "Stoker Gallery" and naming the woman vampire Diane Le Fanu to the more elaborate novelties of having her make her home in the desert or demonstrate a taste for raw chicken.
>
> The eclectic style of this film—day-lit desert landscapes and a final chase through downtown Los Angeles providing a contrast with low-lit interiors full of unnatural colours—encompasses some imaginative narrative turns [including scenes in which] the vampire [uses] her strength to overpower and kill an unsuspecting mugger . . . [and one sequence in which the vampire's] body "float[s]" down an escalator [during] the chase scene . . . (116)

Thus Rothman's protagonist is in control (to a certain degree) of her vampiric destiny, and manifests external signs of this control through transgressive reinscription of gender "norms" (beating up the would-be mugger), and dialectical transcendence of cinematic Gothic tradition. One has only to consider Lambert Hillyer's *Dracula's Daughter* (1936), in which Gloria Holden plays a doomed lesbian vampire who reluctantly drains the blood of young women to survive, in contrast to Celeste Yarnall's energetic and highly eroticized destruction of her victims in *The Velvet Vampire*, to see how Rothman's performative countertestimony of the feminine vampire ethos culturally transfigures previous incarnations of the movie vampire. Indeed, the film's promotional materials promised a linkage of sexual fusion and the *mise en abyme* of vampiric destruction with the words "climax after climax of terror and desire . . ." (Weldon, 750). In Stephanie Rothman's *The Velvet Vampire* this eroticized encounter finds one of its most fully realized expressions: through the mediating agency of the female gaze, Rothman's vampiric Diane Le Fanu (the protagonist of *The Velvet*

Vampire) becomes one of the few representations of the lesbian vampire to be created by a woman, and this aggressive reconstitutive figuration of desire is one of the most intriguing incarnationist tropes in Gothic cinema.

Alice Guy, one of the pioneering directors of the cinema, was a transgeneric figure, moving with ease from comedy to farce to tragedy. She directed the astounding total of *seven hundred* one-reel films in France and the United States between 1896 and 1913, as well as numerous feature films. Sadly, more than 95 percent of these films are lost today. Within the province of this text, what interests me during her American period (as head of her own production company, Solax Films) is her direction of *The Pit and the Pendulum* (1913). Guy's pioneering film gives us a death trope of enunciative automourning, or narrative as epistemological example. In contrast to the bound feminine corpus unfortunately so familiar to generic conventions of the patriarchal horror film, Guy's bound male in agony displays a profound slippage of the libidinal economy at work within the genre of Gothic horror.

It is beyond the province of this text (and indeed, it has been persuasively argued elsewhere, particularly in the historical/theoretical work of Slide and Heck-Rabi; see bibliography) to argue that had the development of cinema followed a non-sexist trajectory in its formative years (when directors such as Guy, Kathlyn Williams, Lois Weber, Cleo Madison, and others flourished at such major studios as Carl Laemmle's Universal Pictures before 1920), contemporary configurations of cinematic desire, loss, and metanarrative structures would probably be altogether different. Until 1920, women functioned relatively freely as directors (albeit with a degree of interference, not unlike their male colleagues of the era), and the visions of the filmmakers mentioned above differ markedly from that of D. W. Griffith, Edwin S. Porter, J. Searle Dawley (director of Edison's 1910 *Frankenstein*), and other contemporary male cinéastes. The panache and style with which Guy attacked the production of *The Pit and the Pendulum* suggests that had she lived today, she would be working comfortably alongside Bigelow, Rothman, and Peterson; indeed, only the total intervention of a transgressive patriarchal power-grab sufficed to de-center women from the director's chair (in large measure) between 1920 and 1980, although some brave individualists, among them Ida Lupino and Dorothy Arzner, continued to fight to create their vision on the screen. This process of reclamation is still going on as we speak, although for the most part, men still occupy the position of director in Hollywood.

Yet Guy's vision in her many films (a major exhibition of her existing works was mounted in Créteil, France, in the Film de Femmes Festival in the spring of 1993) offers the contemporary viewer an alternative vision to a world of predetermined heterotopic hegemonic moments, comprising a means of figuration that de-centers the feminine and consigns the female body, particularly in Gothic horror, to the realm of subjective malaise. Guy's instinctive opposition to the gendered specificity of desire encoded within patriarchal generic constructs stands as eloquent performative testimony to the artificial strictures of male genre "requirements."

Perhaps the most problematic genre of the postmodern horror film practice is the "slasher" film, and it is perhaps both paradoxical and appropriate that this section of the text should conclude with a brief examination of Amy Jones's *Slumber Party Massacre*, a little-cited film scripted by Rita Mae Brown, author of *The Rubyfruit Jungle*. (In 1996, Jones directed the suspense film *The Rich Man's Wife*, starring Halle Berry, a film that also contained more than the usual quotient of violence.) Until recently, it has been argued that such a brutally misogynist enterprise went against the grain of anything that could conceivably be labeled feminist film practice. However, in her ground-breaking book *Men, Women and Chainsaws*, Carol Clover has persuasively foregrounded the figure of the "Final Girl" within the narrative structure of the slasher film, thus re-claiming the film as an act of resistance and reconstructive/agential theory. The killer in *Slumber Party Massacre* is introduced precisely because he is to be resisted, destroyed, transcended. Clover writes:

> Valerie in *Slumber Party Massacre* . . . takes a machete-like weapon to the killer, striking off the bit from his [overtly phallic] power drill, severing his hand, and finally impaling him [and causing his death]. (37–38)

Certainly the killer's violent end is richly deserved within the context of the film, and Jones, Brown, and Clover, using generic appropriation and transgressive reinscription filtered through the agency of an existing metronomic structure, have taken one of the most despicable genres of the horror film and transformed it into a vision of feminist retribution and reconstitution. While it would be naive to suggest that the film was produced for these reasons, with this film Brown and Jones have pulled off one of the most subversive acts in postmodern cinema history: they have taken a thoroughly disreputable and marginalized area of cinema discourse and reclaimed it, transforming the conventional victims of the genre into Final Girls who decisively take matters into their own hands, without application to any external authority for help. Teresa de Lauretis further states that:

> The idea that *a film may address the spectator as female*, rather than portray women positively or negatively, seems very important to me in the critical endeavor to characterize women's cinema as a cinema for, not only by, women. (148)

These new horror films perform precisely this function, positing the viewer as a female giver/bearer of the gaze, creating a performative gendered specificity of desire in their articulation of feminist alterity.

Groundbreaking works of Queer cinema such as *Nancy's Nightmare* (1988), a video by Azian Nurudin, construct an ideal viewer, such as the one buried in Narudin's depiction of:

> a hard-core, lesbian S-M sex act in full leather regalia. Tightly framed and occasionally shot in split-screen, the film begins after the sex has begun and ends while it is still underway, situating the viewer discomfortingly inside the work . . . (Viegener, 124)

And yet perhaps "discomfortingly" is not the correct word in this case. *Nancy's Nightmare* has been created as an in-your-face performance that bears witness to a locus of desire unaddressed by conventional cinematic practice—why should it not be addressed here as a consensual act documented without judgment, beyond the power of the viewer to intervene? In this newly configured world, "female murderousness is a partner in crime with hetero lesbianism; male sexual exclusion and/or the risk of total annihilation become the most exciting things possible" (Williams 1993, 113).

The removal of the male from this scenario of sensual pain and violence can be seen as the ultimate—or at least logically so for the moment—fetishistic retextualization of the horror film. Richard Dyer's comment that "stereotypes mean differently for different groups, and especially for those who are members of the stereotyped group as compared to those who are not" (89) demonstrates that the only truly effective means of seizing control of these stereotypical images is to seize control of their creation, and thus their dissemination.

As Chris Straayer notes in her article "The Seduction of Boundaries: Feminist Fluidity in Annie Sprinkle's Art/Education/Sex,"

> Within this multiplex creativity, numerous boundaries are licked clear. Art melts into porn, porn accommodates life, life becomes art. Breathing orgasms into non-genital sex, and spirituality into orgasms, Sprinkle seduces deconstruction. Exercising a "queer" ideology arising from contemporary gay and lesbian subculture, she confounds pornography's boundaries, transgresses ours, and wraps us in her own. Pornography's naturalist philosophy spreads outward, margins private and public realms, simultaneously intensifying and diffusing the pornographic sensibility. (156)

Thus is it also with the horror film—it is a genre operating upon the margins of representation, it questions existing codes of authority, and it cries out for reconfiguration by a new group of skilled practitioners. In both cases, these new practitioners (in porn and/or horror) have been heretofore cast almost solely as the victims, the acted upon, the object of the gaze, the object to be possessed or defiled. Now, these genres are in the process of reinvention as part of a seemingly new (yet demonstrably ancient) process of transgenderal reinscription.

In 1944, in a film entitled *The Cry of the Werewolf*, Nina Foch was cast as the matriarchal head of a tribe of Gypsy werewolves (much in the manner of the nomadic vampires in *Near Dark*), who during World War II conducted a reign of terror from their traveling camp in and around New Orleans. There are many remarkable sequences in the film—Foch's determination to save her tribe from its enemies; her tears after she is forced to kill to protect the pack; a "Val Lewtonesque" sequence in which, transformed into a werewolf, Foch stalks a young man intent on exposing the activities of the werewolf band. But *Cry of the Werewolf* was directed by a man, Henry Levin.

How much differently might the film have been constructed had it been directed, say, by Dorothy Arzner, who was still active in Hollywood during this period (and at the same studio, Columbia Pictures)? Is there not an enormous difference between the male-centered exploitation film *The Vampire Lovers* by Roy Ward Baker, and *The Velvet Vampire* by Stephanie Rothman, in their respective use of scenes of seduction, the narrative structure of the film, and the display of the feminine body? Isn't *Near Dark* a classic of its kind because it neatly inverts all of our generic expectations of the vampire film, while simultaneously hot-wiring vampiric love into the superficially unrelated generic territory of the contemporary western? I would argue that the answer is decisively yes in all the cases argued above, and in the production of all the other films discussed within this section. Only when the tools of representation are seized will the representations change. This is happening now, and will continue to happen, as women increasingly move into the horror genre, with commercially and aesthetically satisfying new works.

CHAPTER FOUR

Spectacles of Impoverishment: Recycling the Image Bank

THE SILENT CINEMA OF JOHN H. COLLINS

Cinema history is littered with tragedies: careers cut short through death or illness, careers that never really got off the ground because of studio politics or personal problems, careers thwarted by sexism or racism or undervalued by the rigidity of canonization. Women, particularly, have been victims of historical neglect; one has only to look at the enormous number of films made by silent pioneers Lois Weber and Alice Guy (among others) to see that the work of silent women directors has been unjustly neglected in the rush to canonize Porter, Griffith, and other male contemporaries of these talented women.

The career of silent film director John H. Collins contains aspects of all of these unfortunate circumstances. Most cinema histories completely ignore his work; even the new edition of the late Ephraim Katz's *Film Encyclopedia* fails to cite Collins's films. Several of his features are listed in *The American Film Institute Film Catalogue of Motion Pictures Produced in the United States, Vol. F1; Feature Films 1911–1920*, edited by Patricia Hanson, yet complete information on this early auteur remains spotty at best: of Collins's best-known films, the 1918 Metro production of *Blue Jeans* (which starred Collins's wife,

Viola Dana) is often times cited as the highlight of the director's career, but few mentions are ever made of Collins's *The Cossack Whip*, a 1916 Edison production, produced with color tints as a five-reel feature; or the 1915 Edison production *Children of Eve* (also five reels in length); or the 1917 Metro production of *Girl Without a Soul* (another five reel feature), which Collins directed and also scripted. These are just a few of the films Collins directed, although his career credits are not extensive. For just as Collins's career was getting off the ground, he was caught up in the Spanish influenza epidemic of 1918, and died in October of that year. As chronicled in *Magill's Survey of Cinema Computer Data Base*, Collins's early years were productive and eventful, and laid the foundation for what would be an extremely short yet highly prolific career:

> Collins started working at Edison in 1905 as a young-ster of fourteen. His first job there was errand boy, then stenographer, casting director, stage manager, and assistant director. By 1914, he was at last given his first directorial assignment, with a one-reel picture. He made many important contributions to the Edison Studios, among them, the establishment of a library for costume and set research and the buildup of a special effects laboratory.
>
> In 1915, Collins chose Dana for the lead in *The Stone Heart*, a one-reel film about a young girl working in a sweat shop. He began using her as a leading lady when he soon started directing feature-length pictures. That same year they got married and became a complete team. He directed her in six features at Edison before they were offered more money at Metro.
>
> Collins and Dana began turning out a series of very interesting pictures [at Metro, though some of these features were actually copyrighted by Columbia Pictures "for the Metro Company," as will be discussed]. They had made ten five-reel features before they began work on *Blue Jeans*, which became a seven-reel picture and their first "special." Metro was so pleased by *Blue Jeans* that they gave the team a new contract. They made six more features after *Blue Jeans*, when in October, 1918, Collins died of the Spanish influenza.

Dana went on as a Metro star for the next six years. Her films rose in popularity with each release, even though they no longer had Collins's artistic touch. She changed her screen image to that of a baby vamp, and used F. Scott Fitzgerald stories as the basis for two of her features, *A Chorus Girl's Romance* (1920) and *The Off-Shore Pirate* (1921). [Her career ended in 1929, with the feature film *One Splendid Hour.*]

Dana had a sister who was also a film star, Shirley Mason, a Fox star for five years. They both retired at the advent of sound and remained very close until Shirley died in 1979. Dana then moved to the Motion Picture Country House in Woodland Hills, California. [Viola Dana died on July 3, 1987.] (anonymous, *Magill's Survey of Cinema Computer Data Base*, entry on *Blue Jeans*)

Behind these bare facts lie a number of interesting details. Collins's long apprenticeship at the Edison Studios, working his way up the ladder, demonstrates that he was a conscientious and hard-working craftsperson who understood all aspects of the film production process. Once he got his first directional break at Edison in 1914, he rapidly moved on to feature production, and once established as a feature director, he began turning out feature films at a terrific pace. Between 1915 and his death in October, 1918, Collins directed more than twenty feature films—an enormous output for such a short period of time. All this work is in addition to his 1914 one-reel short films.

Viola Dana had been working at the Edison Studios since 1910, playing mostly "unbilled bits" (Katz, 323) until she became a stage star with the Broadway production of *Poor Little Rich Girl* in 1913. Born Virginia Flugrath on June 26, 1897 (Katz, 323), Dana met Collins at the Edison Studios, and their romantic and professional alliance blossomed soon after. When Collins graduated to features with *Cohen's Luck* in 1915, he cast Viola Dana as Minnie Cohen, the daughter of Abe Cohen (played by William Wadsworth), the protagonist of the film. The film ran four reels in length, and was based on the play *Cohen's Luck* by Lee Arthur, who also wrote the screenplay for the film. As the *AFI Film Catalogue 1911–1920* notes, "This film was the first made under Edison's new policy of releasing four reel pictures at regular intervals on the General Film program. William Wadsworth played his role on stage with Annie Russell. Some exteriors for the film were shot in the 'ghetto' sections of New York's City's Lower East Side" (Hanson, 154). The film itself is a slight comedy of errors, but it is significant that Edison would entrust the launch of his new program to Collins, who had only directed one-reelers for Edison up until that time. The film was widely reviewed, and received favorable, if not ecstatic, notices, and Collins's career was truly launched. More than anything else, Collins had demonstrated his ability to bring a film in on time and on budget, and he began a whirlwind pace of film direction that would occupy him until his death.

Collins's next film was *On Dangerous Paths*, starring Viola Dana as Eleanor Thurston. Another Edison four-reel feature, the film was released through the General Film Company on July 23, 1915 (Hanson, 671). The film is a modest production contrasting the values of the wicked city against the idyllic country lifestyle, and again the film met with considerable critical and commercial success. *The Ploughshare*, which followed from Edison/General on October 1, 1915 (Hanson, 721), was a historical melodrama set in the deep South, and a film in which Viola Dana did not appear. The four-reel film details the adventures of William Lawrence (Robert Conness), "who inherits his father's estate and becomes guardian of Jim, his mischievous half-brother" (Hanson, 721). This is only the beginning of a series of improbable and picaresque plot turns resolved in the final reel of the film. The screenplay for *The Ploughshare* was written by Mary Imlay Taylor.

Immediately after this film, Collins plunged into the direction of *Gladiola*, billed as a Thomas A. Edison "special" production, and released on October 15, 1915, at a length of four reels. Viola Dana played the title role of Gladiola Bain, in a romantic drama in which Gladiola must choose between city slicker Ned Williams (Robert Conness, fast becoming a member of the Collins "stock company") and faithful country bumpkin Abner (Pat O'Malley). Gladiola falls for Ned's blandishments and moves to the city against her father's wishes, where the couple are "married." However, after becoming pregnant, Gladiola discovers that Ned is really already married, and Gladiola leaves Ned, returning to her farm. Gladiola endures the ostracism of the small farm community she grew up in to give birth to the child out of wedlock, and brings the child up by herself. In the meantime, Ned Williams's wife has died, and Ned tries to recapture Gladiola's affections, but it is too late. Gladiola has decided to make it on her own, and the film ends with Gladiola, Abner, and Gladiola's child (Eldean Stewart) walking dreamily through the Gladiola fields of her father's farm (Hanson, 334). Based on the story by Mary Rider, the film's early message of feminist self-reliance is a welcome change from stereotypical women's roles of the period, and recalls the defiant heroine of Cleo Madison's *Her Defiance* (1916), a Universal/Rex two-reel film of the same era, which Madison directed and starred in. The film was shot by Ned Van Buren, who would also shoot Collins's next film *Children of Eve* (although other sources credit John Arnold as cameraman for the film [Hanson, 138–139]), a five-reel Edison film distributed through the Kleine-Edison Feature Service, and released on November 10, 1915 (Hanson, 138–139).

Collins wrote both the screenplay and the story for *Children of Eve*, which stars Viola Dana as Fifty-Fifty Mamie, and Robert Conness as Henry Clay Madison. In his first year as a feature director, Collins was already on his fifth film as a director, and he was now taking on the added chore of scenario writer, as well. *Children of Eve* is a rather heavy social drama, with a complicated plot involving prostitution, social reform, child labor laws, and the operation of a hideously unsafe cannery staffed by underage workers. The cannery has no fire escape, and when it catches fire, many of the children workers are killed in the ensuing conflagration. Although tied to a somewhat melodramatic plot, *The Children of Eve* is effective social criticism, in the tradition of Griffith's *A Corner in Wheat*. According to the *AFI Film Catalogue 1911–1920*, "the scenes of a building burning in this film were shot at Fort Schuyler, NY, by a number of cameramen" (Hanson, 138–139), probably as newsreel footage. Ambitious and well-made, according to contemporary reviews, the film was a real step up in Collins's brief career.

This film was followed by *The Innocence of Ruth*, a five-reel (4,839 feet) feature from the Edison Studios, released through the Kleine-Edison Feature Service, directed by Collins from a story by William Addison Lathrop. Released on January 26, 1916, the film is less sweeping in scope than *Children of Eve*, and involves the adventures of orphan Ruth Travers (Viola Dana) as she attempts to make her way in the world. The young Ruth moves in with "young millionaire Jimmy Carter" (Edward Earle) (Hanson, 455–456), but is nearly raped by one Mortimer Edwards (Augustus Philips), who was also conveniently responsible for the financial ruin of Ruth's father. After several predictable complications, Ruth and Jimmy fall in love, and decide to get married. The film received respectable reviews, and by this time, one can discern a pattern in Collins's work. More personal projects like *Gladiola* and *Children of Eve* are followed by frank potboilers, such as *The Innocence of Ruth*, evidence that Collins wanted a degree of artistic freedom in his work, but was also aware of the needs of the box office.

Collins's next film, *The Flower of No Man's Land*, represented another step upward for the young director, as he left the employ of the Edison Studios to work for Harry Cohn's fledgling Columbia Pictures Corporation, then distributing its films through Metro Pictures Corporation. At five reels, the film was written and directed by Collins, and again starred Viola Dana, who made the jump to Columbia along with Collins. Released on June 26, 1916, it would be nice to say that the film represented an artistic advance for the director, but *The Flower of No Man's Land* is a wildly improbable "Eastern western" of sorts. Viola Dana plays Echo, a young orphan girl who has been brought up by her Native American foster father Kahoma (Mitchell Lewis). Echo falls in love with opera singer Roy Talbot (Duncan McRae) who has come to the West to restore his health. Without thinking twice, Echo drops her longtime boyfriend Big Bill (Harry C. Brown). Unbeknownst to Echo, Talbot is already married, but he still takes Echo back East, fills her head with tales of the big city, and then forgets all about her to concentrate on his career. Enraged at Talbot's treachery, Kahoma murders Talbot, and Echo is free to return to the West, and the embraces of Big Bill, whom she plans to marry (Hanson, 288).

The Light of Happiness, which followed on September 4, 1916, was another Columbia/Metro five-reel film, with script and direction by Collins. Again, Viola Dana stars in the film, this time as Tangletop, "daughter of the town drunk" (Hanson, 518). The plot involves a complicated impersonation scheme, but predictably everything is settled by the final reel, in which Tangletop marries a young minister she has been taken with, the Reverend Clyde Harmon (Robert Walker). *The Cossack Whip*, one of Collins's most famous films, found him back at the Edison Studios, now a proven talent in the commercial feature market. Released on November 13, 1916, from a scenario by Paul H. Sloane, *The Cossack Whip* tells the tale of Darya (Viola Dana), whose sister Katrinna (Grace Williams) has been whipped to death on the orders of Russian Prefect of Police Turov (Frank Farrington). Darya vows revenge, and flees to England, where she establishes herself as a ballet star. When Darya's troupe tours Russia, Turov is smitten with her, and Darya pretends to go along with his seduction of her. In a rather risqué climax, however, Darya convinces Turov to chain himself in a prison cell for some passionate lovemaking. The moment that Turov has his wrists in chains, Darya begins whipping him, until a confederate ends Turov's torture by shooting him to death (Hanson, 165–166). Still available today in 35mm format for theatrical exhibition, *The Cossack Whip* is one of Collins's most interesting and bizarre films, and gives contemporary audiences a taste of the director's penchant for curious plot twists and unexpected denouements.

The Gates of Eden found Collins back at Columbia/Metro, in a five-reel feature written and directed by Collins from a story by the Reverend William E. Danforth. Released on October 30, 1916, the film is a religious drama centering on the Shaker sect, and the trials of two young lovers, Eve (Viola Dana) and William (Robert Walker). Dana plays a dual role in the film, portraying Eve's mother, Evelyn, as well as Eve. As Hanson notes, "the film was shot in one of the few Shaker villages remaining in the United States" (315), thus adding to the realism of the piece. *A Wife by Proxy*, released on January 6, 1917 by Metro for Columbia, was another five-reel feature directed and written by Collins, although, according to some sources, June Mathis either wrote or co-wrote the scenario for the film (Hanson, 1036). This time, however, Viola Dana does not appear in the film, which is a tale of family problems, inheritances, and deceptions that are neatly resolved by the end of the film's fifty-minute running time.

Rosie O'Grady followed this production in release pattern, although it had actually been shot some time earlier. Copyrighted by the Thomas A. Edison Studios on March 20, 1916, the Apollo Pictures production was not released until February 1, 1917 by Art Dramas, Inc.; it had been shot and copyrighted under the working title His Sister's Champion (Hanson, 789). This "prize fighting"/action film is unusual for Collins; although it is five reels long, it ends abruptly when the protagonist of the film, Rosie O'Grady (Viola Dana) wakes up and discovers that the entire film has been a dream. God's Laws and Man's, a Columbia/Metro five-reel film released on April 23, 1917, was directed and written for the screen by Collins from the novel A Wife by Purchase, written by Paul Trent. This colonialist tale of British India stars Viola Dana as Ameia, who is saved from being a human sacrifice to Krishna by the intervention of Dr. Claude Drummond (Robert Walker), who buys Ameia to be his wife (Hanson, 337). Predictable complications follow, until a rather contrived conclusion in which Ameia is found to be the daughter of a British major general, and therefore fit to marry Britisher Claude by the final fade out.

Lady Barnacle, produced and distributed by Metro Pictures Corporation and released on June 4, 1917, is another British colonial adventure set in India, again starring Dana. This time she is Lakshima, a young native girl in love with Krishna Dhwaj (William B. Davidson). Once again, the plot is full of surprises and melodramatic convolutions; at the film's end, all obstacles to romance are overcome, and Lakshima and Krishna are wed (Hanson, 495). The film was partially shot in Florida for exterior work to simulate the Indian landscape. The film is a comedy, in contrast to the drama of God's Laws and Man's, although many of the locations and concerns of God's Laws and Man's are evident in the burlesque construction of Lady Barnacle.

Aladdin's Other Lamp, a Rolfe Photoplays production distributed by Metro Pictures as "A Metro Wonderplay" (Hanson, 9) was released at a length of five reels on June 25, 1917, with Collins credited as "supervisor" of the production. June Mathis wrote the script for the film, based on Willard Mack's short play *The Dream Girl*. In this peculiar fantasy film, Viola Dana plays Patricia Smith ("Patsy"), who comes into possession of a magic lamp through a series of complex plot machinations. As with *Rosie O'Grady*, much of the film's action is revealed to be a dream. *The Girl Without a Soul*, another Metro Wonderplay, released on August 13, 1917, and written and directed by Collins, is a rustic drama featuring Viola Dana in a dual role as both Whity and Priscilla Beaumont, the daughters of Dominic Beaumont (Henry Hallam). The five-reel film is another tale of domestic strife and impersonation, resolved to everyone's satisfaction at the last minute (Hanson, 332). *The Mortal Sin*, a Columbia/Metro five-reel feature released and copyrighted on March 12, 1917, tells the story of "struggling young author George Anderson [Robert Walker]" (Hanson, 636–637), who has almost completed his novel *The Mortal Sin*. However, George's publisher refuses to issue the book unless Jane Anderson (Viola Dana), George Anderson's wife, will agree to become the publisher's mistress. This Jane does, but when George finds out, he strangles her to death. Sentenced to die for Jane's murder, George is on his way to be executed when, as in an increasing number of Collins's films, George "wakes up and realizes it was all a dream" (Hanson, 637).

This "it was all a dream" ending was being employed by Collins at this point with frustrating regularity, perhaps indicating the difficulty Collins had with such a hurried and prolific production schedule. As writer and director of most of his films, Collins now found himself thoroughly ensconced in the Hollywood production system, already (even at this early time) turning into a cinematic conveyor belt to churn out features on a regular basis to satisfy the public. Viola Dana and Robert Walker were now the two mainstays of Collins's group of actors; John Arnold usually served as director of photography. Collins was working at a terrific pace to keep audience demand satisfied, and seemed to have formed a solid home at Columbia.

Blue Jeans was yet another step up for Collins; produced and distributed by Metro Pictures Corporation, the film was seven reels long, the longest film Collins had ever directed. Released on December 10, 1917, the film was produced by B. A.

Rolfe, directed by Collins, and written for the screen by June Mathis and Charles A. Taylor from Joseph Arthur's classic melodramatic play, also entitled *Blue Jeans*. As a play, *Blue Jeans* had been a great success when produced in New York City (the play opened on October 6, 1890), and Collins was sure that this old-style melodrama could still command an audience. Photographed by John Arnold and William H. Tuers (Hanson, 84), the film was a huge hit, and is still revived at cinema conventions to this day. Hanson notes that "according to reviews, the film contained subtitles printed [over] stills [freeze-frames] of [the film's] action. *The Motion Picture Magazine* reviewer complained that 'these are very offensive to our artistically trained eyes and seem to interrupt the action rather than facilitate it . . .'" (Hanson, 84). While manifestly offering the public nothing new in the way of narrative structure, Collins's film subversively and effectively embraced the past of both filmic and stage melodrama, complete with a final conclusion in which the hero, Perry (Robert Walker) is saved by the heroine, June (Viola Dana), after he has been tied to a huge log which is being fed into a buzz saw. Yet even in this recycled plot structure, we can see Collins neatly inverting the generic conventions of the 1890s melodrama: June rescues Perry, rather than the other way around. This embrace of feminist politics went unnoticed by most contemporary audience members. The film thus provided action thrills to undiscerning yet approving audiences, and Collins's future seemed ever-more-promising, particularly since he had made the jump from a five-reel to a seven-reel feature with such ease and assurance.

But although he had no way of knowing it, time was running out for John H. Collins. *The Winding Trail*, a western, was Collins's next released production, a five-reel film premiered on January 14, 1918. Curiously, early publicity for *The Winding Trail* listed Tod Browning, who would later create *Dracula* (1931) and *Freaks* (1932), as the proposed director of the film (Hanson, 1043), but Collins replaced Browning just before shooting commenced. Viola Dana stars as Audrey Graham in this rather routine film, which was followed by *A Weaver of Dreams*, another Metro five-reel film of seething domestic drama. Viola Dana was again top-billed in this production as

Judith Sylvester, a young woman enmeshed in a complex and melodramatic series of events, including a train wreck, a shattered marriage, and, for once, a conclusion where everything does *not* end happily. Judith is engaged to Dr. Carter Keith (Clifford Bruce) at the start of the film; by the end of *A Weaver of Dreams*, Judith has seen the destruction of her future dreams of happiness as a rival, Margery Gordon (Mildred Davis) claims Carter's affections. Although Judith is instrumental in reuniting two separated lovers (whose lives are developed in a subplot), she herself is unable to find personal happiness, and "left alone . . . grimly resolves to make the best of her life" (Hanson, 1007). This somewhat more realistic ending was a new departure for Collins (although it works back to the raw feminist transcendence of 1915's *Gladiola*, one of Collins's most unconventional films), but Collins would direct only four more films before his career was abruptly and tragically truncated.

Riders of the Night, a Metro five-reel film directed by Collins from a scenario by Albert Shelby Le Vino is a Kentucky mountain drama which echoes the rural simplicity of *Blue Jeans*. Released on April 29, 1918, the film starred Viola Dana as Sally Castleton, a sweet young girl "who lives in a Kentucky mountain cabin with her kindly grandfather and cruel aunt" (Hanson, 773). *Opportunity*, another Metro five-reel feature directed and adapted for the screen by Collins (from Edgar Franklin Stearns's short story of the same title), was released on June 28, 1918; it starred Viola Dana as Mary Willard and Hale Hamilton as Anthony Fry, in a romantic "comedy/drama" involving "boxing . . . male impersonation, mistaken identity [and] detectives" (Hanson, 681) in an unconventional drama set against a big-city backdrop.

Flower of the Dusk, a Metro five-reel feature written and directed by Collins (from Myrtle Reed's novel of the same name) was released on August 12, 1918, the last summer of Collins's life (Hanson, 288). At the time, the film must have seemed another routine project for the by-now ceaselessly busy and highly respected writer/director, but this melodrama and *The Gold Cure* were Collins's last two completed films. *The Gold Cure*, a five-reel Metro feature once again directed and scripted by Collins (from Alexine Heyland's short story, "Oh, Annice!," which was also the film's working title [Hanson, 339]), was yet another film of picaresque impersonation and mistaken identities. *The Gold Cure*, in any event, was not released until after Collins's death in October of 1918; Metro held on to *The Gold Cure* until January 6, 1919, when it was finally released to the public (Hanson, 339).

After completing *The Gold Cure*, Collins began work on the Metro five-reel feature *Satan Junior* in September/October of 1918, but when Collins became ill, the production was shut down for four weeks to allow time for Collins to recover. However, "after an illness of less than a week, Collins cited by [*Motion Picture World*] as 'probably the youngest director of note in the country' died of pneumonia in New York" (Hanson, 802–803). Herbert Blaché, best known to posterity as the estranged husband of pioneering director Alice Guy (Blaché), took over production of *Satan Junior* at the end of the four-week shutdown, completing it in workmanlike but unremarkable style. The film was released to the public on March 11, 1919.

From the start of Collins's public career, with the release of *Cohen's Luck* on May 28, 1915, to the posthumous release of *Satan Junior* on March 11, 1919, Collins had been a feature film director for slightly less than four years. During that time, John H. Collins directed more than twenty features, or an average of six feature films a year, many of which he also wrote, or adapted from plays, short stories, or novels. Although he had a decided taste for melodrama, Collins was also a cinematic stylist of considerable verve and invention, particularly in his first features for Edison, which retain much of their energy and style even today. To direct more than twenty feature films in less than four years takes talent, luck, skill, and craftsmanship. Collins had the good fortune to work with the gifted John Arnold as his director of photography, and was blessed with a productive relationship with his wife, Viola Dana, who went on to a long career as an actress after Collins's death; her last film was *One Splendid Hour* (1929). John Arnold went on to photograph *The Big Parade* (1925) and *The Wind* (1928) among other projects; Arnold retired from active cinematography in 1929 "to become president of the American Society of Cinematographers (1931–36) and head of the MGM camera department (1931–1956)" (Katz, 51). Arnold also photographed some scenes for *Lust for Life* in 1956. Viola Dana's last film was the 1929 production *The Show of Shows*; she later married "screen cowboy Maurice 'Lefty' Flynn" (Katz, 323), and died in 1987. For both Dana and Arnold, working with John H. Collins had been one of the highpoints of their respective careers.

There is no way of telling what Collins would have done had he been allowed a longer span of life; perhaps he would have settled into a rut as a director of program pictures, perhaps he would have retired (as Dana did) with the advent of sound, or perhaps Collins would have eventually broken free of the chain of five-reel features that dominated most of his brief life (as he did with the seven-reel *Blue Jeans*) to accomplish something truly extraordinary. At the present moment, some seventy years after Collins's death, his work is undergoing a revival of interest and being favorably compared, in some quarters, to that of D. W. Griffith, Cleo Madison, Lois Weber, and other silent cinema pioneers.

It is to be hoped that more of Collins's work will be shown to the public, so that his body of work as a whole can be judged more accurately. But even if all of Collins's films are excavated and shown (assuming that all of them still exist), we still have only the beginning of a promising career. What would John H. Collins have accomplished beyond the four short years he was allowed as a director of feature films? Surely John H. Collins deserves more attention in cinema history than he has gotten in most mainstream cinema history texts. Three-quarters of a century after Collins directed his last film, his work, and his name, are at last entering the filmic canon.

WORKING AT THE MARGINS: ROGER CORMAN

Another figure in need of a fresh critical reappraisal is the oft-maligned, oft-misunderstood director Roger Corman. Any current appreciation of Corman seems confined to his work as a mildly interesting 1950s curiosity, who made a lot of quick and cheap films with extreme violence and poor acting. To most critics and historians, Corman is considered a visionless hack. Corman's near legendary respect for the production dollar and his incredible speed in shooting (Corman directed the main sections of his film *The Terror* [1963] in two days on sets left over from *The Raven* [1963]), coupled with the inexorable sleaziness of his material seem superficially to back up this opinion. But speed in production, coupled with stringent production economy and extremely topical subject matter, are three of Corman's chief assets as a director in these early films.

Corman's career started in earnest in 1955 with his direction of the interesting "chamber western" *Five Guns West*. Before that, Corman had been a studio runner at 20th Century Fox and a literary agent. His first script sale, *Highway Dragnet* (1953, dir. Nathan Juran), was followed by a few years of fast writing and finally his production of *It Crawled the Ocean Floor* (1955, dir. Wyott Ordung). On *Five Guns West*, Corman began his long association with cinematographer Floyd Crosby, who assisted Corman's early predilection for dollies with a wide angle lens shooting base. Working quite often in black-and-white CinemaScope, Corman needed as much room as the cramped, rented sets could give him. But even though Corman was already laying down the general rules that were to guide him brilliantly through fifteen years in this first modest film, it is essential to realize that the primary consideration was always one of product.

Corman's first films were mostly for American International Pictures (AIP). Except for the now-defunct production companies of Monogram and Producers' Releasing Corporation, it is impossible to find a cheaper, more opportunistic operation. Throughout its brief but highly incandescent career, AIP had a simple formula for making a successful feature film: (1) spend no money on production, or as little as possible (this changed somewhat with *The House of Usher* (1960) and the subsequent films in the AIP Poe series); (2) play up the basest, most sensationalistic angle to reach the widest possible audience; (3) exaggerate wildly in the advertising, far beyond the bounds of normal Hollywood hyperbole (creating, in fact, the demand for a spectacle when none was actually forthcoming, particularly in such films as the woefully impoverished Corman production of *The Voyage of the Viking Women to the Waters of the Great Sea Serpent* (aka *The Viking Women and the Sea Serpent* [1957]);

and (4) finally, book each film in as many theatres at once as possible to forestall negative word-of-mouth. This last idea, dubbed saturation booking, is the only film distribution scheme that implies that the film is worthless, kind of a sweeping arc on the way to the trash can; AIP's strategy has now become an industry-wide standard for major commercial fare.

As a director, Corman jumped right in and began turning out feature films at a torrid pace, all of them stamped with his own peculiar vision and haphazard production values, as if Corman had to get his vision on the screen no matter what compromises were made in physical production standards in the process. In 1957 alone, he directed nine feature films, on schedules averaging five shooting days, some in CinemaScope. Starting in 1955, Corman directed *Five Guns West* (1955), *The Oklahoma Woman* (1955), *Apache Woman* (1955), *The Day the World Ended* (1956), *Swamp Women* (1956), *Gunslinger* (1956), *It Conquered the World* (1956), *Not of This Earth* (1957), *The Undead* (1957), *Naked Paradise* (aka *Thunder Over Hawaii* [1957]), *Attack of the Crab Monsters* (1957), *Rock All Night* (1957), *Teenage Doll* (1957), *Carnival Rock* (1957), *Sorority Girl* (1957), *The Viking Women and the Sea Serpent* (1957), *She Gods of Shark Reef* (1958), *War of the Satellites* (1958) (in which Corman appears as a NASA technician), *Machine Gun Kelly* (1958), *Teenage Caveman* (1958), *I Mobster* (1959), *A Bucket of Blood* (1959), *The Wasp Woman* (1959), *Ski Troop Attack* (1960), *The Little Shop of Horrors* (1960), *The Last Woman on Earth* (1960), and *The House of Usher* (1960) (AIP's first "super-production").

But are these films worthy of our attention? Firstly, it seems simplistic and essentialist to dismiss Corman simply because he was a hack. Poe himself was the meanest of hacks. Working with amazing speed under the worst possible personal circumstances, Poe nevertheless managed to transcend the limitations of his macabre genre with his own impetuous vision. While there are thousands of truly valueless artists working in every field, to consider work-for-cash immediately second rate is inexcusably shortsighted. Actually, most inspired "hackery" has a desperate, straining air to it, and Corman's is no exception. And secondly, an appreciation of Corman, as with any other artist, demands an acceptance of certain conditions. Working under such skull-cracking speed, certain priorities must be established and pursued, while other considerations must be abandoned altogether. Corman's sets were cheap and tacky. His actors were hired by the day. One must look beyond these financially imposed limitations for something larger; it is not unlike extending the grace of extenuating circumstances to Jack Smith's *Flaming Creatures* (1963).

Consider *The Undead*. The film was part of Corman's cinematic outpouring in 1957, a year of excessive production and bargain-basement spectacle for the director, and Corman's favorite visual component at the time was the flashy tracking shot. Corman's early tracking shots prefigure the exaggerated hysteria contained in the kind of sensibility apparent in Samuel Fuller's *Underworld, U. S. A.* (1961), a film in which camera moves become part of the spectacle itself, inextricably wedded to images presented on the screen. It may be more than coincidental that in both cases, the film in question is the work of a producer/director. Fuller wrote his scripts as well, and Corman always worked in close concert with his scenarists. In both films, the camera drags the spectator almost bodily into the center of the action. It points hysterically. It spirals in on the most fearful object. In the beginning of *The Undead*, the camera falls back in total surprise during the first major character entrance. Yet, somehow, it had gravitated to the doorway in unconscious anticipation. There is a hasty, uncollected raggedness to these tracking shots. Missing is the classical polish Ophuls lent to even the most pedestrian tracks in *La Ronde* (1950). There is a constant tension to the framing; every movement is a thrust, which fits perfectly the uneasy, unrealistic tension in the acting.

In the opening scenes of *The Undead*, idealistic young psychiatrist Richard Garland visits the seedy office of his former professor, which is located in a particularly rundown area of Sunset Strip. On the way to his former teacher's office, Garland has picked up a rather frightened and curiously innocent young streetwalker (Pamela Duncan). The prostitute sits in a corner, smoking nervously, while Garland spills out a mad scheme of personality regression and time travel through hypnosis. Duncan, blasé and fatalistic after years of abuse and objectification, seems the perfect subject for Garland's experiment; against their better judgment, Garland persuades both his former professor and the streetwalker to go through with the experiment, and the film is properly underway. At this point, the camera is bouncing off the walls with nervous anticipation, looking for some sort of exit, some new source of visual energy to exhaust. Release finally comes, but only through the agency of the streetwalker's imagination, and a lengthy lap dissolve. Even after the next scene is completely established (in an indoor "exterior" set), the memory of Corman's trapped camera lingers. As the film progresses and we return to the psychiatrist's office again and again, one has the feeling that the camera has been running all the time in between, still combing the set for some unseen revelation.

Any prop will do. It seems almost as if the ideas inherently expressed in any shot are more important than the physical realities of the set. Indeed, every scene in these early films looks completely fake, as though some overall sense of image substitution were at work. An example, one of many possible: as *The Undead* progresses, a brainwave energizer is brought in; it is nothing more than an ordinary 35mm magnetic film transfer machine. Yet Corman's frenzy makes us indifferent to this obvious fraud, and there are no apologies forthcoming from anyone. The camera lingers on the machine solemnly, then falls back rapidly to view the entire tableau. The blinds are drawn on the only window in the room, obscuring, incidentally, the non-existent street outside.

In this film, as in many others of his early period, Corman is obsessed with time, particularly with that moment just before an action becomes irrevocable. In daily practice, this is the moment just before you cut your finger on the paring knife. In the conclusion of *The Undead*, Corman gives us one of his most complex visions of this alternative instant. The streetwalker has escaped punishment for witchcraft in a former life only to discover that, unless she dies, all her future selves will cease to be. She is finally convinced she must surrender herself to the ax, but before she does the camera stops before her face in a moment of almost religious contemplation. We hear the voices of a string of future personalities, all begging her for the chance to live. We see her death, but there is nothing to be seen in her face. Whatever her thoughts, her reasons for sacrifice, they remain an enigma. It brings to mind the last moments of Falconetti's visage amidst the flames in Dreyer's *La Passion de Jeanne d'Arc* (1928), or the motives of Robert Bresson's protagonists in his many films. Motivation is unknowable; all spectacle is ephemeral, presented only to be undermined, or withdrawn.

To further compromise the physical reality, or perhaps to heighten the inherent unreality of his productions, Corman rarely reshot. During the shooting of one scene in *Little Shop of Horrors*, a little two-day quickie shot on pre-lit sets, Jack Nicholson and Jonathan Haze were fighting a life-or-death struggle in a dentist's chair when Nicholson accidentally knocked over a huge drill. Corman jumped into the scene to save the rented prop from destruction and put an end to the shot. Much to Nicholson's shock, Corman went right on to the next scene with nary a retake. In the finished film, it seems precisely the right place to dissolve to the next sequence. In short, Corman knew what he had. Since the first take is likely to be the only take, all the actors in a Corman film pour themselves into their roles with genuine frustration. Whatever they do, good, bad or indifferent, will probably be kept. It is sometimes held that the true test of an actor is to shine in a rotten vehicle, but here we have a Pirandellian touch: rotten acting fits these films and in *no way* detracts from them. The brilliance of Corman's films does not rely on individual performances. Indeed, one actor can play several parts within an early Corman film, with minimal makeup; as a cost-saving measure, Corman even cast his brother, Gene (now a producer) in several roles in one film (*Machine Gun Kelly*).

This sort of thing reaches a peculiar zenith in *The Terror* (1963): Corman whipped up the script in one night and shot the bulk of the action in the next two days on sets left over from *The Raven* (1963), with the actors improvising much of the dialogue as the cameras were rolling. The crew rushed from set to set furiously, trying to get the film shot before the carpenters struck the impressive sets. Boris Karloff had just starred in *The Raven*, but finished his work ahead of schedule because of Corman's speed and facility, and thus owed the director several days of work. Reluctantly, Karloff signed on to *The Terror* with only a fragment of a script in hand, protesting all the while that the finished film would never coalesce into anything remotely resembling a finished project; at the same time Corman had Monte Hellman, Francis Ford Coppola, Jack Hill, Dennis Hopper, and Jack Nicholson out filming other material. In a sense, Karloff's predictions were accurate: when Corman finally cut the film together, it made absolutely no sense. Undaunted, Corman brought back Nicholson and Dick Miller, told them the plot, and neatly disposed of most of *The Terror*'s narrative framework with a few minutes of straightforward exposition. The film was released under Corman's Filmgroup company banner to respectable reviews and excellent returns at the box office.

All of this would be merely an interesting anecdote were it not for the fact that *The Terror* seems, in its final version, a remarkably cohesive enterprise. This is more than good luck, or the vindication of the Kuleshov experiment in sync sound. Corman's brooding mood piece takes advantage of the nebulousness that inevitably surrounds any such ill-defined enterprise, and feeds it back into an exercise in audience/performer interpretation/reception. Having just completed *The Raven* in twelve days, Corman's cast and crew were fully primed to do something else. *The Terror* is thus a vehicle for Corman's surplus narrative structure, and serves as a combined mimetic gesture on the part of both actors and the director. The dialogue is sparse but evocative. The speeches are delivered with an air of genuine uncertainty. So many different sets of input are at work in the film that the film becomes, in the best sense, a collaborative effort, much like Wayne Wang's *Blue in the Face* (1996), shot in a few days on the leftover sets of *Smoke* (1996). As with the actors and technicians used in *Smoke*, Corman realized he was working with professionals—and he banked on it. In addition, he had the good sense to realize that only when his stock company had already been taken through one completely pre-planned film could they hope to wholly improvise one.

To my knowledge, the only other director to capitalize on the possibilities of such role identification is Andy Warhol. Warhol, however, carried it several steps further by using non-actors, then throwing them into a completely contrived situation. The end result in such Warhol films as *Vinyl* (1965) and *My*

Hustler (1966) is a kind of curious phenomenon that might be termed, "people acting actors acting people acting." Corman picked up on this and incorporated it into *The Wild Angels* (1966) and *The Trip* (1967).

While Corman may deal in image substitution when it comes to sets and props, one of the things that he does not traffic in is symbolic substitution. When he does, it seems contrived and false, as in *The Masque of the Red Death* (1964). Identities may be shared or blurred, but the audience is always informed precisely of what is happening. The connection is always clear and simply stated: a troll turns into a spider and back again in *The Undead*, a witch slinking atop a rock is transformed into a tigress, and so on. Sometimes these transmutations are accompanied by a burst of light. The theme that is often the dramatic center of the film (who is that, whom do they speak and act for, what is their real identity?) is disposed of right in front of our eyes, as if in preparation for some greater illusion (or allusion) that is much less obvious. These clearly stated transformations result not so much in simplicity, but in complicity between director and viewer. The real mysteries in Corman's films must be solved jointly by both spectator and maker.

Yet, while Corman had to make the most of many unfavorable situations, one would have to go back to Orson Welles to recall such an opportunity to speak with film. As a very young man, everything was handed to Corman, and he went to work. The energy and brashness these two men have in common is not surprising. The transcendent comparison between Welles and Corman has been made before, and in both cases, the directors incite us not through exhortation, but through sincerity and purpose. Jean-Marie Straub, to take a completely opposite example, is also uninterested in conventional standards of acting excellence and seems to take a perverse delight in the cheap props and sound he employs. Straub arrives at his destination through minimalist concentration—Corman and Welles through impatience.

Corman was keenly aware of what the competition was up to. Outside of William Castle (creator of *Strait-Jacket* [1964], *Homicidal* [1961], and *House on Haunted Hill* [1959], among other films), no other director used as much gimmickry as Corman did. His subject matter was every bit as tawdry as the realities of the filming situation. Again, Corman accepted the challenge enthusiastically. He was right in there with a synthetic cyclone full of werewolves, stand-up comics, juvenile delinquents, sadists, gunslingers, power-crazed scientists, vampires, high school cheerleaders, motorcycle gangs, and irresponsible acid-heads. While Godard views his scheming pop-star monsters in *Masculine/Feminine* (1966) with fashionably cool detachment (even if at very close range), Corman leaps into his characters' world. There is respect and even admiration for the outlaw, the outcast. Every gesture is left intact, every scream, every agony is fully shared. There are no softly lit interludes, no Chantal Goya pleading with the ceiling while Jean-Pierre Leaud makes clumsy advances in the semidark. Much too precious. If there is a possibility of redemption (a word Corman would probably despise in this context), it exists in the personal reality, which is never exposed in real life and so is left uncharted here. Yet the internal struggle is as real as Bresson's, and it stands in the same mute agony.

At the time Elia Kazan was fashioning a much more reasonable system of relationships for James Dean in *East of Eden* (1955), Corman proved in *Teenage Doll* and *Rock All Night* that no such neat pattern existed. Corman's work seems ultimately so difficult to pin down because his moral stance shifts from film to film, unerringly identifying with the codes of his protagonists. Just as *Dirty Harry* (1971) is clear-cut and straightforward in its protofascist political bent, Ted Post's *Magnum Force* (1971) receives relatively little critical attention because it completely vitiates the first film's basic precept. Although Post's direction seems needlessly bloodthirsty, and is perhaps less crucial to the success of the project than John Milius's screenplay, *Magnum Force* is targeted because it operates on the same principle of total and shameless involvement that Corman uses in all of his work as a director. It is this direct connection to the spectacle being presented, and to the characters who bring it to flickering, uncertain half-life, that is objected to, because it offers no way out. Even in such a completely successful work as Alfred Hitchcock's *Psycho* (1960), the structural artifice of the shower murder distances us from true emotional identification;

Corman's technique is always at the service of his protagonists, who seem to burst through the frames of his films, demanding our collective attention.

Different concepts are expressed in different ways. The fact that Corman is often criticized for a supposed "lack of visual style" (read "easy to identify") is a result of this. It seems to me more than a coincidence that the critical fascination in the 1970s and early 1980s with structuralism came during a period of baroque criticism, when the first line of auteurs were dying off at an alarming rate, and the next generation had yet to be firmly established. Visually, there is very little comparison between the setups in Corman's *Bloody Mama* (1970) and his film *The St. Valentine's Day Massacre* (1967); the first is crazed with a frenzy of identification for its dimwitted protagonists, while the latter is presented as history, in which all of the already-deceased characters are introduced (though the medium of a voice-over), with their birth and death dates neatly included, before they perform a single act within the film. But there is indeed a similarity between Corman's camerawork in *Machine Gun Kelly* and *Bloody Mama*; both films side with the outlaw instinct. Although Corman had to stop working in black and white (for purely economic reasons—resale to all-color television), the visual style of both avoids the kind of glossy sentimentality that pervades Arthur Penn's much praised yet infinitely inferior *Bonnie and Clyde* (1967). The romance of crime is not alien to Corman, as he proves in *The St. Valentine's Day Massacre*, which is partly nostalgia and partly love letter. But it, too, draws the line at real violence, and this is presented with a vengeful insistence.

Still, it would be silly to claim purely aesthetic reasons behind this. As the fifties ended, Corman's budgets got increasingly bigger, and Corman finally struck out on his own away from AIP (which he had done before with William Shatner's compelling performance as a vicious Southern racist agitator in *The Intruder* [1962], after which he immediately returned to AIP). And here, in a very sad and real sense, we begin to sense boredom and uncertainty. Working for 20th Century Fox on *The St. Valentine's Day Massacre*, was, from all accounts, not particularly fulfilling. By the time of *The Wild Angels*, the atmosphere has become almost completely detached: long parallel tracks of the Angels out on the highway, cool West Coast horizons, and a little bit of subjective handheld camera now and then. Where before every shot seemed to be a subjective shot, merely by virtue of the intense involvement between the director and his audience, here the camera cuts at the crisis point to the character's view point, and she or he is left alone to deal with, for the most part, an unending spectacle of atavistic death and violence. The feeling is that of Nazi footage spliced into a World War II Air Force documentary to give "the other side" of the film's narrative structure.

In *The Wild Angels*, Corman as spectator/participant seems thoroughly jaded. There are instances of liberation: during a picnic, the Angels careen around wildly on their bikes, and the camera joyously joins them—but the feeling is of temporary liberation. The climax of this new detachment is revealed during the rape of a nurse, seen from the victim's point of view. The scene is shot handheld and underexposed, as though Corman is unwilling to let us see what is happening. At first, the camera flails around, trying to focus on some object, any object. Then, as the struggle becomes hopeless, the camera "gives up," and stares at the ceiling. Then a horrible thing happens: we cut to the street outside. This *could* be a usage of imagined violence vs. a visualization of (fictionalized) violence, but it isn't. What is happening here is avoidance of communication, a lack of empathy. This unhappy tendency continues right up to the climactic funeral/orgy sequence, where the camera stumbles around the interior of a church for over five minutes, reeling uncertainly, no cuts, as blindly stoned as the Angels are, unable to do anything more than record.

At this point, the spaces between Corman's films got longer and longer, and finally, with *Von Richtofen and Brown* (1971), the flow stopped. And quite appropriately so, for the world of *Von Richtofen and Brown* is one of unrelieved pessimism and inevitable failure. The opening set-ups are rife with complex dolly/zooms and very "depthy" photography enhanced with judicious use of a wide angle lens. The interior sets flooded with late afternoon sunlight and the immaculate costuming set up expectations of heroic immortality. By the final third of the film, however, life has become a surreal but continually lethal game of aerial tag: thus we are subjected to nearly twenty minutes of unceasing din as the German and British flying corps literally rip each other to shreds. Even at the end, the same sunlight spills carelessly into the same rooms. Now, however, we see those same rooms as tacky and confining, where before they held the promise of power and an infinite future. Corman made a brief return to the director's chair with the disastrous *Frankenstein Unbound* (1990), but the film was half-hearted, lacking the energy and vitality that distinguished his earlier work as a director. Since then, Corman has functioned solely as a producer (for his company, Concorde/New Horizons) and sometime actor (most memorably as a slimy lawyer in Jonathan Demme's *Philadelphia* [1993]). As an artist, Corman's current curiosity reputation works against the possibility of a fairer assessment of his works, outside of cult "fringedom," as well as against the availability of his early work on home video in original format (letterboxed, as it should be for such films as *Machine Gun Kelly* and *The Last Woman on Earth*). Contemporary reviews of his films have become the films themselves. This is the final twist: Corman's early films, originally the most exploitable movies in existence, have lost their market. Yet their value remains, as with any work, outside of critical estimation. Corman's vision has influenced a host of contemporary filmmakers, and Corman himself seems to have been marginalized in the shuffle. This is doubly sad, for Corman's films, arguably more so than those of any other director of the late 1950s and early 1960s, have much to tell us about the fabric of American society during this tumultuous period.

THE ROMANCE OF VIOLENCE

Corman worked primarily in the horror and science fiction genres, although he strayed upon occasion into the realm of crime narratives (*Machine Gun Kelly, I Mobster, The St. Valentine's Day Massacre*), presenting the routine circumstances of daily criminal existence as a series of eruptions and stylishly composed set pieces, with each of his performers in his films allowed a portion of the spectacle as her/his own territorial domain. This leads me to an examination of the spectacle of the crime film, as constructed from a series of events which have entered the domain of apocryphal legend. As numerous critics and historians have observed, the conventions of the gangster film long ago, for better or worse, became schematized as generic "stations of the cross." The St. Valentine's Day Massacre, Dion O'Bannion's assassination in his flower shop, the drugstore phone booth killing of Mad Dog Coll, the raid on the Hawthorne Inn: all of these factual incidents of criminal history have long assumed the mythic status usually assigned to duels between the gods. Films such as Howard Hawks's *Scarface* (1932), Roger Corman's *The St. Valentine's Day Massacre* (1967), Corman's *Machine Gun Kelly* (1958), Hawks's *The Big Sleep* (1946), William Wellman's *Public Enemy* (1931), Brown's *Doorway to Hell* (1930), and many, many other crime films, have elevated rather grisly, ordinarily shabby events in the lives of a number of psychopaths, murderers, bank robbers, rapists, and hired guns to the realm of popular fable. Indeed, most of the "famous" incidents in the history of crime are clustered around the 1920s in Chicago. There are, of course, many films in the crime and gangster genre that have nothing to do with Al Capone's reign on the North Side, but for the purposes of fabulation, most crime films have traditionally turned to the Roaring Twenties.

Reasons for this association are many and have been the source of a good deal of speculation into the public's fascination with crime films. At least part of the appeal of crime films seems to reside in their portrayal of people and situations which inherently exist outside of the structure of daily, "lawful" events. Viewers of all films participate in the action they see unfolding before them; the implications of this are frequently disturbing, as one ponders the public's interest in the protagonists of such films as *Friday the 13th Part Five* (1985), the remake of *Scarface* with Al Pacino (1984), or *The Evil That Men Do* (1985), the Charles Bronson action film by J. Lee Thompson. In all of these films, the extreme depiction of graphic violence forces the viewer to be either victim or murderer, because the entire "plot line" of these films is a string of violent, sadistic murders. If there is romance in these films, it eludes me. Romance is related to the domain of past events. Crime films are essentially cheerfully lurid, decadent entertainments, but their romantic allure is a function of their enshrinement and re-enactment of events that have become part of our national outlaw history.

We know the outcome of crime films from the first frame, particularly if the film in question is a *noir*. The action will be a downward spiral, with momentary high spots on the inevitable road to destruction. Earlier crime films such as William Wellman's pioneering and generally underrated film *Public Enemy* (1931) followed a rise-and-fall approach to the gangster's life. Whether the film starts with the rise to the top or the fall to the gutter, most crime films end in the gutter, or the cemetery, or the morgue. Where is the romance in a rendezvous with destruction? It resides in the element of risk that all crime films contain.

The schematic structure of the crime film, its repetition of predestined events, is something that had long ago been isolated. Early film criticism in the 1960s, and before that in the prescient writings of James Agee and Parker Tyler, as well as Andre Bazin and later Truffaut, Godard, and Marker, fastened on the ritualistic element of the gangster film as a signifier to the romantic instinct in these films. Peter Wollen's excellent volume *Signs and Meanings in the Cinema*, a classic of iconic deconstructionalism in film studies, identifies the gangster as one of several filmic character "icons" operating in the world of the crime film. This primitive system of inventing an instant history for each person in a film through visual typing assists the audience in identifying with the characters. Through the audience's perception that the image of the criminal is a series of gestures and attitudes, costumes and ritualized role-playing, the audience is encouraged to believe that by isolating these stylistic elements of the criminal imitating them, one may vicariously participate in participatory risk. Certainly, most of us, whether or not we care to admit it, can to an extent identify with the use of violence as the arbiter of events. But as Fritz Lang observed in Jean-Luc Godard's film *Contempt* (1963) (itself not a crime film at all), "Murder, killing, is no solution." Thus, the violence we see on the screen, though momentarily cathartic, does not offer any lasting release, or freedom, or promise of personal renewal in daily life.

On the romantic side of our spectator personality we may guiltily revel in scenes of carnage and destruction, but simultaneously, for most people, a sense of checks and balances inculcated in us since childhood signals that retribution must, inevitably, follow. Because of this, embrace of violence in crime films is an act of romantic defeatism; it seeks to entice us into a cozily nihilistic situation. As we sit in the theatre, we know that we are not actually seeking to control events through the use of force. Yet, removed from the risk of any consequences, we can step aside from and avoid our implicit moral responsibility at the end of the tale. Clumsily inserted speeches in Hawks's *Scarface* admonish the audience that criminals are "rats," that there is no "decency" in "glorifying the activities of hoodlums," but the rest of the film mitigates against any sense of humanism by depicting its frequent scenes of murders, explosions, car crashes, and the like with obvious, Eisensteinian relish. *Scarface* is a furiously kinetic film, because *Scarface* is first and foremost an action picture, and it operates in a world where *action* is the precondition of all ideas. Ben Hecht's script is a litany of famous gangland incidents, told with some modification of names and places, but certainly true to the spirit of the events it covered. Hecht's script was hammered out with legendary speed; its approach to tis subject resembles an in-depth character article one might find in *The Sunday New York Times* or *The New Yorker* or, more luridly, in the *New York Post* or the London *Sun*. While we do not like Tony Camonte, and find his approach to life repellent and self-destructive, the sweep of events entices the audience to become at the very least a fascinated observer of Tony's life. Whatever we may think of Tony and his methods, he certainly deals effectively with each situation that confronts him. His eventual collapse into gibbering hysteria in the final reel of the film encourages the audience to lose sympathy for Camonte, however, and as viewers, we step back from Tony to view his final moments of cowardice with disdain and disgust.

Because *Scarface* is one of the first sound gangster films of real distinction, along with *The Criminal Code* (1930), *The Big House* (1930), and a handful of other films of the early 1930s, its penchant for romanticizing events is somewhat limited by its inherent lack of historical perspective. Paul Muni's Tony Camonte can hardly be called an Anti-Hero, nor can Edward G. Robinson's Rico Bandello in *Little Caesar* (1931); they are hoodlums, gangsters, men of violence. They shoot their way to the top of the heap with monomaniacal aggressiveness, yet once there, they inevitably get "picked off" by the next ambitious young guy on the way up.

Things have mellowed considerably by the time of Corman's *St. Valentine's Day Massacre* (1967). Here, Jason Robards portrays Al Capone (no longer fictionalized as Tony Camonte) in a performance that has not traditionally been received with much warmth. Rod Steiger's version of the gangster in *Al Capone* (1960), Muni's Tony, even Ben Gazzara's Capone in *Capone* (1970) received more supportive contemporary reviews, but for me, Robard's Capone is an interesting departure from what one might have expected in the role. (Corman had originally thought of using Orson Welles, and although Welles was willing, even enthusiastic about the possibilities of the role, 20th Century Fox apparently insisted on Robards, much to Corman's dissatisfaction.) Corman's Chicago in *St. Valentine's Day Massacre* is a construct of rigidly "factual" reportage, a minute-by-minute, event-by-event re-enactment of the events leading up to Capone's mass execution. While none of Robards's henchmen is particularly attractive in Corman's film (including George Segal in a rather good performance as Jake Gusenberg), Corman has a good deal of "fun" with the iconic, mythic, and romantic structures at work within the world of the gangster, or, at least, the world of the gangster as reincarnated more than thirty years after the events themselves occurred. Although Corman's film can be called mechanical, even heartless in its inexorable rush to the destruction of all its players (indeed, the film ends with a zoom into oblivion on the tombstone of Al Capone), Corman's view of past events is still quite sentimental. All of the members of the various mobs seem to have a fine time until they are cut down in the unavoidable hail of bullets, which, given the peculiarities of a gangster's life, seems more or less an unavoidable pitfall. John Agar smiles from ear to ear as Dion O'Bannion; less than sixty seconds later, still smiling, he is shot to death in the front room of his flower shop by his "associates and friends." Robards, as Capone, plays his role in the film with an unusual dryness; his responses to the press when questioned about his role in the slayings are amusingly straightforward. The massacre itself is depicted with uncompromising vengeance, including the climactic shots fired in the raid from a sawed-off shotgun at close range, but along the way to their *Götterdämmerung*, the hoods seem to have a good time.

Corman's *Machine Gun Kelly* (1958), with an early performance by Charles Bronson, is far grittier than *St. Valentine's Day Massacre*; indeed, in a series of letters exchanged between Roger Corman and myself this past year, Corman indicated that he very much disliked the completed film of *St. Valentine's Day Massacre*, deriding it as both mechanical and sentimental. The "romance" in private eye crime films, as opposed to gangster crime films, is a matter of long record. Bogart's trench coat and snap-brim hat, his hip flask and retractable gun rack in his coupe, long ago passed into our visual collective memory index as the unmistakable visual hallmarks of a *noir* detective. But this is another kind of "romance," and not the province of this discussion. For the rest, for the public's seemingly insatiable need to identify with acts of violence against society, and to act in these circumstances as if in the grip of a Shelleyan dream—as if she or he will be entirely divorced from any result of their actions, and will thus avoid the cycle of mythic decay common to all romantic fabulation—this will certainly continue. Though rendered more graphically, the allure and escapism of crime films will simply be re-created anew, in film after film, spun from nearly the same rigidly catalogued series of events.

THE CONFIGURATION OF THE "OTHER"

This consideration of various archetypes of the classical Hollywood gangster films leads us into a further examination of the motion picture "heavy." Ian and Elisabeth Cameron's book *The Heavies* offers an interesting, if jocular, overview of the world of

Hollywood's classic male villains; that volume and the Camerons' companion work on female villains, *Dames*, offer two fairly exhaustive galleries of cinematic "types" of evil. What sets these heavies apart from the protagonists of Hollywood cinema (those individuals "blessed" with perfect features—even teeth, a stylishly slim build) is their essential Otherness, their marginalization, their lack of certain characteristics that mainstream society prizes.

In a sense, the heavies discussed here represent the triumph of the disenfranchised. Those scarred, legless, sociopathic, disfigured, truncated, racially proscribed, marginalized figures whose elimination from the dominant discourse of "mainstream" (white, Anglo-Saxon, male) society has given them only one recourse: victory through a liberating embrace of those structures that seek the destruction of that ruling class. Indeed, since the white male hierarchy that informs the structure of Hollywood filmmaking creates most heavies on the grounds of iconic unsuitability alone (that most superficial system of values, the very cruelty of which is merely a matter of luck in life and the circumstances of birth), there seems to be no other avenue open to these individuals.

These heavies contain the characteristics of the dreaded Other, that which the ruling group is most afraid of within their own characters, displayed in triumph and revolt against that group. Furthermore, many heavies lack a certain element, in their emotional makeup, which makes it impossible for them to participate in the dominant societal structure, even if they were not already denied admittance on the grounds of their physical unsuitability alone. There are also heavies whose "deviance" is hidden from the rest of the cast members, and at times even from the audience, until the climax of the film's narrative structure. The identifying characteristics of these villains is that they have no recognizable physical, emotional, or intellectual shortcomings: they have infiltrated the class that they seek to undermine.

When one considers that the stereotyping of heroines and heroes in classic Hollywood cinema is so insistently rigid, it should come as no surprise that there are more than enough different types of heavies to keep the viewer interested. Heroes had to be tall; conventionally handsome, albeit with a rugged look for an appropriate virile screen presence; with hair and teeth well maintained; their speech correct but not overly refined; white (this requirement still survives; even as Hollywood became slightly more unconventional in its iconic typing in the 1970s, major black stars were still few and far between); free from disease or blemish.

Women were also typed in a very narrow range. Conventional beauty was the most exclusive prerequisite. As with leading men, height was a consideration—typically, 5'5" to 5'10"; hair and teeth must be well taken care of; they had to have proper speech, and be white and "clean." During World War II, when most men were eager to join the war effort, the Hollywood studios (particularly the smaller outfits, such as PRC and Monogram) were forced to use leading women and men who skirted the boundaries of this cookie-cutter mentality, and the studios saw their films suffer at the box office because of it. With such A-level leading men as Clark Gable and Tyrone Power actively seeking combat assignments, one might see the wartime rise of the Cover Girl simply as a survivalist studio strategy. Hollywood's pin-up girls were the major studios' only uncompromised icons. The studios would have to wait until after the war to get their leading men back.

As for the heavies, female and male, glyphic unsuitability remained their chief asset, enhanced precisely by those social graces they did *not* possess. George Macready (best known as Rita Hayworth's bisexual husband in *Gilda* [1946]) and Henry Daniell (whose most perfect work may arguably be seen in *The Four Skulls of Jonathan Drake* [1959] and *The Chapman Report* [1962]) lacked warmth; Laird Cregar's (in *Hangover Square* [1945] and *The Lodger* [1944]) gross obesity put him firmly outside the spectrum of commercialized sexual desire; pug-ugly Ted de Corsia (in *Lady from Shanghai* [1948] and *The Naked City* [1948]) lacked breeding; Lee Marvin's sociopathic frenzy (in *The Big Heat* [1953]) marked him as one who has abrogated the codes the dominant culture so fervently (perhaps desperately) embraces. As E. Ann Kaplan notes in her discussion of Dan Duryea's performance as Johnny in Fritz Lang's *Scarlet Street* (1945), the classic Hollywood heavy is not only cut off from society, he is cut off from the possibility of divine redemption. "Johnny, like many characters in more typical noir films, is a 'fallen' creature in a world view that sees evil as a matter of individual distance from God rather than as something socially conditioned" (36).

Many of the more potent Hollywood heavies distance themselves not only from God and society, but from the very acts that inform the structure of their existence. Thus, the distinction between "action heavies" (those who do the bidding of their superiors) and "brain heavies" (who concoct, at a distance, the schemes their minions carry out, and then dispassionately review the consequences of their machinations) must be drawn. For such veteran action heavies as Kenne Duncan, Bud Geary, Roy Bancroft, and George J. Lewis, unquestioning allegiance forms the fabric of their lives.

Action heavies never question the roles they have been assigned; rather, they rush through the films they inhabit in a frenzy of fist-fights, car crashes, and bombings, all in the service of an authority whose instructions they must, of generic necessity, never question. For their part, it is enough for the brain heavies to hear the results of their destructive pursuits. As Stephen Heath notes: ". . . one might recall Sade's comment that, for the true libertine, it is the sensations communicated by the organ of hearing which are the more gratifying and whose impressions are the keenest (thus his libertines listen to long narratives, construct machines to amplify sound, achieve orgasm on hearing cries)" (176). Removed as they are from the events they set in motion, the essential relationship between the brains and action heavies is one of tale-teller and auditor. The criminal mastermind of pulp fiction, contemplating the rupture of society from his isolated lair, must of narrative necessity wait for the reports of his lieutenants, just as his lieutenants must return to him, time after time, for admonishment and further instruction.

The very grossness of a heavy such as Robert Emhardt (most particularly in Samuel Fuller's *Underworld U.S.A.* [1961]), the result of years of criminal lassitude, precludes his active role in any deviant enterprise. In *Strangers on a Train* (1951), Robert Walker's character Bruno Antony, marginalized from society (as typified by his father's disgust with Bruno's homosexuality), is willing to perform Guy Haines's (played by Farley Granger) "murder," but prefers to distance himself from his own proposed homicide, and not only for reasons of avoiding detection. A variant of the brains heavy, Walker's Bruno Antony is both active and passive, but he becomes an active agent only when carrying out the will of others. A further refinement might then be drawn from this. Elisha Cook, Jr., can be seen as an action heavy, as he seldom hatches the plans he is called upon to carry out in film after film; yet he is an active agent who is, in turn, acted upon, assuming the role of the fall guy in most of his cinematic portrayals. (Cook even made a film in 1947 for director Reginald LeBorg with the title *Fall Guy*: the title, of course, referred to Cook's position with the narrative.) It is hard to overestimate the value of iconic typecasting in a case such as Cook's: the actor's baby face, directly at odds with the monotonal, disinterested delivery he affords his lines, creates a wholly satisfying archetype of the *noir* victim. The fastidious Sam Jaffe, neatly clad in homburg and gloves in John Huston's *The Asphalt Jungle* (1950), is as removed from the mechanics of crime as the brutal, unkempt Aldo Ray is involved in them: by their faces, their clothes, as well as their actions, will we know them.

But even as action, brains, and fall guy heavies are defined by their actions, dress, social and sexual grounding, and their distance from theist and humanist values, they are also limited by their adherence to these inverse conventions. Thus, even the most kinetic of heavies emerges, finally, as a curiously static figure, a victim of the ineluctable modality that Sartre refers to as the "practico-inert." All their acts do not advance them. Heavies exist, rather, in a downward spiral, and each blow they strike against the dominant cultural discourse serves only to ensure their ultimate destruction. The Hollywood film, then as now, embraces triumphant closure to the literal exclusion of all other value systems. As Dana Polan commented, even playfully subversive attacks on the dominant societal structure strengthen rather than undermine ruling social codes. Discussing a "drag act" in Michael Curtiz's *This Is the Army* (1943), Polan affirms that ". . . such moments occur always on the stage of the show within the film; [these] playful moments suggest no more than a feigned, fictive, fleeting disturbance of order that ultimately leaves it really undisturbed" (132). Acts against the empire encourage those who have no choice but to subscribe to that empire's continuance. Only those who have no choice would even consider joining an essentially deviational structure which cannot, within the generic codes Hollywood so rigidly enforces, succeed.

There is, however, a type of heavy who masks his or her intent in mock obeisance to the cultural structure he or she seeks to destroy. This may be either an act of will or the result of psychosis. Anthony Perkins's Norman Bates in *Psycho* projects a mask of quiet complacency that temporally obscures murderous, misogynistic homicidal rage, yet Hitchcock makes Norman a victim of his sexual repulsion/attraction, rather than the master of it. Lionel Atwill's characters, on the other hand, usually moved with ease in the upper reaches of the cinematic ruling classes. Atwill's Eric Gorman, for example, in A. Edward Sutherland's *Murders in the Zoo* (1933), consciously hides his obsessive possessiveness of his wife, and the antisocial acts he "must" concomitantly commit in order to retain his hold on her, beneath the facade of a millionaire big game hunter, who donates wild animals to the municipal zoo and, even in the depths of the Depression, resides in a house that silently testifies to his affluence and social standing in the community.

In *The Archaeology of Knowledge*, Michel Foucault begins his discussion of the perceptual dominances which shape cultural discourse with a frank admission that his work, as Karlis Racevskis puts it, "is an endeavor that seeks to evade traditional patterns" (131). But Foucault does not seek to replace these "traditional patterns" with an alternative locus; rather Foucault agrees that "my discourse, far from determining the locus in which it speaks, is avoiding the ground on which it could find support. It is trying to operate a decentering that leaves no privilege to any center" (205). This is exactly the same sort of operation that the classical cinema heavy also seeks to perform.

One might argue that a new locus in any such individual process inevitably arises—the locus of the operational intellect. Certainly this is not incompatible with the goals of the heavy. Above all, the heavy seeks to enshrine her- or himself as the sole

structure of a newly charted universe, one which willfully discards any conventionally agreed-upon precepts. The physical
location of this alternative structure must, of course, be spa-
tially removed from the society it seeks to undermine. Dr.
Frankenstein operates in a lonely mountain eyrie; forties gangsters, active and/or passive, reside in subterranean squalor or
splendor; Lex Luthor, Superman's nemesis, exists in solitary
grandeur in a literally "underworld" hideout. Indeed, the appellation "underworld" benefits the villain's fallen status. As with
Lucifer, the more memorable forties heavies certainly do not
lack imagination or initiative. Many of them have even par-
taken of the same privileged social status that Lucifer himself
enjoyed.

Noir films, particularly, abound in men and women whose
talent, skills, and social acceptability should have afforded them
unlimited access to the ruling circle. Typically, egotism, unal-
loyed ambition, or a "deviant nature" (remembering that the
forties marked the beginning of Hollywood's long and profitable
love affair with psychoanalytic apparatus) have consigned them
to the ranks of the acted-upon. Is it any wonder, then, that these
potent, often scintillating personages seek to abolish the order
which promised them so much, only to abruptly drop them
from the ranks, often at the moment when their social status
seemed most assured?

No doubt the reader has noted that this discussion of the
heavy has been confined only to men; this sexual exclusion, or
foreknowledge of sexual difference, is certainly not new. As Ian
and Elisabeth Cameron note in their pioneering study *Dames*,

> Feminists could find evidence of discrimination in the
> paucity of women in the front rank of 'heavies.' Unless
> clearly stated otherwise, it's a man's world in the movies.
> Indeed, when female 'heavies' do turn up, they are often
> pushing wives of the Lady Macbeth type or are tormenting
> their menfolk, whether with infidelity, greed or lust for
> power. Hollywood offers its ladies few chances to carry out
> murder contracts, plan heists, or lead lynch mobs. (3)

The Camerons continue with a rudimentary categorization of

varying types of feminine villains: Molls, Tarts, Singers ("really Tarts in code," we are told), and Phenomena (Jane Russell and Jayne Mansfield are offered as the two prototypes of this classification).

The essential difference between the male and female heavy, at least in a cinema that is almost exclusively the product of masculine imagination, is that viewed from this male-dominant perspective, female heavies are often more sexually desirable then the "good girl," with whom the male protagonist will ostensibly "partner." If they are not slatterns (Ann Sothern in *Lady in a Cage* [1964]) or bitches (Rosalind Ivan in *Scarlet Street* [1945]), they are gross (Kate Murtagh in *Farewell, My Lovely* [1975]) or domineering (Rosalind Russell in *Craig's Wife* [1936]). If they are none of these archetypes, then the female heavy is most typically seen as Joan Bennett's Kitty in *Scarlet Street* (1945), or Barbara Stanwyck's Jessica Drummond in Samuel Fuller's *Forty Guns* (1957): a sexually rapacious predator who promises satiety of the flesh, coupled with the male's ultimate destruction. Thus, Stanwyck's Phyllis Dietrichson in *Double Indemnity* (1944) hooks Fred MacMurray with the promise of sexual satisfaction, but in agreeing to Stanwyck's plan to murder her husband, the male pays for the quenching of his lust with his life. The most blatant manifestation of this "mechanics of lust" may be Carol Forman's performance in Spencer Gordon Bennet and Fred C. Brannon's *The Black Widow* (1947), a Republic serial in which Ms. Forman plays the brains heavy who continually dispatches her henchmen to certain doom. They obey her, we are told, because they are enslaved by their desire for the image she projects. The justly notorious Ilsa films, *Ilsa: She-Wolf of the S. S.* (1974) and *Ilsa: Harem Keeper of the Oil Sheiks* (1978), both directed by Don Edmunds and starring the pseudonymous Dyanne Thorne as Ilsa, portray this theme of desire/castration-fear in utterly graphic terms. Ilsa castrates every man who "dares" (her word) to have sexual intercourse with her. The mere act of submitting (if this is the proper word) to Ilsa's enticements is more than enough cause for these ritual castrations. Indeed, the tag line of the film is simply "no man spends a night with me and lives!"

These role positionings, as demeaning and destructive to

women as they are to men, guarantee not only a perpetual state of frustration in classical Hollywood cinema (and, not incidentally, a great deal of narrative drive in the "struggle for possession of the woman" which informs the structure of most '40s and '50s cinema), but encode, none too subtly, the message that satisfying sex means certain death, at least for the male of the species. Ilsa and the Black Widow represent desire both as exhaustion and annihilation: as they allow a series of men to sexually "possess" them, they remain distant, contemptuous, relishing only the impending doom of their mates. Opposed to this in the cinema of the '40s and '50s is the icon of "the good girl," who, though perhaps not as enticing as "the woman better left alone," nevertheless represents moderate sexual fulfillment and safety. This, of course, further posits that fulfilling sexual encounters must always be illicit; marriage is the cradle of both safety and boredom.

Margaret Hamilton may be the 1930s cinematic personification of the "unfeminine" woman. Her indelible portrayal of the Wicked Witch of the West in *The Wizard of Oz* (1939) typecast her forever as the hateful crone. Even in such innocuous films as *Meet the Stewarts* (1942), Hamilton's shrewish housekeeper remains unattractive, shrill, judgmental to a fault, and entirely outside the realm of sexual attractiveness. Ann Savage, memorable in Edgar G. Ulmer's *Detour* (1946), was forever after typecast as the hard, unforgiving, vengeful shrew, who led men on to their Langian doom. Mercedes McCambridge, motivated by the desire to possess Sterling Hayden, is nearly responsible for the death of Joan Crawford in Ray's *Johnny Guitar* (1954); Fay Spain, memorable as Hel in Corman's *Teenage Doll* (1957), seeks the destruction of her archenemy, Barbara Bonnie (played by June Kenney; Hel refers to Barbara throughout the film as "you cheap little slut"), simply because she is a "nice girl," and thus a mocking representative (down to a staunchly Republican father) of the society that has rejected Hel. Audrey Totter, whom the Camerons refer to in *Dames* as a "parboiled version of Alice Faye" (131) stalked through such films as *The Set-Up* (1949) and *Lady in the Lake* (1947) radiating both allure and menace; any man who dared to possess her would certainly find himself a victim. Claire Trevor, at her best in Robert Wise's all-but-forgotten *Born to Kill* (1947) and Minnelli's *Two Weeks in Another Town* (1962), was a destructive agency of a different sort. Abused and discarded, Trevor seemed propelled towards her own destruction, even as she sought the demise of those around her. As for Jayne Mansfield and Jane Russell, whom the Camerons include in *Dames*, I find it hard to consider them heavies. It seems clear now that they are far more victimized than victims. Yet an undeniable aspect of self-abasement clings not only to Mansfield and Russell, and all female heavies, but to all heavies irrespective of sex. The stance taken by these marginalized women and men against the dominant value structure that classical Hollywood cinema espoused ensured, as I have noted, the doom of the heavy. Narrative closure (not to mention the Breen/Hays Production Code Office) required that they be held responsible, ultimately, for all their acts.

Yet, there is a certain charm and gentle antiquity to the heavy of the '40s and '50s. The reluctant humanoid figure of Frankenstein's monster and the supernaturally blood-lusting figure of Dracula, both introduced in the 1930s, were sufficiently Other to warrant ritual and repeated resurrection up until 1945, when Universal, sensing that the actuality of wartime events had deconstructed their monsters, gathered all their filmic outcasts (the Wolfman, Dracula, the Monster, and others) together into two neat packages, *The House of Frankenstein* (1944) and *The House of Dracula* (1945), before abandoning the series. Today, audience demand for continued opposition to the societal contract requires the creation of such graphically violent figures as Jason, the mute and inexorable executioner of Camp Crystal Lake in the *Friday the 13th* films (from 1980 on); Freddie Krueger, the hideously scarred child-murdering sociopath of the *Nightmare on Elm Street* series (from 1984 on); Pinhead, the torturing nemesis from another dimension in the *Hellraiser* series (from 1987 on); as well as the British figure of the Funnyman (1995) from the film of the same name—to say nothing of the collection of randomly assembled serial killers in such films as *Se7en* (1995), *The Glimmer Man* (1996), and many others. In these later films, the imaginative horror of off-screen violence first posited by Lang has been replaced by synthetic, artificially constructed close-ups of various limbs, head, intestines, and other constructed body parts, none of which seems even remotely real; all these graphic glyphs are copies without an original.

RIPPING THE FABRIC OF SOCIETY

Concomitantly, the dominant order is now more easily subverted. The first *Nightmare on Elm Street* (1984), for example, ends with the triumph of the disruptive, when Freddie rips the gauzy fabric of the film's parodic happy ending asunder in the film's final moments. As Polan suggested, the heavies of the '40s and '50s existed primarily to enhance the victory of those who were privileged to hold the center of the narrative locus. The heavies of the late 1980s, and, one suspects, of the 1990s, may confirm deviance as the dominant mode or informing structure that governs current humanist commerce. Even within the world of supposedly "normative" human social intercourse, one should consider the case of Otto Preminger's film *Tell Me That You Love Me, Junie Moon* (1970), in which a group of societal misfits—designated as Other because of various accidents, scars, birth defects and the like—abandon the artificial fabric of ordinary social commerce for a rundown summer house on the edge of town. There, separated from the rest of society, the protagonists of the film attempt to construct what one of the characters describes as "a normal life." Liza Minnelli, as Junie Moon, has had her faced permanently scarred by battery acid, poured on her by a male attacker who is homicidally furious at being rebuffed; Junie Moon comes to realize, as the film progresses, how much of her former life was based entirely on the surface of her appearance. With this supposedly normative value removed, Junie's interior being is arguably negated by the disfigurement of her face until she rejects the society that has rejected her, and finds community and companionship with others whom society has marginalized. This is spectacle at the most basic level: the spectacle, or specter, of one's public appearance. We are all required to re-construct ourselves daily through a variety of fabrics, belts, blouses, earrings, and makeup before we "face the world" each morning of our lives; spectacle thus becomes a personal statement of identity and identification within the tribe, in which we are all urged to "put on our best face" for the world each working day.

As with our social appearances in the public sphere, films are more ephemeral than ever before, because of the twin exigencies of nitrate decomposition and fading color stocks. Yet simultaneously, they are ubiquitously available, twenty-four hours a day, on such cable networks as Encore, Turner Classic Movies, and American Movie Classics, "uncut and uninterrupted," just as our presence is required at the multitude of political, social, and business functions which dominate the greater portion of our waking existence. Matters of personal appearance and style have become all-encompassing attributes or defects, encouraged by the overpowering omnipresence of televisual culture. The artificially perfect collective consciousness of the movies has become our consciousness, even within the confines of our homes; no longer do we need to make the decision to venture forth from our domestic sphere to witness the socializing spectacle which the cinematic construct has come to present. With ever-rising budgets, state of the art filmmaking is no longer a populist enterprise, if it ever was; the days when Roger Corman, Edgar Ulmer, Ida Lupino, and others could create a modestly budgeted feature film in the $100,000 range and be assured of theatrical distribution for the resultant work are gone forever, replaced by straight-to-tape video releases and cable and TV "original movies." Because of this economic straitjacket, populist concerns in the cinema have increasingly been marginalized.

Yet while our choice in theatrical cinema spectacles is now limited, particularly outside the larger cities, to multi-million dollar spectacles of death and destruction, a choice for the viewer does remain. The smaller screen of televisual reception has become larger; so large, that in some extreme cases, it can actually be said to the size of a small theatrical film projection screen. With the proliferation of films on tape—to say nothing of the smaller public domain tape specialists who keep the more esoteric films in print long after commercial distributors have lost interest in them, content to flood the shelves of their video rental stores with multiple copies of the latest dominant-cin-ema release—home viewers now have both the means and the distribution mechanism to create their own programming. While cable systems and satellite dishes offer a spurious pleni-tude of imagery, their programming is, ultimately, reducible to a serial repetition of a few time-worn (and thus profitable) gen-res. The alternative home programming I'm discussing offers the truly interactive viewer an alternative to the oligarchy of the dominant media, while simultaneously enriching the visual memory of the subject with alternative voices of cinema/video discourse. The films of Iran, of China, of the nations of Africa, offer us a rich new image bank of alternative visions, if we will only embrace them, while the endless repetition of Hollywood films of the '30s, '40s, '50s, and '60s offers us only the unyield-ing and unchanging terrain of the already-known, ceaselessly repeated without variation, losing resonance and recognition, until the narrative of these films crumbles beneath the weight of their newfound omnipresence. Already, both in the manner in which they are programmed and in the public reception of these films which is encouraged by the various cable channel "hosts" who present them, these archetypes of the dominant cinema look more like home movies of the tottering ruling class than anything else, pointing up nothing so much as the various zones of omission and marginalization in which they traffic, their racism and sexism readily apparent. Looking at *Public Enemy* (1931), for example, are we viewing a William Wellman gangster film from Warner Brothers in the 1930s, or are we viewing home movies of the studio system at work in the early days of the sound era, with James Cagney as the featured player? And when we watch Alan Crosland's sublime silent film *Is Life Worth Liv-ing?* (1921), does the film's narrative of a young man and a young woman saving each other from mutual suicide through sheer determination and capitalistic commercial enterprise (a decid-edly Maoist/Bressonian premise) command our attention? Or do the views of Central Park before skyscrapers dominated Man-hattan, of pawnshops poorly lit and poorly ventilated, of Fifth Avenue during rush hour in the 1920s, or of the dingy tenements where the film's protagonists must live out their lives?

Comparing the fading, dying vision offered by films of the

dominant cinema which strip-mined American popular culture in the first half of the twentieth century with a film such as Cheick Oumar Sissoko's 1995 film *Guimba the Tyrant*, a film from Mali which documents the overthrow of a political tyrant and effectively urges the audience to continually overthrow, rather than acquiesce to, the existing social order (as do such films as Renny Harlin's *A Long Kiss Goodnight* [1996]), one is immediately struck by the impoverishment, and also the suffocating opulence, of the American cinema. When considering the vigor and economy of such films as *Guimba the Tyrant*, Sarah Maldoror's Angolan film *Sambizanga* (1972), Mahama Johnson Traoré's Senegalese indictment of Koranic schools, *Njangaan* (1974), Ousmane Sembene's Senegalese film *Guelwaar* (1993) (which documents the contemporary clash between cultures and religious beliefs in present-day Africa), or Zhang Yimou's Chinese films *Raise the Red Lantern* (1992) and *The Story of Qui Ju* (1993), the paucity of imagination and/or risk in Hollywood cinema becomes readily apparent. The transparency of spectacle in the Hollywood cinema in the last days of the twentieth century, more than one hundred years after the birth of the medium in the late 1880s, is the translucence of collapsing narrative structures, signification systems exhausted through ceaseless recycling, and a star system which cannibalizes all who participate in it (even as it removes these shadow protagonists from contemporary culture and places them within a medieval firmament of faces, gestures, and intonations which both circumscribe and delimit the potential rupture of their utterances and actions).

Keanu Reeves in *Chain Reaction* (1996) is as much of a construct as are the digital special effects that surround him. In the opening scene Reeves escapes on a motorcycle from the confines of an exploding manufacturing plant; it is a thing of bits and pieces, none real, all synthetic, with the two-dimensional non-solidity of computer-generated wreckage strewn about the screen with careless, heedless abandon. None of it holds our attention or engages our imagination for a nanosecond. *Independence Day* (1996), *Twister* (1996), *The Frighteners* (1996)— the list goes on, a procession of empty pantomimes which both eviscerate and scorn individual imagination and talent, in pursuit of a crushing, all-consuming surplus of spectacular production. Peter Jackson's *Heavenly Creatures* (1994) uses computer-generated imagery, but subsumes it within a narrative framework that is both immediate and accessible, grounded in the mundane realities and exigencies of everyday existence. Deprived of his homeland's influence, cut adrift on the sound stages of Universal, and lumbered with the presence of the affable yet vague Michael J. Fox, Jackson had no hope of repeating the success of *Heavenly Creatures* with *The Frighteners*: the latter film lacks any cultural context beyond the narrow strictures imposed by the Hollywood genre machine, and emerges as a succession of ghoulish yet curiously unconvincing special effects: spectacle without substance. Even as we are delighted with the lack of limitations afforded us, as spectators, by the generation of digitally created imagery, as we are offered more, we take away less. Since everything is possible, nothing is surprising. Astonishment pales before a mechanism which reveals, ultimately, nothing so much as the poverty of our collective imagination. Perhaps this is why Antonin Artaud ultimately deserted the cinema; the spectacles which it presented were ultimately so ephemeral, so bankrupt from their inception, that only works on paper (specifically, Artaud's newly collected and preserved drawings) and his performances as part of the Theatre of Cruelty would satisfy his desire for a spectacle which at once entrances and transports the viewer. Spells, incantations, meditations, and transformations—these were the elements of Artaud's universe, a domain of phantoms that we most commonly associate with the cinema. Now, all that is left is the monotonous morphing of this into that, one into the other, all the same and yet simultaneously reconfigured, an endless landscape of meaningless, continual transubstantiation.

DIGITAL REPLACEMENT OF THE REAL

Not surprisingly, the new realm of digital imagery has been embraced by advertising interests, and not just in the anticipated manner of creating increasingly cost-effective special effects for conventional televisual commercials. A digital imaging firm in Princeton, New Jersey, has successfully created and implemented a new advertising scheme in which the company logos of major American industries (Coke, Chrysler, and the like) are digitally superimposed onto the playing fields of baseball, football, and soccer games on an international basis, via satellite hookup, using a different corporate logo for each broadcast area. Thus, viewers of a baseball game in New York might see an advertisement for Miller Beer behind the batter's box; the same viewer in France might see the Citroen corporate logo in the exact same location. Each country, or corporate zone, would receive the digital advertising image that would most maximize sales within that geographical region.

Furthermore, these images are so "real" that it is impossible to distinguish them from the actual play being presented during televised sports events; for a football game viewed in Los Angeles, a gigantic circular Coke logo might magically appear in center field, dominating both viewer and player space, as the participants in the game proceed with their appointed tasks, oblivious to the commercial intrusion. "Floating Ball" logos are also being implemented under this scheme. They seem to float magically in the air above the fifty-yard line, casting an electronically perfected shadow on the playing area beneath. As the originators of this system point out, the use of digital imaging here allows the same commercial space to be sold over and over again, many times during a game, and with differing sponsors for each broadcast location; it enhances revenues to both teams and advertisers. The only participants adversely affected, of course, are the viewers, who are now deprived of even the illusion of verisimilitude when watching a sporting event. And since these corporate logos can be so deftly and artificially introduced into the sphere for sporting activity, what is to stop cost-conscious team owners from creating "dream players" to hype up the spectacle of sport? And who can ever again trust an instant replay?

The spectacle presented by the new digital imaging systems is one of continuous consumption, artificial perfection, an airbrushed world of serenity and plenty, in which no one is hungry, or ill, or ever grows old. The present becomes eternal, manipulated by pixels and the whim of a sponsor. The ruling ideology of computer-generated imagery in both business and entertainment practice is above all that of a synthetic creation, spun out like so much cotton candy on demand, melting into nothingness even as it is presented and instantly consumed. The humane, arguably direct, spectacle afforded one by such a film as Robert Bresson's *Les Dames du Bois de Boulogne* (1945), involving as it does the pageant of human desire, of love, betrayal, regeneration, and faith, is no longer a marketable, or even a desirable item; there are simply too many rough edges begging to be rounded off. It is almost as if the human dimension of the moving image, in both commerce and art, never existed, since it is so readily being dispensed with.

And yet the tide of this change seems irrevocable, unstoppable, as we enter a new century of moving image production, distribution, and presentation with an entirely new (and more cloistered, and splintered) audience, held in thrall by the images in the dark. Our viewing is more casual with the medium of the televisual apparatus, but it is also more urgent. Our connection to the world has become one of images rather than contacts, of surfaces rather than interior motivation. As we survey the films of the coming millennium, I would suggest that we would do well to jettison the hold of the mainstream cinema over our hearts and minds, and turn instead to the non-narrative, responsive films which sprang up in Paris in the 1920s, and in New York and San Francisco in the 1960s: personal cinema. One such artist who has chosen this path is Craig Baldwin, whose films *Wild Gunman* (1978), *RocketKitKongoKit* (1986), *Tribulation 99* (1991), *O No Coronado!* (1992), and *Sonic Outlaws* (1995) gesture towards, as Baldwin himself puts it, new "methods of creative resistance"—and perhaps the hope of an "electronic folk culture"—in the midst of an all-consuming electronic environment under increasing corporate control" (Baldwin).

In his appropriation of found images, clips from old science fiction movies and instructional films (which reflect Baldwin's schooling under avant-garde pioneer film collagist Bruce Conner), Baldwin lays bare the construct behind the conceit of cinema/video spectacle. Any image will suffice to advance his paranoid narrative structures (all spectacles being equal, both impoverished and lavish), and Baldwin revels in the grotesque, the paranoid, and the apocalyptic in his choice and manipulation of found images, taking back the dominant construct of the passive spectacle and repositioning the viewer as an interactive archivist of our collective cinematic memory. For the choice is clear: we must create a communal spectacle in which all may participate, composed of images that speak to us personally, without mediation, images that we are required to interpret and reconstruct entirely for ourselves; or we become passive viewers at the service of a narcotizing series of images that seek to control and pacify our emotions, reducing our lives to an extension of the visions we see within the domain of the televisual, rather than apportioning the production of spectacle a small segment of our corporeal consciousness. If spectacle is transparent, it is perhaps because the very opacity of light thrown on a screen through a series of colored dyes, gels, or pixels manipulated by laser beams and the like is always an ephemeral construct, living and dying from moment to moment as the images we see are projected in front of our eyes. Constantly bursting forth in light, constantly decaying into momentary, flickering darkness, the transparency of the cinematic/video construct is at once alluring and dangerously seductive, a spectacle that we must control, before it controls us.

BIBLIOGRAPHY

Acker, Ally. *Reel Women: Pioneers of the Cinema 1896 to the Present.* New York: Continuum, 1991.

Acker, Kathy. "The End of the World of White Men." In *Posthuman Bodies*, Judith Halberstam and Ira Livingston, eds. Bloomington: Indiana University Press, 1995, 57–72.

Albrecht, Lisa, and Rose M. Brewer, eds. *Bridges of Power: Women's Multicultural Alliances.* Philadelphia: New Society, 1990.

Alexander, Karen. "Julie Dash: *Daughters of the Dust*, and a Black Aesthetic." In *Women and Film: A Sight and Sound Reader*, Pam Cook and Philip Dodd, eds. Philadelphia: Temple University Press, 1993, 224–231.

Allen, Richard. "Representation, Illusion and the Cinema." *Cinema Journal* 32.2 (Winter 1993): 21–48.

Altomara, Rita Ecke. *Hollywood on the Palisades: A Filmography of Silent Features Made in Fort Lee, New Jersey, 1903–1927.* New York: Garland Publishing, Inc., 1983.

———. Anonymous. "Lively: The Danziger Brothers." *Financial Times* (April 14, 1965).

———. "Viewpoint: A Question of Economics." *Kinematograph Weekly* 2827.7 (December 7, 1961): A.

———. "Danziger Wins Control." *Daily Mail* (May 1, 1958).

———. Entry on "Blue Jeans." *Magill's Survey of Cinema Computer Data Base*, n.d.

Arasoughly, Alia, ed. and trans. *Screens of Life: Critical Film Writing from the Arab World*. Quebec: World Heritage Press, 1996.

Arthurs, Jane. "Thelma and Louise: On the Road to Feminism?" In *Feminist Subjects, Multi-Media, Cultural Methodologies*, Penny Florence and Dee Reynolds, eds. Manchester: Manchester University Press, 1995: 89–105.

Atkinson, Michael. "The Eternal Return." *The Village Voice* (Film Special Section) (November 21, 1995): 4–5.

Attile, Martina, and Maureen Blackwood. "Black Women and Representation: Notes from the Workshops held in London, 1984." In *Films for Women*, Charlotte Brunsdon, ed. London: BFI, 1987, 202–208.

Auty, Martyn, and Nick Roddick. *British Cinema Now*. London: BFI Publishing, 1985.

Bakhtin, M. M. *The Dialogic Imagination*. Caryl Emerson and Michael Holquist, trans. Michael Holquist, ed. Austin: University of Texas Press, 1981.

Baldwin, Craig. Essay on his work as a filmmaker on *The Flicker Pages*, curated by Scott Stark, located on the World Wide Web at: <http://www.sirius.com/~sstark/mkr/cb/cb-bio.html>.

Ball, Eustace Hale. *Photoplay Scenarios: How to Write and Sell Them*. New York: Hearst's International Library Co., 1917.

Bart, Peter. "The *Other* Arnold." *GQ* (October, 1995): 89, 90, 94.

Barthes, Roland. *S/Z*. Richard Miller, trans. New York: Hill and Wang, 1974.

Bataille, Georges. *The Accursed Share: An Essay on General Economy*, vol. 2, *The History of Eroticism*; vol. 3, *Sovereignty*. New York: Zone, 1993.

Baudrillard, Jean. *The Gulf War Did Not Take Place*. Paul Patton, trans. Bloomington: Indiana University Press, 1995.

Bauman, Zygmunt. *Intimations of Postmodernity*. London: Routledge, 1992.

Bertsch, Marguerite. *How to Write for Moving Pictures: A Manual of Instruction and Information*. New York: George H. Doran Co., 1917.

Bhabha, Homi K. "The Other Question—The Stereotype and Colonial Discourse." *Screen* 24.6 (November/December 1983): 18–36.

———. *The Location of Culture.* New York: Routledge, 1994.

Blaché, Alice Guy. *The Memoirs of Alice Guy Blaché.* Roberta and Simone Blaché, trans. Anthony Slide, ed. Metuchen: Scarecrow Press, 1986.

Blackwood, Maureen, ed. *The Sankofa Papers.* Unpublished, held at the offices of the Sankofa Collective, London, n.d.

Blum, Daniel. *A Pictorial History of the Silent Screen.* New York: G. P. Putnam's Sons, 1953.

Bobo, Jacqueline. "*The Color Purple*: Black Women as Cultural Readers." In *Female Spectators: Looking at Film and Television,* E. Diedre Pribram, ed. London: Verso, 1988, 90–109.

Bordwell, David, Janet Staiger, and Kristen Thompson. *The Classical Hollywood Cinema: Film Style and Mode of Production to 1960.* New York: Columbia University Press, 1985.

Braidotti, Rosi. *Nomadic Subjects: Embodiment and Sexual Difference in Contemporary Feminist Theory.* New York: Columbia University Press, 1994.

British Film Institute. *British Film Institute Production Catalogue.* London: BFI Publishing, 1991.

Byg, Barton. *Landscapes of Resistance: The German Films of Danièle Huiller and Jean-Marie Straub.* Berkeley: University of California Press, 1995.

Bynum, Caroline Walker. *Fragmentation and Redemption: Essays on Gender and the Human Body in Medieval Religion.* New York: Zone, 1992.

Cameron, Ian, and Elisabeth Cameron. *The Heavies.* London: Praeger, 1967.

———. *Dames.* London: Praeger, 1969.

Campbell, Craig W. *Reel American and World War I: A Comprehensive Filmography and History of Motion Pictures in the United States, 1914–1920.* Jefferson, NC: McFarland, 1985.

Campbell, Loretta. "Reinventing Our Image: Eleven Black Women Filmmakers." *Heresies* 16 (1983): 58–62.

Carr, Catherine. *The Art of Photoplay Writing.* New York: The Hannis Jordan Co., 1914.

Carroll, Noel. *The Philosophy of Horror, or Paradoxes of the Heart.* New York: Routledge, 1990.

Case, Sue Ellen, Philip Brett, and Susan Leigh Foster, eds. *Cruising the Performative; Interventions into the Representation of Ethnicity, Nationality, and Sexuality.* Bloomington: Indiana University Press, 1995.

Caute, David. *Joseph Losey: A Revenge on Life.* Oxford: Oxford University Press, 1994.

Cheshire, Godfrey. "Where Iranian Cinema Is." *Film Comment* 29. 2 (March-April 1993): 38–39.

———. "Iran, the Art Film's Last Stand." *The New York Press* (April 24–30, 1996): 46–47.

Ciment, Michel. "*Accident.*" In *The International Dictionary of Films and Filmmakers,* vol. 1, 2nd ed., Nick Thomas, ed. Chicago: St. James Press, 1990, 8–10.

Clover, Carol J. *Men, Women and Chainsaws: Gender in the Modern Horror Film.* Princeton: Princeton University Press, 1992.

Cook, David A. *A History of the Narrative Film.* 3rd ed. New York: Norton, 1996.

Curtis, David, ed. *A Directory of British Film and Video Artists.* Luton, Bedfordshire, UK: John Libbey, 1996.

Curtis, Robert. *Edgar Wallace—Each Way.* London: John Long, 1932.

Davis, Sally Ogle. "7322 Major Films—14 Directed by Women." *San Francisco Chronicle* (Datebook) (January 25, 1981): 17.

Debord, Guy. *The Society of the Spectacle.* New York: Zone, 1994.

de Sade, Marquis Donatian Alphonse François. *Les 120 Jours de Sodome.* Vol. 1. Paris: Union Generale d'Editions, 1975.

Deivert, Bert. "Shots in Cyberspace: Film Research on the Internet." *Cinema Journal* 35.1 (Fall 1995): 103–124.

de Lauretis, Teresa. "Rethinking Women's Cinema: Aesthetics and Feminist Theory." In Diane Carson, Linda Dittman, and Janice R. Welsch, eds. *Multiple Voices in Feminist Film Criticism.* Minneapolis: University of Minnesota Press, 1994, 140–161.

Derrida, Jacques. "Racism's Last Word." Peggy Kamuf, trans. *Critical Inquiry* 12 (1985): 290–299.

Diawara, Manthia. *African Cinema: Politics and Culture.* Bloomington: Indiana University Press, 1992.

———. *Rouch in Reverse.* Video: 1995, UK/US/Mali. 51 minutes. Color. Parminder Vir, Producer. In French and English, with English subtitles. Distribution: California Newsreel.

di Bernardo, Giovanni. "Roberto Rossellini: Marx, Freud and Jesus: An Interview, Summer 1976." In *The Cinéaste Interviews on the Art and Politics of the Cinema,* Dan Georgakas and Lenny Rubenstein, eds. Chicago: Lake View Press, 1983, 149–154.

Dixon, Wheeler Winston. Interview with Maureen Blackwood at the offices of the Sankofa Collective, London, March 23, 1994, London.

———. Telephone interview with Isaac Julien, at Testing the Limits, New York, November 15, 1994.

———. Telephone interview with David Lawson, at Normal Films, London, November 15, 1994.

———. Telephone interview with Rachel Talalay, Los Angeles, spring, 1995.

———. *It Looks at You: The Returned Gaze of Cinema.* Albany: SUNY Press, 1995.

Dollimore, Jonathan. *Sexual Dissidence: Augustine to Wilde, Freud to Foucault.* Oxford: Clarendon, 1991.

Doyle, Jennifer, Jonathan Flatley, and José Estaban Muñoz. *Pop Out: Queer Warhol.* Durham, NC: Duke University Press, 1996.

Duncan, Jody. "Quick Cuts: Maximum *Speed.*" *Cinefex* 59 (September 1994): 89–92.

Dyer, Richard. *The Matter of Images: Essays on Representations.* London: Routledge, 1993.

Ehrlich, Linda C., and David Desser, eds. *Cinematic Landscapes: Observations on the Visual Arts and Cinema and Japan.* Austin: University of Texas Press, 1994.

Eisenstein, Sergei. *The Film Form: Essays in Film Theory.* Jay Leyda, trans. and ed. New York: Harcourt, Brace, 1949.

———. *The Film Sense.* Jay Leyda, trans. and ed. London: Faber and Faber, 1943.

Erens, Patricia, ed. *Sexual Strategems: The World of Women in Film.* New York: Horizon, 1979.

Everett, Anna. "Africa, the Diaspora, Cinema and Cyberspace: Are We Ready for the 21st Century?" *Screening Noír* 1.1 (Spring 1995): 1, 10.

Everson, William K. *American Silent Film.* New York: Oxford University Press, 1978.

Florence, Penny, and Dee Reynolds, eds. *Feminist Subjects, Multi-Media, Cultural Methodologies.* Manchester: Manchester University Press, 1995.

Fontana, Benedetto. *Hegemony and Power: On the Relation Between Gramsci and Machiavelli.* Minneapolis: University of Minnesota Press, 1993.

Foster, Gwendolyn Audrey. Unpublished interview with Kristine Peterson, 1991.

———. *Women Film Directors: An International Bio-Critical Dictionary.* Westport, CT: Greenwood, 1995.

Foucault, Michel. *The Archaeology of Knowledge.* Alan Sheridan, trans. London: Travistock, and New York: Pantheon, 1972. (Originally published as *L'archaelogie du savoir.* Paris: Gallimard, 1969.)

———. *Discipline and Punish: The Birth of the Prison.* Alan Sheridan, trans. New York: Vintage, 1979.

Frow, John. *Cultural Studies and Cultural Value.* Oxford: Clarendon, 1995.

Fusco, Coco. "Sankofa Film/Video Collective and Black Audio Film Collective." In *Discourses: Conversations in Post Modern Art and Culture,* Russell Ferguson, William Olander, Karen Fiss, and Marcia Tucker, eds. Cambridge: Massachusetts Institute of Technology and The New Museum of Contemporary Art (N.Y.), 1990, 17–43.

Garbicz, Adam, and Jacek Klinowski. *Cinema, the Magic Vehicle: A Guide to Its Achievement. Journey One: The Cinema Through 1949.* New York: Schocken, 1983.

Gifford, Denis. *The British Film Catalogue 1895–1970: A Guide to Entertainment Films*. Newton Abbot, Devon: David & Charles, 1973.

Giroux, Henry A. *Disturbing Pleasures: Learning Popular Culture*. New York: Routledge, 1994.

Glover, David. "Looking for Edgar Wallace: The Author as Consumer." *History Workshop Journal* 37 (1994): 143–164.

Goulding, Daniel J., ed. *Post New Wave Cinema in the Soviet Union and Eastern Europe*. Bloomington: Indiana University Press, 1989.

Grantham, Mark. "Life on the Cheap with the Danzigers." Manuscript in the British Film Institute Archives, n.d.

Graves, Gaye L. "True Guys: Digital Domain, the First Year." *Cuts* (September 1994): 32–33, 35, 38, 41.

Greene, Graham. "Edgar Wallace." In *Collected Essays*. Harmondsworth: Penguin, 1970, 169–173.

Habermas, Jürgen. *The Past as Future*. Interview by Michael Haller. Max Pensky, trans. and ed. Foreword by Peter Hohendahl. Lincoln: University of Nebraska Press, 1994.

Halberstam, Judith, and Ira Livingston, eds. *Posthuman Bodies*. Bloomington: Indiana University Press, 1995.

Hampton, Benjamin B. *History of the American Film Industry from Its Beginnings to 1931*. New York: Dover, 1970. (Originally titled *A History of the Movies*.)

Hanson, Patricia King, and Stephen L. Hanson, eds. *The Film Review Index*. Vol. 1, 1882–1949. Phoenix: Oryx Press, 1986.

Hanson, Patricia King, ed., with Alan Gerinson. *The American Film Institute Catalog of Motion Pictures Produced in the United States*, Vol. F1; *Feature Films, 1911–1920, Credit and Subject Indexes and Film Entries* (2 vols). Berkeley: University of California Press, 1988.

Hart, Trevor Ray. "The Brit Pack." *Time Out* 1231 (March 23–30, 1994): 18–23.

Heath, Stephen. *Questions of Cinema*. Bloomington: Indiana University Press, 1981.

Heck-Rabi, Louise. *Women Filmmakers: The Critical Reception.* Metuchen: Scarecrow, 1984.

Heller, Scott. "Scholars Contemplate the Future of Film Studies in a World of Fast-Changing Technology." *The Chronicle of Higher Education* (October 27, 1995): A17.

Hill, John. *Sex, Class and Realism: British Cinema 1956–1963.* London: BFI Publishing, 1986.

Hill, John, and Martin McLoone, eds. *Big Picture, Small Screen: The Relations Between Film and Television.* Luton, Bedfordshire: John Libbey, 1995.

Hirsch, Foster. *Joseph Losey.* Boston: Twayne, 1980.

Hope, Ted. "Indie Film Is Dead." *Filmmaker* (Fall 1995): 18, 54–58.

Horwitz, Rita, and Harriet Harrison, with Wendy White. *George Kleine Collection of Early Motion Pictures in the Library of Congress.* Washington, DC: Library of Congress, 1980.

Huhtamo, Erkki. "Seeking Deeper Contact: Interactive Art as Meta-commentary." *Convergence* 1.2 (Autumn 1995): 81–104.

Hutcheon, Linda. "Colonialism and the Postcolonial Condition: Complexities Abounding." *PMLA* 110.1 (January 1995): 7–16.

Issari, Mohammad Ali. *Cinema in Iran, 1900–1979.* Metuchen, NJ: Scarecrow, 1989.

Jackson, Lynne, and Jean Rasenberger. *"The Passion of Remembrance:* An Interview with Martina Attile and Isaac Julien." *Cinéaste* 14.4 (1988): 23–37.

Julien, Isaac. *Frantz Fanon: Black Skin, White Mask.* Video: 1996, UK. 50 minutes. Color. Mark Nash, producer. In English and French, with English subtitles. Distribution: California Newsreel.

Juno, Andrea, and V. Vale, eds. *Angry Women.* San Francisco: Re/Search Publications, 1991.

Kakutani, Michiko. "Designer Nihilism." *The New York Times Magazine* (March 24, 1996): 30, 32.

Kaplan, E. Ann. "Ideology and Cinematic Practice in Lang's *Scarlet Street* and Renoir's *La Chienne.*" *Wide Angle* 5.3 (1983): 32–43.

Katz, Ephraim, with Melinda Corey, George Ochoa, et al. *The Film Encyclopedia.* 2nd ed. New York: HarperCollins, 1994.

Kinder, Marsha. *Blood Cinema: The Reconstruction of National Identity in Spain.* Interactive CD-ROM. Los Angeles: Cine Disc, 1996.

Kirkham, Pat. "The Personal, the Professional and the Partner(ship): The Husband/Wife Collaboration of Charles and Ray Eames." In *Feminist Cultural Theory: Process and Production*, Beverly Skeggs, ed. Manchester: Manchester University Press, 1995, 207–226.

Kneale, J. Douglas. "Voice and Letter in *The Prelude.*" *PMLA* 101.3 (May 1986): 351–361.

Koning, Dirk. "No Sex, Please: Congress and the Courts Threaten Censorship of Cable Access, Internet." *The Independent* 18.10 (December 1995): 6, 7.

Koszarski, Richard, ed. *Hollywood Directors: 1914–1940.* New York: Oxford University Press, 1976.

———, ed. *The Rivals of D. W. Griffith.* Minneapolis, MN: Walker Art Center, 1976.

Kristeva, Julia. *Powers of Horror: An Essay on Abjection.* Leon S. Roudiez, trans. New York: Columbia University Press, 1982.

Kroker, Arthur, and Marilouise Kroker. *Hacking the Future: Stories for the Flesh-Eating 90s* (with accompanying CD). New York: St. Martin's, 1996.

———, eds. *The Last Sex: Feminism and Outlaw Bodies.* New York: St. Martin's, 1993.

Kruger, Barbara. "Sankofa Film/Video Collective and Black Audio Film Collective [at] the Collective for Living Cinema." *Artforum* (September 1988): 143–144.

Kuhn, Annette. "A Credit to Her Mother." In *Feminist Subjects, Multi-Media, Cultural Methodologies*, Penny Florence and Dee Reynolds, eds. Manchester: Manchester University Press, 1995: 58–72.

Lacan, Jacques. "Seminar on 'The Purloined Letter.'" Jeffrey Mehlman, trans. In *The Purloined Poe: Lacan, Derrida and Psychoanalytic Reading*, John P. Muller and William J. Richardson, eds. Baltimore: Johns Hopkins University Press, 1988, 28–54.

Lahue, Kalton C. *Dreams for Sale: The Rise and Fall of the Triangle Film Corporation*. South Brunswick and New York: A. S. Barnes and Company, 1971.

Landy, Marcia. *British Genres: Cinema and Society 1930–1960*. Princeton University Press: 1991.

Lane, Margaret. *Edgar Wallace: The Biography of a Phenomenon*. London: Heinemann, 1938.

Larkin, Alile Sharon. "Black Women Filmmakers Defining Ourselves." In *Female Spectators: Looking at Film and Television*, E. Diedre Pribram, ed. London: Verso, 1988, 157–173.

Lauritzen, Einer, and Gunnar Lundquist. *American Film Index, 1908–1915*. Stockholm: Film-Index, 1976.

———. *American Film Index, 1916–1920*. Stockholm: Film-Index, 1984.

Leahy, James. *The Cinema of Joseph Losey*. London: Zwemmer, 1967.

LeMoncheck, Linda. *Dehumanizing Women: Treating Persons as Sex Objects*. Totowa: Rowman and Allanheld, 1985.

Lofts, W. O. G., and Derek Adley. *The British Bibliography of Edgar Wallace*. London: Howard Baker, 1969.

Lyotard, Jean-François. *The Postmodern Condition: A Report on Knowledge*. Geoff Bennington and Brian Massumi, trans. Minneapolis: University of Minnesota Press, 1984.

MacDonald, Myra. *Representing Women: Myths of Femininity in the Popular Media*. London: Edward Arnold, 1992.

Magill, Frank N., ed. *Magill's Survey of Cinema. Silent Films*. Englewood Cliffs, NJ: Salem Press, 1982.

Margulies, Ivone. *Nothing Happens: Chantal Akerman's Hyperrealist Everyday*. Durham, NC: Duke University Press, 1996.

Mavor, Carol. *Pleasures Taken: Performances of Sexuality and Loss in Victorian Photographs*. Durham, NC: Duke University Press, 1995.

Meisler, Andy. "And Now, Here's . . . Ummm . . . Space Ghost." *The New York Times* (Sunday, November 20, 1994): sect. 2, 44–45.

Milne, Tom. *Losey on Losey.* Garden City, NY: Doubleday, 1968.

Minh-ha, Trinh T. *Framer Framed.* New York: Routledge, 1992.

Morrison, Toni. *Playing in the Dark: Whiteness and the Literary Imagination.* New York: Random House, 1992.

Mossman, Tam. *The Unabridged Edgar Allan Poe.* Philadelphia: Running Press, 1983.

Mueller, Roswitha. *Valie Export: Fragments of the Imagination.* Bloomington: Indiana University Press, 1994.

Munden, Kenneth, ed. *American Film Institute Catalog of Feature Films, 1921–1930.* New York: R. R. Bowker, 1971.

Munsterberg, Hugo. *The Photoplay: A Psychological Study.* New York: D. Appleton and Company, 1916.

Murphy, Kathleen. "Abbas Kiarostami Retrospective." *Stagebill* (April 1996): WR 2–6.

———. "Recent Iranian Cinema: Program Notes for the Walter Reade Theatre." *Stagebill* (April 1996): WR 2, 7–11.

Murphy, Robert. *Sixties British Cinema.* London: BFI Publishing, 1992.

Nichols, Bill. *Blurred Boundaries: Questions of Meaning in Contemporary Culture.* Bloomington: Indiana University Press, 1994.

Niver, Kemp R. *The First Twenty Years: A Segment of Film History.* Los Angeles: Locare Research Group, 1968.

Nolan, Jack Edmund. "Edgar Wallace." *Films in Review* 18.2 (February 1967): 71–85.

O'Brien, Geoffrey. *The Phantom Empire.* New York: Norton, 1993.

Paglia, Camille. *Sexual Personal: Art and Decadence from Nefertiti to Emily Dickinson.* New York: Random House, 1990.

Parish, James Robert. *Hollywood Character Actors.* New Rochelle, NY: Arlington House Publishers, 1978.

Parisi, Paula. "Monster Job for Digital Domain." *The Hollywood Reporter* (October 7–9, 1994): 1, 29, 32.

Parry, Benita. "Problems in Current Theories of Colonial Discourse." *Oxford Literary Review* 9.1–2 (1987): 27–58.

Pauer, Florian. *Die Edgar-Wallace-Filme.* Munich: Goldmann, 1982.

Pettigrew, Terence. *British Film Character Actors: Great Names and Memorable Moments.* London: David and Charles, 1982.

Pines, Jim. "The Cultural Context of Black British Cinema." In *Blackframes: Critical Perspectives on Black Independent Cinema,* Mybe B. Cham and Claire Andrade-Watkins, eds. Cambridge, MA: MIT Press, 1988: 26–36.

Pinter, Harold. *Five Screenplays.* London: Methuen, 1971.

Pirie, David. *A Heritage of Horror: The English Gothic Cinema 1946–1972.* London: Gordon Fraser, 1973.

Pitt, Peter. "Elstree's Poverty Row." *Films and Filming* 360 (September 1984): 15–16.

Polan, Dana. *Power and Paranoia: History, Narrative and the American Cinema 1940–1950.* New York: Columbia University Press, 1986.

Prokop, Tim. "Closeup: Adding Teeth to *Wolf.*" *Cinefex* 59 (September 1994): 97–106.

Rabinovitz, Lauren. *The Rebecca Project.* Interactive CD-ROM. New Brunswick: Rutgers University Press, 1996.

Racevskis, Karlis. *Michel Foucault and the Subversion of Intellect.* Ithaca and New York: Cornell University Press, 1983.

Rahimian, Behzad, ed. *Film International: A Cross Cultural Review* 3.1 (Winter 1995): WWW < http://gpg.com/film/issue1/index.html >.

Redhead, Steve. *Unpopular Cultures: The Birth of Law and Popular Culture.* Manchester: Manchester University Press, 1995.

Roland, William. "Danzigers Sell Studio for £300,000." *Evening Standard* (October 26, 1969).

Roper, Jonathan. "The Heart of Multimedia: Interactivity or Experience?" *Convergence* 1.2 (Autumn 1995): 23–28.

Ross, Scott. "The Digital Domain." *The Red Herring* (December 1993): 30–32.

Rossell, Deac, and Klaus Eder, eds. *New Chinese Cinema.* Dossier 11: National Film Theatre. London: BFI Publishing, 1993.

Rowan, Geoffrey. "Seeing Is Disbelieving." *The Globe and Mail: Report on Business* (August 15, 1994): sect. B, B1, B3.

Russo, Vito. *The Celluloid Closet*. Revised edition. New York: Harper and Row, 1987.

Sáez, Ñacuñán. "Torture: A Discourse on Practice." In *Tattoo, Torture, Mutilation and Adornment: The Denaturalization of the Body in Culture and Text*. Frances E. Mascia-Lees and Patricia Sharpe, eds. Albany: State University of New York Press, 1992: 126–144.

Said, Edward. *Culture and Imperialism*. New York: Knopf, 1993.

——. *Orientalism*. New York: Vintage, 1979.

Sarris, Andrew. *The American Cinema: Directors and Directions*. New York: Dutton, 1968.

Scarry, Elaine. *The Body in Pain: The Making and Unmaking of the World*. Oxford: Oxford University Press, 1985.

Scheuer, Steven, ed. *Movies on TV and Videocassette: 1993–1994*. New York:Bantam, 1992.

Schneider, Tassilo. "Finding a New Heimat in the Wild West: Karl May and the German Western of the 1960s." *Journal of Film and Video* 47.1–3 (Spring–Fall 1995): 50–66.

Seltzer, Mark. *Bodies and Machines*. New York: Routledge, 1992.

Shaviro, Steven. *The Cinematic Body*. Minneapolis: University of Minnesota Press, 1993.

Shay, Don. "Mayhem Over Miami." *Cinefex* 59 (September 1994): 34–79.

Silver, Alain, and James Ursini. *The Vampire Film: From Nosferatu to Bram Stoker's Dracula*. New York: Limelight, 1993.

Skeggs, Beverly, ed. *Feminist Cultural Theory: Process and Production*. Manchester: Manchester University Press, 1995.

Slide, Anthony. *Aspects of American Film History Prior to 1920*. Metuchen, NJ: Scarecrow, 1978.

——. *Early Women Directors*. New York: Da Capo, 1984.

Snead, James A. "Image of Blacks in Black Independent Films: A Brief Survey." In *Blackframes: Critical Perspectives on Black Inde-

pendent Cinema, Mybe B. Cham and Claire Andrade-Watkins, eds. Cambridge, MA: MIT Press, 1988: 16–25.

Snider, Michael. "Video Game Ratings Present a New Difficulty Level." *USA Today* (March 3, 1994): 4D.

Sontag, Susan. "The Decay of Cinema." *The New York Times Magazine* (February 25, 1996): 60–61.

Stacey, Jackie. "The Lost Audience: Methodology, Cinema History and Feminist Film Criticism." In *Feminist Culture Theory: Process and Production*, Beverly Skeggs, ed. Manchester: Manchester University Press, 1995, 97–118.

Stam, Robert. *Subversive Pleasures: Bakhtin, Cultural Criticism and Film*. Baltimore: Johns Hopkins University Press, 1989.

Stein, Elliott. "Focus, Please!" *The Village Voice* (Film Special Section) (November 21, 1995): 5.

Stein, Gertrude. "Why I Like Detective Stories." In *How Writing Is Written*. Santa Barbara: Black Sparrow Press, 1974.

Steinberg, Don. "Joe Piscopo Lives." *GQ* (October, 1995): 113–114.

Straayer, Chris. "The Seduction of Boundaries: Feminist Fluidity in Annie Sprinkle's Art/Education/Sex." In *Dirty Looks: Women, Pornography and Power*, Pamela Church Gibson and Roma Gibson, eds. London: BFI, 1993, 156–175.

Suárez, Juan A. *Bike Boys, Drag Queens and Superstars: Avant-Garde, Mass Culture, and Gay Identities in the 1960s Underground Cinema*. Bloomington: Indiana University Press, 1996.

Suárez, Juan, and Millicent Manglis. "Cinema, Gender, and the Topography of Enigmas: A Conversation with Laura Mulvey." *Cinefocus* 3 (1995): 2–8.

Suleiman, Susan Rubin. *Risking Who One Is; Encounters with Contemporary Art and Literature*. Cambridge: Harvard University Press, 1994.

Tasker, Yvonne. *Spectacular Bodies: Gender, Genre and the Action Cinema*. London: Routledge, 1993.

Taubin, Amy. "Unseated." *The Village Voice* (Film Special Section) (November 21, 1995): 8–9.

Taylor, Kenneth. Letter to the author, February 13, 1997, and telephone interview, March 2, 1997.

Thomas, Bob. *King Cohn: The Life and Times of Harry Cohn.* New York: G. P. Putnam's Sons, 1967.

Thompson, Kristin, and David Bordwell. *Film History: An Introduction.* New York: McGraw Hill, 1994.

Todorov, Tzvetan. *The Morals of History.* Alyson Waters, trans. Minneapolis: University of Minnesota Press, 1995.

Trotsky, Leon. *Trotsky's Diary in Exile.* Elena Zarudnaya, trans. Cambridge, MA: Harvard University Press, 1958.

Vernet, Marc. "The Look at the Camera." Dana Polan, trans. *Cinema Journal* 28.2 (Winter 1989), 48–63. (Translation of "Le regard à la camèra: figures de l'absence." *Iris* 1.2 (1983): 31–45.)

Viegener, Matias, "The Only Haircut that Makes Sense Anymore: Queer Subculture and Gay Resistance." In *Queer Looks: Perspectives on Lesbian and Gay Film and Video,* Martha Gever, John Gregson, and Pratibha Parmar, eds. New York: Routledge, 1993, 116–133.

Virilio, Paul. *The Art of the Motor.* Julie Rose, trans. Minneapolis: University of Minnesota Press, 1995.

Wallace, Edgar. *Writ in Barracks.* London: Methuen, 1900.

———. *The Four Just Men.* London: Tallis, 1905.

———. *The Nine Bears.* London: Ward Lock, 1910.

———. *Sanders of the River.* London: Ward Lock, 1911.

———. *The Fourth Plague.* London: Ward Lock, 1913.

———. *The Admirable Carfew.* London: Ward Lock, 1914.

———. *The Man Who Bought London.* London: Ward Lock, 1915.

———. *Those Folk of Bulburo.* London: Ward Lock, 1918.

———. *The Adventures of Heine.* London: Ward Lock, 1919.

———. *The Man Who Knew.* London: Newnes, 1919.

———. *The Books of Bart.* London: Ward Lock, 1923.

———. *Captains of Souls*. London: John Long, 1923.

———. *Chick*. London: Ward Lock, 1923.

———. *The Dark Eyes of London*. London: Ward Lock, 1924.

———. *The Black Avons*. London: G. Gill, 1925, 4 volumes.

———. *Barbara On Her Own*. London: Newnes, 1926.

———. *The Day of Uniting*. London: Hodder and Stoughton, 1926.

———. *People*. London: Hodder and Stoughton, 1926.

———. *The Square Emerald*. London: Hodder and Stoughton, 1926.

———. *The Brigand*. London: Hodder and Stoughton, 1927.

———. *This England*. London: Hodder and Stoughton, 1927.

———. *Again Sanders*. London: Hodder and Stoughton, 1928.

———. *Elegant Edward*. London: Readers Library, 1928.

———. *Four Square Jane*. London: Readers Library, 1929.

———. *The Iron Grip*. London: Readers Library, 1929.

———. *The Lone House Mystery*. London: Collins, 1929.

———. *Planetoid 127*. London: Readers Library, 1929.

———. *Red Aces*. London: Hodder and Stoughton, 1929.

———. *The Calendar*. London: Collins, 1930.

———. *The Devil Man*. London: Collins, 1931.

———. *On the Spot*. London: John Long, 1931.

———. *When the Gangs Came to London*. London: John Long, 1932.

Wallace, Pat. "Edgar Wallace Directs." *The Picturegoer* (August 1929): 17–18.

Wallace, Penelope. *A Brief Life of Edgar Wallace*. Pamphlet, n. pag. Oxford, 1965.

Warren, Patricia. *British Film Studios: An Illustrated History*. London: Batsford, 1995.

Weaver, John T., ed. *Twenty Years of Silents, 1908–1928*. Metuchen, NJ: Scarecrow, 1971.

Weldon, Michael. *The Psychotronic Encyclopedia of Film*. New York: Ballantine, 1983.

Whitehead, John. "T. S. Eliot and Edgar Wallace." *Notes and Queries* 36.2 (June 1989): 203–204.

Wice, Nathaniel. "Once Upon a Time in Chinatown." *The Village Voice* (Film Special Section) (November 21, 1995): 14, 17.

Wiegman, Robyn. *American Anatomies: Theorizing Race and Gender*. Durham, NC: Duke University Press, 1995

Will, David, and Paul Willemen, eds. *Roger Corman: The Millennic Vision*. Edinburgh: Edinburgh Film Festival, 1970.

Willemen, Paul. "Letter to John." *Screen* 21.2 (Summer 1980): 53–66.

Willemen, Paul, and Jim Pines. *Questions of Third Cinema*. London: BFI Publishing, 1989.

Williams, Linda. *Hard Core: Power, Pleasure, and the "Frenzy of the Visible."* Berkeley: University of California Press, 1989.

———. "Sisters Under the Skin: Video and Blockbuster Erotic Thrillers." In *Women and Film: A Sight and Sound Reader*, Pam Cook and Philip Dodd, eds. Philadelphia: Temple University Press, 1993, 105–114.

Wolstenholme, Susan. *Gothic (Re)Visions: Writing Women as Readers*. Albany: SUNY Press, 1993.

Zavarzadeh, Mas'ud. *Seeing Films Politically*. Albany: SUNY Press, 1991.

ABOUT THE AUTHOR

Wheeler Winston Dixon is the Chairperson of the Film Studies Program and Professor of English at the University of Nebraska, Lincoln. His most recent books are *It Looks at You: Notes on the Returned Gaze of Cinema* (SUNY Press), *The Films of Jean-Luc Godard* (SUNY Press), and *The Exploding Eye: A Re-Visionary History of the American Experimental Cinema* (SUNY Press). Dixon is the author of more than fifty articles on film theory, history, and criticism, which have appeared in *Cinéaste, Interview, Literature/Film Quarterly, Films in Review, Post Script, Journal of Film and Video, Film Criticism, New Orleans Review, Classic Images, Film and Philosophy, Popular Culture Review*, and numerous other journals. A member of the editorial board of *Film Criticism, The Journal of Film and Video, Literature/Film Quarterly, Popular Culture Review*, and *The Journal of Popular British Cinema*, and editor of the SUNY Press series, *Cultural Studies in Cinema/Video*, Wheeler Winston Dixon's films and videotapes have been screened at Anthology Cinema Archives, the Museum of Modern Art, the Museum of the Moving Image of the British Film Institute, the Whitney Museum of American Art, and elsewhere. A retrospective of his films was presented by invitation at the Millennium Film Workshop in New York City in May, 1997.

INDEX

207